Sexy Dressing Etc.

Sexy Dressing Etc.

Duncan Kennedy

HARVARD UNIVERSITY PRESS
Cambridge, Massachusetts
London, England
1993

Robert Hale, "Coercion and Distribution in a Supposedly Non-Coercive State," *Political Science Quarterly* 38 (1923): 472-473, reprinted by permission of the Academy of Political Science.

Excerpt from *The History of Sexuality* by Michel Foucault. Copyright © 1976 by Éditions Gallimard. English translation copyright © 1978 by Random House. Reprinted by permission of Georges Borchardt, Inc.

This book is printed on acid-free paper, and its binding materials have been chosen for strength and durability.

Library of Congress Cataloging-in-Publication Data

Kennedy, Duncan, 1942-
    Sexy dressing etc. / Duncan Kennedy.
      p. cm.
    Includes index.
    ISBN 0-674-80294-2
    1. Law—Social aspects—United States. 2. Sociological
jurisprudence. 3. United States—Social conditions—1980-   4. Group
identity—United States. 5. Sex role—United States. I. Title.
KF213.K38 1993
340'.115—dc20   93-1206
                                  CIP

Contents

Preface

I wrote these essays for different occasions, with no thought that they might make a book. After the fact, they seem to have a great deal in common. It is not that they share a single theme, but rather that each develops in its own way a cluster of themes and aspirations that has preoccupied leftist intellectuals in recent years.

The Theme of Group Identity

All four essays are about groups and at the same time about cultural "identities." (It's interesting how groups have become identities.) But the approaches are very different.

"Radical Intellectuals in American Culture and Politics, or My Talk at the Gramsci Institute" offers an account of American national identity. It is at the same time a "postcolonial" settling of accounts with the Europe I spent time in as a youth in the 1960s, and a cultural pluralist interpretation of American life.

"A Cultural Pluralist Case for Affirmative Action in Legal Academia" asserts the culturally specific character of the black community and its intelligentsia as the basis for race-conscious decision making, by mainly white law faculties considering African-American applicants, against the claims of color-blindness.

"The Stakes of Law, or Hale and Foucault!" is mainly about the impact of law on the distribution of power and welfare between "workers" and "owners," but it also scouts the terrain in search of a theory of how law constitutes group identities as well as arbitrates among them.

"Sexual Abuse, Sexy Dressing, and the Eroticization of Domination" endorses the radical feminist theory that the eroticization of domination is crucial to heterosexual identity in patriarchy, but also tries to find something redemptive in the peculiar interchange between female sexy dressers and the male part of their voyeuristic audience.

In all the essays, I'm saying that one can't (shouldn't) deny the importance of group affiliation, or identity, in all aspects of life. But I also affirm that groups and identities are contingent and fluid, that each person is likely to be internally contradictory rather than the same all the way through. My view is that the identities celebrated both in modern multicultural rhetoric and in the traditionalist rhetoric of the mainstream are best seen as "positions" or "situations" within which people operate as free agents. Of course, the freedom is relative to the position or situation. But freedom does mean that we sometimes get to choose how to handle things after taking our identities into account. It does not mean that we can get beyond contextual constraint and do or be anything we want. And we can also choose to be loyal and true to our constrained identity positions, choose to be as little free as possible.

This postmodern line on identity goes beyond the valuable insight that generalizing about, say, men and women may suppress the differences between black men and white men, between gay women and straight women, and so forth. That insight suggests that subcategorization might solve the problem of apparent essentialism, by moving us closer to what people are like "as individuals."

But subcategorizing may take us further from the particular truth of a consciousness rather than nearer to it, not because the truth is situated at the level of the universal, but because the seductive specificity of "straight, white, upper-middle-class male" hides as much as it reveals. I subcategorize myself in this way not because these attributes reveal who I am but because they enable readers of these essays to use (and misuse) their own social knowledge of my "type" to understand what I am saying, to get at the level of connotation, the conscious and unconscious undercurrents of meaning that we all build into whatever we say or write.

These essays accept the structure of categories and subcategories, and then describe yet further sub-subcategories. Their strategy is to represent more and more "realistically," and thereby undermine, by a kind of *reductio* of specificity, the very hope, the very need, of realistic representation.

The Critique of Regime Theories

Another theme of these essays is that social life in the West today is ordered by what we might call in a rough way a capitalist, patriarchal, white supremacist "regime," but that the regime is neither structurally coherent—it has no "system logic"—nor capable of totalitarian control—opposition in its interstices is a viable option.

The essays attack, piecemeal, different claims to have discovered system logics, whether put forward by liberal political theorists, by radical feminists, by Marxists, or even by postmodernists, and whether proposed as description or as prescription. But even though my attitude toward regime *theory* is unrelentingly critical, I use constantly and even hope to develop the basic notion of a regime. I don't aim to demonstrate that grand theory is impossible or that we shouldn't try to generalize—that would itself be a kind of grand theory. Rather, each essay nibbles away at grandness, or tries to gnaw it from within, tries to appropriate it without being appropriated.

Whether or not it has a logic, the essays argue in different ways that the system exercises less control over life than intellectuals think it does. The illusion of control comes partly from overestimating the rationality of the system, which gives rise to paranoia or to apologetic smugness, depending on one's politics. But it comes also from day-to-day experiences in which it seems at the local level that everything has already been determined from somewhere else.

The general idea of attacking generality is to shore up the intuition that small-scale resistance is possible, in the sense that it is not precluded by the hegemonic power of the regime. In the absence of a coherent scheme of social order imposed on everyone or chosen by everyone, individual cells of the social organism can be up for grabs and can influence one another. The renunciation of theoretical grandness, and of the intelligentsia's sense of connection to what Europeans call "the State," is depressing only if you think you know what needs to be done, and know some people who could do it if only they could get hold of the necessary power over everybody else.

The Positive Themes

In spite of the negative critique of system logic and central control, my enterprise as a whole is eminently positive, both in the sense of descriptive and in the sense of upbeat. The essays are full of moralizing and prescription, advocating local institutional political struggle and local institutional theoretical projects, and all kinds of changes in legal rules.

At the descriptive level the essays develop, and exemplify in different situations, a general sociology, a jurisprudence, and a sociology of law. The general sociology presents the United States as a land of contending communities with intelligentsias deploying ideologies. I spend a lot of time developing the notions of community, intelligentsia, and ideology.

The jurisprudence, derived from legal realism, emphasizes the amazing plasticity of basic legal concepts like property or contract. Under the general rubrics of property and contract we refer to a multiplicity of quite specific subrules that structure conduct. The content of the subrules can't be derived from the abstractions, but has to be decided case by case.

The sociology of law presents these legal rules, and also private institutional rules and informal social norms, as "rules of the game" of cooperation and conflict between the different communities. Intelligentsias deploy the ideologies to influence the content of the rules. Quite specific rules of the game, applied at the local level, exercise an invisible but profound influence on who gets what, and how much of it. This is equally true for the interactions between men and women, whites and blacks, gays and straights, workers and bosses, pro-sex postmodernist and neopuritan feminist identity politicians.

All the essays attempt to mix and meld European and American theory, without letting either dominate. Legal realism is a pervasive American influence, along with its kindred movements, pragmatism and institutional economics. A central problem is how people like me can (should) relate to American black liberation theory and American radical feminism.

The Continental "fancy theory" is based in Freud and Marx, but I am mainly conscious of trying hard to assimilate, to cannibalize and then actually *use,* structuralism, neomarxism, phenomenology, existentialism, and postmodernism (and, I suppose, whatever else may come into fashion). "Radical Intellectuals in American Culture and Politics" is homage to Gramsci; "A Cultural Pluralist Case for Affirmative Action," to Sartre, Althusser, and Derrida; "The Stakes of Law," to Foucault; and "Sexual Abuse, Sexy Dressing, and the Eroticization of Domination," to Saussure, Lévi-Strauss, and again Foucault.

One peculiarity of legal intellectuals, whatever our politics, is that in our academic culture, which is marginal vis-à-vis both legal practice and "real" academia, it is acceptable to be a "generalist" in a way that is discredited in history, literature, economics, psychology, philosophy, and so forth. Thus we feel free to write about, say, Althusser, or to "do" economics, as underinformed amateurs. In the process we often make elementary mistakes—as I undoubtedly do in these essays—but we also sometimes produce stuff that is interesting and that would never be produced by people operating within the conventional disciplinary boundaries. My ambition here—to write in a way that keeps popular culture and local institutional practice in play simultaneously with many different kinds of theory—derives from that of wedding the rebellious, ironic, exhibitionist, irrationalist, ecstasy-tending project of cultural modernism/postmodernism to the more earnest, objective, and preachy project of leftism or *political correctness.*

"Radical Intellectuals in American Culture and Politics, or My Talk at the Gramsci Institute" was first published in 2 *Rethinking Marxism* (1988); "A Cultural Pluralist Case for Affirmative Action in Legal Academia" was first published in the *Duke Law Journal* (1990); "The Stakes of Law, or Hale and Foucault!" was first published in 15 *Legal Studies Forum* (1991); "Sexual Abuse, Sexy Dressing, and the Eroticization of Domination" was first published in 26 *New England Law Review* (1992).

I want to thank the editors of those journals for their help. I have made minor changes in this version of the texts. Peter Gabel helpfully criticized early drafts of three of the essays. Thanks to Patricia Fazzone and Mopsy Strange Kennedy.

Sexy Dressing Etc.

1

Radical Intellectuals in American Culture and Politics, or My Talk at the Gramsci Institute

I am going to paint with a very broad brush, indeed parody, the American and European intellectuals' picture of American culture, and of the role of left intellectuals in American politics, during the period roughly from 1945 until 1970. This is the view that I grew up with and that still predominates, particularly among older intellectuals. I will then offer, tentatively, a different picture, a "postimperial" analysis of American culture and politics that has somewhat different implications for left practice. My thought is not to discard the more familiar view, but rather to add an angle.

American Culture

We begin with a set of general characterizations of U.S. culture. It is individualist (cowboys), materialist (gangsters), and philistine.

Philistinism is not a minor, superstructural feature. Intellectuals, left, right, and center, get access to American politics through culture, and the quality of culture is therefore a factor determining

This essay is an elaboration of a much shorter talk I gave at the Gramsci Institute in Rome on April 4, 1987; I thank Giovanna Cavallari for organizing that event.

1

their influence. The charge of philistinism can be divided into sub-charges:

> There is absence of culture in the sense of a lack of ancient objects widely understood to be beautiful.
>
> There is absence of culture in the sense of a lack of interest in literature and the arts, and a low level of cultural accomplishment where there is interest (possible exceptions include Hemingway/Fitzgerald/Faulkner, jazz, abstract expressionism, and some other random favorite of the speaker).
>
> There is "bad taste" in the production of daily life, whether in the private sphere of commercial artifacts or in the design of public buildings and spaces, including in both spheres a bad attitude toward natural beauty, with commercial advertising the paradigm of desecration.
>
> There is a hostile attitude toward culture, in the sense not of bad taste but of a distinct antipathy toward high cultural accomplishment and the milieux that produce it, both of which are dismissed as impractical, elitist, too difficult, useless, or whatever.
>
> There is the manipulation of mass consciousness by mass media, which seem to shape taste and cultural choice with relatively little resistance either from folk habits and customs or from elites, and to have low cultural standards in exercising this power.
>
> There is "one-dimensionality" in the sense identified by the Frankfurt School: the reactionary political effect of the manipulation of mass culture is that capitalism substitutes passive modes of depoliticized consumption for the higher forms (active, individual but also public, high-quality, potentially transcendent of any given social reality) through repressive desublimation.

I think most American and European left intellectuals see these traits of American culture as a development within (or a degeneration of) Western European culture as a whole, and as closely tied to the transformations of capitalism. Moreover, we tend to regard American capitalism as the most advanced in the world, so that developments here give indications of probable or at least quite possible events in the less advanced capitalisms of Western Europe (though this view is certainly far less prevalent today than it was twenty years ago).

The idea that the philistinism of American culture is a threat to Western Europe is one of the bonds uniting left and right in the Old World. It owes some of its force to the developmental theory just sketched, in which the United States is to Europe as California is to the East Coast. It also relies on imageries of addiction and sacrilege, with an analogy being perhaps the Chinese mandarin reaction to Western culture during the period of the opium trade. The cover of the book Critique of Commodity Aesthetics by W. F. Haug, a German, published in Britain in 1986, is a photo showing the Piazza San Marco scattered with pieces of black trash that spell the words "Coca-Cola."

American Politics

American and European left intellectuals tend to have much the same image of American politics. The salient traits of our politics are:

There is no working-class party.

There is neither a socialist nor a communist party.

The presidential campaigns that epitomize American politics are determined by how skillfully rival candidates within the political center spend millions of dollars "marketing" themselves, like soap powders, through intellectually contentless advertising and vacuous campaign speeches designed to play a few seconds on the local television news.

The single most important fact explaining these traits is American economic growth over the twentieth century.

The connection is that the American working class has struck a deal with the American ruling class, renouncing political radicalism in exchange for economic well-being.

American culture as described above has a complex role in this deal. First, it is both the product and the cause of economic development: endless economic expansion and the opportunities for advancement it offers breed the individualism, materialism, and philistinism that in turn provide the spiritual fuel, the true "spirit of capitalism" the system needs to keep going.

But this is also a culture of false consciousness in the service of capitalist stability. The main costs of American-style development are grotesquely exaggerated disparities between rich and poor—rendered particularly repulsive by the vulgarity of self-made economic elites—and the absence of safety nets, so that the squalor at the very bottom is worse than anything Western Europeans will tolerate for their (native-born) poor.

Individualism, materialism, and philistinism all bolster fantasies in the mass of workers that they too will one day become millionaires, or at least escape economic marginality. These fantasies pacify them in the face of the conspicuous consumption of the rich and reconcile them to the dreary, culturally empty quality of everyday existence in America.

What is perhaps even more sinister, the culture of individualism, materialism, and philistinism combined with the appearance of endless opportunity creates an illusion of accountability for one's economic fate. The poor are poor because they lack initiative or talent or because they are ethnically or racially inferior, according to the popular understanding. In this way, popular culture generates self-hatred rather than proud working-class consciousness at the bottom of the heap, as well as indifference among those just above the bottom to the horrible fate of those below them.

Hegemony

America is thus the land of Gramsci. Civil society is not just strong, it is forged of steel. The state can be federal, and decentralized even at the provincial level, because the war of motion—in which capital relies on state violence to back its power in the streets or at the factory gates—is an insignificant aspect of American political life. When political violence does occur, it is likely to be more lethal than in Europe, but disorganized, as in the use of murder and massacre against dynamite in the early labor movement, or the National Guard against unarmed urban rioters (who were looting stores rather than building barricades) in the 1960s.

Consent to capitalist rule, the surrender of radicalism in return for economic growth, is the defining characteristic of the whole society. The organic intellectuals of the ruling class enforce the bargain through the media, exercising a degree of cultural control that was unthinkable when there were still peasant cultures, and local elites in daily contact with the masses.

Hegemony is intensified by an odd trick: the political elites of the United States, whether liberal or conservative, reject virtually all of what Europeans see as normal political discourse. Even in the age of Reagan, the media devoted a surprisingly large amount of time and energy to denouncing as equally pernicious "extremists of the right and left." The crucial dichotomy, in the official ideology, is the one between pragmatism and ideology; and the dichotomy is fundamental to the point of defining alternative modes of being.

Ideologues, according to the ideology, are "true believers," who are likely to be psychologically rigid, doctrinaire, prone to "orthodoxies," self-righteous, often violent when others refuse to submit to their plans, perennially willing to justify evil means by noble ends—in short, the legitimate heirs of Hitler and Stalin (who merge in the public mind into a single composite extremist personage). Radical criticism of the system is ideological a priori.

Ideology thus stabilizes in two different ways: the organic intelligentsia of the ruling class persuades people (and of course is itself persuaded) that the existing American system is by a vast margin both the freest and the richest in the world. This same intelligentsia preaches that people who contest this message belong to a dangerous subspecies, the "ideologues," who are legitimately excluded from public discourse because they are compulsive liars and cheats. McCarthyism still lurks just below the surface of American political life.

In this parody of an orthodox view, there is a corner of the canvas reserved for the late 1960s, an interpretation of what might seem the incongruent events of that period that renders them consistent with the rest of the picture. First, the revolt of youth was a combination of self-indulgent, culturally retrograde, repressively desublimatory stuff, like rock 'n' roll and drugs and free love, with serious but self-interested stuff, like opposition to the draft. When the war in Vietnam was over, the cultural dimension was all that remained, and it quickly turned to "me-decade" narcissism.

The civil rights movement, followed by the uprising of the urban black masses, won temporary concessions. When the threat of black violence had been crushed by state force or receded in exhaustion, white society went back to its business, and the black community split into a deteriorating underclass and a co-opted bourgeoisie.

Left Intellectuals

The tale of the left intelligentsia in this America is a sad one quickly told.

Left intellectuals have little or no access to the cultural consciousness of the masses, since this is to be had only through the mass media, which are controlled by organic intellectuals of the ruling class who believe that left intellectuals are either crazy or evil, but in either case won't help sell anything to a philistine audience.

Left intellectuals have little or no hope of participating in the exercise of state power, since this is to be obtained only through a party system that does not include working-class or ideologically left formations.

Insofar as they accept this state of affairs and attempt to build their prestige directly with the masses, circumventing both the media manipulators and the state apparatus, left intellectuals find themselves up against an individualist, materialist, and philistine popular culture that quite simply won't listen to them. Our most characteristic attitude is that of prophets without honor in our own country.

There is nonetheless a collection of left niches, now well enough defined and funded so that at least a few young people can aspire to a career. For example, there are radical social critics (mainly in universities) who despair of exercising any kind of state power, but play Jeremiah against capitalist decadence (for example, Noam Chomsky, Christopher Lasch). There are radical policy intellectuals, "pragmatists" who nudge social democratic state managers and union officials to the left (for example, the staff of the Institute for Policy Studies, Michael Harrington), and outsiders formulating socialist critiques and programs (for example, Barry Bluestone). And there are "social activists" who define themselves as spokespeople for politically marginal groups and causes—minorities, women, the environment, peace, consumers, inhabitants of neighborhoods ignored by city hall, and so forth—that are collectively to play the traditional role of the people, or the proletariat, but are for the moment disenfranchised (for example, Ralph Nader, Acorn). Finally, there are thousands of jobs, teaching sociology or political science or anthropology, in the American system of decentralized mass higher education, far from power but with at least some hope of tenure.

This situation may at first appear to be essentially one of impoverishment and impotence. On second glance, it may be one of privilege, at least in the future. This possibility is bound up with that of a "postindustrial" interpretation of current developments in the West. By this I mean the hypothesis that the economies of these countries will be increasingly white collar, knowledge based, and decentralized, with less and less clear distinction between state and private activity. It also depends on a critique of the implicit contrast with Europe that runs all through and indeed determines this description of the United States.

European Culture

The intellectuals' picture of American culture is very much constructed by way of contrast with Western European culture, rather than with, say, the way of life of Nigeria or Singapore. When we say the United States is materialist, individualist, and philistine, we mean to contrast it with Denmark or Italy.

We think of Denmark and Italy as relatively spiritual, communal, and cultured.

Spirituality seems an odd category for the left, but it is very much what the left cares about. It doesn't (usually) mean religion, but it does mean a humanist ideology of spiritual uplift, in which the living out of political or personal ideals is imagined to count for more and material possessions to count for less than they do in the United States.

The communal dimension means that Europeans don't treat the (native-born) poor as badly, that they react in a less dog-eat-dog way to social crises than Americans, that they maintain networks of mutual support and caring, familial or geographic, that they imagine would be absent across the Atlantic. It also means that the state is expected to supervise all of life (for example, regional planning) in a way it isn't in the United States.

What the higher level of culture means is that these countries own a stock of high-quality cultural objects, continue to produce high-quality objects and performances, appreciate them, subject the masses to media that honor and inculcate high cultural values under the supervision of a cultural elite, all under conditions of contest, such that no political tendency (or, for that matter, the "no-tendency tendency") controls culture in the interest of the status quo.

This picture of European cultural difference seems to be shared by the European intelligentsia of the left, center, and right. It is something that binds Europe together in opposition to America, no matter what the disagreements on other issues. What it amounts to is that European left intellectuals identify with European high culture in a way that is essentially "national" rather than left-wing. They love their historic European way of life and consider it superior to that of the Russian and American outlanders. The culture, such as it is, of these marginal colossi is either third-rate, or their own in the way that Italian architecture and the Italian contents of the Louvre are French: by purchase, exile, or pillage, and by those means alone. American intellectuals tend to share this view of their own culture.

European Politics

European politics, by contrast with American, consists of contention for state power by political parties that represent coherent interest groups each of which also possesses a coherent political ideology with pretensions to universal validity. The question in European politics is: According to what principles shall society be organized? The role of the state is to implement the social decision of this question by restructuring society to correspond to the chosen ideal.

The right, center, and left possess intelligentsias that staff their political parties and their media, and provide government personnel when they exercise state power. They also provide analysis, or "theory," through which political leaders supposedly interpret current events and formulate strategy. The intelligentsias do these things because it could not well be otherwise: the literate, theoretically trained groups within each of the large divisions of humanity naturally take over the intellectual functions, under the direction, of course, of the mass, whether that consists of business people or the working class. The basic difference between parties is substantive: the working-class parties have numbers, utopian vision, and correct theory (usually Marxism), while the capitalist parties have state power, money, and bourgeois economic and political theory.

Hegemony

Europe is the land of Gramsci according to a different model from that of America. In Europe there are commonly held high cultural standards, and the multifarious vulgarities of the United States are just not permitted, my dear. It is true that culture is conservative, but in a quite different way: institutions like the Catholic hierarchy, the civil service, the military, and the part of the media that is owned outright by capitalist interests use their prestige to endorse reactionary values and positions in the affairs of the day. The battle of the left is to create a socialist culture that will, needless to say, be superior to that of the old guard and of the vulgar new money, meaning that it will be popular and progressive but will nonetheless meet the highest standards of the European cultural tradition.

Left Intellectuals

It is often my impression that Western European left intellectuals are mesmerized by three master images:

  the image of the philosopher-king legitimately entitled to exercise power in society by virtue of his possession of *correct theory* (Plato)

  the image of the intellectual as the ally of aristocracy on the side of cultural refinement against the gross, philistine bourgeoisie from which the intelligentsia springs (Molière)

  the image of the left intellectual as wielder of "the lightning of philosophy" that will "strike into the virgin soil of the proletariat" (Marx in *Contribution to the Critique of Hegel's "Philosophy of Right"*)

These images are none the less powerful for the fact that radical intellectuals profess to subordinate themselves and their theories to the masses or to the outcome of democratic processes. Because of the belief that correct theory (philosophy) gives a claim on political power, because of the alliance of intellectuals with the pretensions of aristocracy, and because of the idea that the intellectual aristocrat is the natural leader of the masses, the subordination of the intelligentsia is, to put it mildly, never close to complete. Indeed, to their American counterparts, European left intellectuals, no matter how radical, seem astonishingly elitist.

In this world of images, the state is the intellectuals' instrument for rationally transforming social life at the behest of the people. The only questions of significance are how to get hold of state power and how exactly to deploy it for their purposes. The basic choices are:

> organizing the working majority into mass parties that will dominate representative democratic institutions while playing by their rules
>
> revolutionary direct action, ranging from guerrilla warfare through terrorism to the organization of a revolutionary mass party
>
> some strategic combination of the above

Euroamerica

I have been describing an understanding of Europe and America that has been around for a long time, at least since the late 1940s, and it is the view I grew up with. In the remainder of this essay I present a different view without trying to supersede tradition altogether. The implications are anarcho-syndicalist; the European theorist who seems closest to my perspective is the Foucault of "Two Lectures" (in *Power/Knowledge*, 1980) and of the methodological discussion in the first volume of his *History of Sexuality* (1978).

A first and elemental feature of the postwar picture is that it is out of date in its hopeful presentation of European cultural autonomy. For forty years Western European culture has been Americanizing even more rapidly than the cultural guardians of left and right feared; by the late 1960s it seemed to me, a youth of twenty five, that Europe had simply succumbed to American cultural imperialism. Today it seems plain that the two continents are far more similar than they were then, and it would be difficult to support such once self-evident propositions as that Yankees are individualist, materialist, and philistine by comparison with Old Worlders.

Let me speak plainly: a very large part of European culture is simply American culture, sometimes imposed by commercial force, but just as often eagerly, addictively absorbed. Because we Americans have been so successful at abuse and seduction, it is more important than it once was that Americans and Europeans develop an intelligent understanding of the roots of our now common situation. The old picture of American culture is little better than reactionary today.

European politics are no longer more ideological or more principled than American politics. The European left intelligentsia has no more realistic hope for state power through left-wing parties and no more real chance to use state power rationally to transform society in the direction indicated by utopian ideals and correct theory than does the American left intelligentsia. We are all basically in the same boat, at this moment in history, and no one has a good idea of where we're going. I am not going to argue any of these obviously controversial propositions. I hope that what I have to say about America will be interesting even to those who reject them out of hand.

Postimperial America

Europe has become more like America, but we were not, to start with, as much like Europe as we seemed, so that the outcome of our rapprochement is conjectural.

American culture differs from that of Western Europe because it is the common property of a heterogeneous postimperial society, rather than of a nation in the European sense. To my mind, the relative impotence of the American left intelligentsia derives less from the absence of culture or from the power of capital than from the independence of the American lower orders—the lower-middle, working, and welfare classes and the racial and ethnic minorities. The origin of that independence is in the nineteenth-century history of the United States as a European colony that happened to be run by the settlers rather than from a metropole.

There are two familiar frameworks for understanding America. One is that of "equal opportunity," the "melting pot," and "everyone in America is or aspires soon to be middle class." The emphasis is on groups in motion from a highly particular ethnic past that differentiates them from everyone else in the society into a more abstract, deracinated, but also modernized American present. The revaluation of ethnicity among the intelligentsia in the last two decades is more an expression of this understanding of America than a contradiction of it—reaffirming it by fighting it strictly on its own terms.

The other framework is that of class, within which we pursue a left-wing critique of capitalist mass society focusing on the western shore of the North Atlantic. Class divisions mean divisions along economic lines, whether in the orthodox mode of "relation to the means of production" or in the sociological mode of "education, income, occupation." The critical premise is that under the surface, behind the apparent hegemony of bourgeois values, there is the dirty secret that the United States is no less riven by class than is Western Europe.

I am proposing that we try to understand the United States and the role of its intelligentsia in yet another way—by analogy to Third World societies constructed in the eighteenth and nineteenth centuries by the European empires.

When we Americans focus on our former colonial status, we sometimes compare ourselves to Argentina and Australia, European "settler" societies that wiped out or marginalized their "small" indigenous populations. But there are two other colonial types that are helpful as analogies in contrasting the United States and Western Europe: the slave societies based on race and racist ideology (Haiti, Jamaica, Brazil), and "composite" societies in which, after conquering a set of contiguous tribes or peoples engaged mainly in agriculture and handicrafts, the European power joined them together in a colony and then encouraged non-European migrants from other cultures to move in to perform economic activities other than farming (Malaya, Madagascar). The United States is a former slave society of the type in which slavery is based on race, and in which there is still mass racial prejudice. It seems unreal to analyze American race relations as though the nation were either a "melting pot" or a straightforward class society with divisions based on economic categories. The culture of a former slave society is bound to be a hybrid in a different way from that in which all cultures are hybrid, with its own special set of privilegings and secret influences.

For example, ethnic divisions among American whites are always understood in the context of a more fundamental division between whites and blacks, and American ethnicity is thereby surely constituted differently from European. (The French are sometimes a different "race" from the Italians, the northern Italians from the southern.) The image of "white woman" in the United States differs from that of "white woman" in Western Europe in ways that are perhaps traceable to the coexistence, in the white American mind, of the white woman with a contrasting slave-descended black woman stereotyped as mammy, maid, or prostitute.

The history of slavery, continuing racial discrimination, and the deindustrialization of the last twenty years have produced a black underclass numbering in the millions. The existence of such a group, massively "different" from mainstream America not in one way—color—but in all the ways of an oppressed culture, reinforces the acute sense of race that helped constitute the group in the first place.

The simultaneous emergence of a large black working class and a substantial black bourgeoisie, integrated with whites at work and living outside the ghetto but socially segregated (and self-segregated), creates new political and cultural possibilities. But what is happening is not reducible to anything as simple as the assimilation of blacks to white society and may, if anything, increase tensions between working-class whites and nonunderclass blacks.

In a former slave society thus organized, the intelligentsia of the "master" race, whether reactionary or progressive, is unlikely to occupy the same position of taken-for-granted legitimate authority vis-à-vis any of the groupings of slave-descended people that the Norwegian intelligentsia, say, occupies in relation to the Norwegian masses. The black underclass, in particular, may be a "natural" constituency for white radical intellectuals, but it is one they approach with little or no claim to be taken seriously as political allies, let alone political leaders.

Moreover, it is easy to see why black intellectuals in a former slave society with a vast, persistently racially prejudiced white majority might occupy an ambiguous, uneasy position vis-à-vis white intellectuals and white people in general, as well as in relation to the black underclass. They are likely to draw the issues of cultural nationalism and political empowerment differently from intellectuals allied with the working class in a society with a feudal past, even though both groups live in class societies that have some equality of opportunity.

The view of the American black community as living in an "internal colony" has been familiar on the (white) American left for about twenty years now, along with a common sense that white radical intellectuals should "organize their own communities" and then engage in coalition politics with groups led by blacks. This approach has something to offer the analysis of the relations between radical intellectuals and other groups in American society.

Managed Heterogeneity

American national mythology emphasizes the agency of immigrant groups, their *choice* to come here rather than accept religious persecution (Puritans, Jews, Armenians), famine (the Irish), or political defeat (refugees of 1848, Cubans, Vietnamese). It emphasizes that the "search for a better life" in America is social as well as economic.

There is a lot of truth in the myth. But it leaves out the agency of the American and Western European ruling classes that *chose* to put capital together with labor in some places rather than others, framed laws that permitted or encouraged immigrant agency, invested in ocean transportation and brand-new slums, paid taxes to build Ellis Island. Through these policies, the nineteenth-century American elite treated the United States as a resource to be developed through intelligent population management, much in the way the European powers treated their colonies.

The relations between American intellectuals and the "masses" are filtered through ethnic differences that have roots in this "market for immigrants" as well as in the slave market. The United States is one of those societies in which the current racial/ethnic mix is what it is in part because in the nineteenth and early twentieth centuries English, French, Belgian, Dutch, German, and American capitalists and state managers took to intentionally moving large populations from racially homogeneous areas with a "labor surplus" (created by the world imperial economy) into mixed areas with labor shortages of various kinds.

Unlike the Byzantine Empire, which forcibly transplanted whole "nations" from one part of Asia Minor to another, the European empires moved people mainly by offering them jobs for more money than they could earn "at home." Then they supported them socially and politically in colonial enclaves under a European commercial and planter elite (the famous "divide and conquer" formula).

I am thinking particularly of Burma, where the British encouraged the settlement of Indians and Chinese along with the ethnic Burmese and the indigenous hill people; of British Guyana, where Indians, blacks, native Americans, and Hispanics coexist; or of Kenya, where there were, before independence, Arabs, Indians, Africans, and white English settlers. Hawaii, with its Hawaiian, Japanese, Chinese, and "white" populations is another example, one that is useful in understanding the continental United States.

We can roughly contrast these composite societies with those of "Great" Britain or the Russian empire, where the rulers hooked up more or less homogeneous territorial groups into a heterogeneous totality that was first a geographic collection and then a "nation." And we can also contrast them with colonies in which a settler group "peoples a new land."

Many of the European immigrants to America fit the mold of settlers, since they arrived hoping to become small or large farmers (yeomen rather than peasants), businessmen, or professionals, bringing at least an early modern form of Western European culture based on education and "liberal" values. These are the northern Europeans from the industrializing imperial countries that were long favored by American immigration laws.

But at one time or another in their history many American immigrant groups have looked more like the groups in the composite colonial societies (or like the Third World "guest workers" in Western Europe today)—they have lived in the United States thinking of themselves as "abroad" or "overseas" to make money, sending a lot of their earnings home and thinking of going home altogether as soon as possible. In the United States, and in the composite societies where they have not been expelled by nationalist independence movements, they have gone through the drama of realizing they will never go home, that home is nowhere, that home is the new land.

At one time or another many Chinese, Japanese, Puerto Rican, and Mexican immigrants have fitted this mold:—here for economic reasons, retaining ties to reference cultures to the West or South, with their own languages and current history, cultures that remain real alternatives to Americanization. The status of Asians and Hispanics is complicated by the facts of "free" migration (no enslavement) and racial prejudice, facts both differentiating them from and linking them with blacks. Neither the rhetoric of abstract Americanism nor that of class captures the reality of Hispanic Los Angeles.

Many European immigrants came from the nonmodern, nonindustrial, nonimperial periphery of nineteenth-century Europe, from peasant societies experiencing labor surpluses. They were Irish, southern Europeans, Slavs and Jews from Eastern Europe, looking for unskilled industrial work in large cities or for small commercial opportunities. They were initially more like the Indian dockworkers of Rangoon than like the German settlers of the Upper Midwest.

European migrants from the periphery, and many of their descendants, still differ from the Yankee/northern Europeans in their consciousness of America in that they don't see themselves as just "owning" it. They have "made it" in America, in their own image of themselves, against enormous odds—defined by their position in Europe before emigration.

And they differ from Asians and Hispanics in their self-definition as white, assimilated, and entitled to their *positions acquises,* ambiguously based on merit and group solidarity in the struggle for upward mobility, in institutions like schools, labor unions, state bureaucracies, and small business. Here the best analogy may be to the *colons* of Algeria (only some of whom were French) or to the Afrikaners of South Africa.

New York—and London—are closer to modern Istanbul, with its collection of ex-Byzantine, ex-Ottoman peoples in enclaves, than to Paris, Rome, or Berlin.

Avant-Garde Rich Peasant

The idea that "the population of the United States is more racially and ethnically heterogeneous than that of Denmark or France" is often invoked to explain why social welfare policies that have worked in Western Europe to confine the worst kinds of nineteenth-century urban squalor to foreign guest workers haven't worked or won't work in the United States. The explanation sometimes has a racist presupposition (heterogeneity equals blacks, and "blacks are hopeless"), but it also sometimes presupposes that there is less class solidarity within the lower groups of American society because of heterogeneity, and more willingness among the white majority to allow the black poor to go to the wall.

But ethnic and racial heterogeneity, understood as a specifically postimperial phenomenon, is also culturally important. Consider American advertising, television, popular magazines and comic books, the Edsel, roadside diners and neon signs, evangelical and fundamentalist religion, the proliferation of plastic objects, asbestos and aluminum siding, hot dogs, Wonder Bread, fast food and fast French food, *Animal House,* "The Dating Game," and commercial dating services. All these in their diversity reflect a dramatic collision of African, Asian, Latin American, and southern and eastern European *peasant and folk* cultures with the stunning material possibilities of the New World industrial revolution.

The outcome of this collision is the popular culture of American modernity, which was originally one of a kind, the only one in which *the decision what to do with extravagant new wealth was largely unconstrained by the power of an existing national high cultural elite that could shape collision along "respectable" lines.* One result is a dramatic difference in the experience of American as opposed to European intellectuals, including radical intellectuals.

Cultural Hegemony of the European Intelligentsia

Spanish or Austrian intellectuals, left, right, and center, relate to the Spanish or Austrian working and lower-middle classes as members of a common culture; the intellectuals happen to possess superior credentials according to a standard of superiority that is racially, nationally, and above all historically shared. They also exercise, whatever their particular origins, an entitlement to deference that comes from centuries of intelligentsia association with aristocratic and then bourgeois class rule.

The European cultural elite has deployed this cultural (as opposed to political) authority to shape the use of industrial power over nature along lines that are continuous with earlier forms of material and social life. The modern working classes live differently and act differently from the European peasantries of the late Middle Ages and the early modern period, but the actual content of those differences seems to have been as heavily influenced by the higher orders—the aristocracies, the bourgeoisie, and the intelligentsia—as by autonomous peasant or worker choice in the uses of wealth.

Of course, European intellectuals have sometimes chosen to define themselves as organic intellectuals of the working class, whether through the vehicle of Marxism or Christian socialism. When they do so, they bring with them to their new allegiance the limited but real Weberian "traditional authority" that their culture has assigned—across class lines—to the roles of artist and thinker, along with the personal attributes associated with their class origins.

The (presumptive) class superiority and prestigious specialized function of the intelligentsia are sources of power over the working class in the shaping of radical projects. But they are also an aspect of the general power of the cultural elite that disciplines each European society to conform to national norms of good taste in the choice of household objects, legitimates existing standards of high culture, reproduces traditional forms from etiquette to religious ritual, in short preserves the cultural hegemony of the intelligentsia (as opposed to the political hegemony of the bourgeoisie).

I have overdrawn this picture for effect. A more nuanced version would emphasize the relative autonomy of the European working classes manifested in, say, Methodist religion, the music hall, the trade union movement, the Paris Commune, or the struggle of household servants to define the daily conditions of their existence. Moreover, class differences between radical intellectuals and workers create distance and resentment within the left, rather than just empowering some over others.

The American Intelligentsia as an Ethnic Group

The English-speaking white settlers of eighteenth- and early nineteenth-century North America had an organic intelligentsia on a similar model. It too had "aristocratic" pretensions based on an unbroken tradition of elite culture, and put forward a claim to political leadership based on its possession of correct theory. It traced itself back both to middle- or upper-class cultural figures and to religious-dissident or political-dissident yeoman or artisan (not peasant) ancestors in England and Scotland. This group was well represented among the Founding Fathers, as it had been in the early leadership of the Massachusetts Bay and Virginia colonies.

The political and business power of the pre-Civil War gentry, the old American ruling class to which the intelligentsia was attached, did not survive the combination of immigration and industrialization. Or rather, betrayed by their own classical liberal laissez-faire ideology, the gentry let new wealth submerge them and then absorb them piecemeal into a new economic elite.

The "native" intelligentsia did better at survival, taking on new groups and ideas without ever altogether losing its English flavor. Today it is part (*perhaps* the dominant part) of the modern American white intelligentsia, which was formed by actual intermarriage as well as by intellectual crossbreeding with northern European and Jewish refugee intelligentsias, and by recruitment of upwardly mobile ethnics (many also Jewish) through the educational system.

It was less successful at the job it chose, or was assigned, of nationalizing the immigrants, working always at a disadvantage, with the tools of the trade—Reason, the prestige of culture, and traditional association with aristocracy. New Americans imitate and aspire, to a certain extent, across America's rigid color line and more fluid ethnic lines, but they also ignore what doesn't appeal to them, and change everything for the worse, from the point of view of the old elite, even when they are trying as hard as they can to assimilate. The American intelligentsia has never come close to occupying, in relation to the postimperial American masses, a role like that of its European counterparts.

There are three reasons for this. First, the intelligentsia formed in the way described has no "traditional" claim to authority over the postimperial racial and ethnic subgroups of the United States, since it is racially and ethnically "other" to those subgroups. Second, the postimperial subgroups came from cultures that did not have intelligentsias, in the Western or northern European nineteenth-century sense, at the time they emigrated. (Some of them came from countries like Ireland and Greece that were then developing intelligentsias through nationalist struggle against the empires.)

Third, the emigrants left their elites behind. No mandarins or Shinto priests came to the West Coast to build railways; neither the ancient landowning families of southern Italy nor the literary/political upper-middle classes of the north figured prominently on Mulberry Street. When peasant or small trader groups reconstituted themselves as "ethnics" in the United States they did so in the mode of *bricolage,* adapting social forms from their home countries to possibilities of social mobility and cultural innovation that had been anathema there. Irish America bears only an oblique relationship to Irish Ireland.

The slavers and the slave owners quite deliberately brought Africans to America with as little cultural baggage as possible. The conditions of slavery made it impossible for blacks to reestablish their specific, highly diverse African social patterns here (though no one could stop them from bringing African culture, reconstituting it, and weaving it into everything American). The structures of prestige and political authority of the modern black community are a new product—there is no "traditional" African elite in the United States that can trace its origins back beyond slavery.

These diverse "decapitated" American communities were not just waiting to hook up as subordinates to the early nineteenth-century political class, bourgeoisie and intelligentsia, to form a new nation on the European model. They generated their own business, political, literary, and social elites at a furious rate, playing the game by mixed rules, inventing hierarchies that dealt with but did not fuse with preexisting structures.

In spite of recruitment across racial and ethnic lines, the intelligentsia in the United States is closer to an ethnic group than to a specialized, hegemonic corps within the division of labor of class society. Relations of the racial and ethnic minorities with the intelligentsia are partly relations of "mass" to "elite," with all the overtones of subordination within a unified cultural matrix, and partly relations across cultures like those of the heterogeneous colonial societies described above.

Functions of the Postimperial Intelligentsia

It is not that the cultural elite of the United States can find no role in what was once "its own" society. It's just that the role is more postimperial than European.

Here are four areas of intelligentsia endeavor that are time-consuming and may keep the wolf from the door:

There is the preservation of a postimperial old settler enclave amidst the alien flood, with the result that Harvard, the Public

Broadcasting Service, the National Endowment for the Humanities, and the *New York Times* sometimes seem like the decolonized polo and tennis clubs in Kuala Lumpur or Cotonou, where civil servants, planters, and merchants once gathered behind "White Only" signs.

There is a *mission civilatrice* (like that of the school system and publishing industry of the French empire), teaching what was once called "American" and is now called "mainstream" culture, as a second language, to those willing and able to pay for assimilation. (In this role the intelligentsia often slides down the social scale into a mere "service" rather than "culture maven" capacity.)

There is "expertise": getting "access" to state managers and public opinion by appealing to science while denying any political or cultural agenda that might conflict with the norm of American pluralism, and exercising great covert power for good or evil through the subterfuge, indeed reproducing in a disguised form the very dominance of class- and culture-specific values that ideology disavows.

There is the life of the cultural *bazaari* peddling absolutely anything that will sell to the enormous mass of would-be upwardly mobile first-, second-, and third-generation postimperial immigrant subgroups. Bazaari work in Hollywood, the music business, commercial television, Madison Avenue, the self-improvement industry, Fashion Avenue, home design and home decorating, the design of recreation vehicles and power boats, and mail-order catalogues everywhere.

Aesthetic Modernism in the Culture Market

It is of the *bazaari* role, shared with inventive entrepreneurs with no high-toned background at all (Cecil B. DeMille, John DeLorean, Crazy Eddie), that the American intelligentsia should be most proud. There are sinister antecedents in the textile and hardware industries of Manchester and Sheffield that created new designs and new products for the colonial markets of the British Empire, destroying native handicrafts all over the world. But the results in America were more benign: a dose of anarchy in the culture market led to a limited triumph of aesthetic modernism, rather than to the one-dimensionality or repressive desublimation that was all the Frankfurt School could see.

The influence of aesthetic modernism on the landscape, the machines, the appurtenances of daily life, from Coke bottles and paper plates to skyscrapers and picture windows, Miami Beach and Las Vegas, is *partly* explained by mundane factors like efficiency in creating a lot of new stuff fast. But the particular forms of the American cult of the new and up-to-date flow also from the conditions of postimperial postpeasant heterogeneity.

There was not much that was genuinely democratic about the aesthetic modernist turn, since millionaires and big capital played the major role, served in the quest for profit by an army of intensely middle-class culture workers. But they were philistine millionaires and big capitalists, selling to a deracinated mass audience. The culture workers lost power as European elite standards receded before the buck, and gained it as there was less and less to inhibit them from gambling that something truly wacky would get backing and sell millions.

The independence of the lower-middle, working, and welfare classes, their émigré freedom from any integrated, hierarchical cultural matrix, made them open to the experimental marketing strategies of new companies with new designs. The notorious conservatism of folk culture was shattered by the very fact of moving to America. When people began to have money, they "bought whatever they wanted" in a way they never would have in the old country, and their children lack even the memory of those constraints.

The result was not that the diverse forms of peasant taste repressed in the hierarchical societies of Europe or Asia or Latin America could finally express themselves through the free market. A Barbie doll is not a shadow puppet liberated from traditional society. The immigrants had no access to the production of American culture except through the medium of a national intelligentsia that was itself an internally diverse rival ethnic group.

My point is that the army of mainly Yankee, northern European, and Jewish culture workers were dealing with a new kind of mass market—one not bound together by any single national culture, one without traditional elites even within its subcultures. The *bazaari* had to innovate because there was nothing "old" that they could expect to have appeal beyond a fraction of the market. When they found their commitment to modernism and an interest in the most sophisticated aesthetic happenings in other places, they could sell the masses Fiestaware, the *art moderne* moviehouse facade, and the Airstream aluminum trailer, if only they made them, by European elite standards, "loud" and "tacky" enough.

Exceptionalist Interlude

What we got, putting peasant and folk culture together with economic growth and aesthetic modernism, was very often horrible. There is much truth to the view that the Americans have simply wasted the part of their natural heritage they haven't desecrated, and made tragically little of their now-shrinking wealth. But the result is also sometimes thrilling. By contrast, European low culture seems to have been dead since the early nineteenth century.

For example, compare German or English with American commercial television. The Yankee product is vulgar, raw, repetitive, extravagant, dead as a doornail for hours at a time, but also bizarre, potentially surprising, genuinely nonelite even though mainly constructed by forsworn elitists pandering to what they regard as the bad taste of the client masses. American television is also visually inventive (for example, the rise of the video art form, its infiltration of the spot advertisement) and full of odd, endlessly evolving faddish beauty.

European television ("Benny Hill" to the contrary notwithstanding) is just plain boring. The reason, I imagine, is that high cultural standards, embodied in national cultural elites who possess real power through state control of broadcasting, simply will not permit the explosion of experimental profit-motivated vulgarity that is the institutional form for progress. Afro-Anglo-American rock 'n' roll is another epochal event that could happen only when the cultural establishment had lost control of the record industry to the vulgarians.

The Intelligentsia Critique of Mass Culture

Both the horrible and the thrilling represent the first large-scale attempt to put aesthetic modernism into practice. Because it was happening only in the United States, it seemed peculiarly American. Because it was driven by postimperial nouveau wealth, it *was* peculiarly American.

But much of the European and the American self-hating critique of this culture is just the traditional aristo-symp intelligentsia critique of peasants everywhere. Individualism, materialism, and philistinism are Molièrean categories with which to flay the vulgar parvenu not far enough removed from the windowless cottage of his ancestors.

A great deal more of the critique is aimed at aesthetic modernism itself, rather than at anything specific to our shores. The Western intelligentsia in general, and the left in particular, has been hostile to its own avant-garde (when the intelligentsia fails to react in this way, the avant-garde has to invent something new to "blow their minds"). Since the avant-garde has exercised more influence over popular culture in the United States than anywhere else, a traditionalist (that is, aesthetically reactionary) left intelligentsia finds American culture particularly hard to stomach.

In spite of the critique, or in blissful ignorance of it, the American fusion of independent mass taste with modernist aesthetics has "taken off." The younger generation of intellectuals tends to see it as an organic national style, with its own internal dynamism, to be hated and appreciated in its particulars rather than deplored as a whole. What was once a crude "pidgin" mixture of two wildly disparate cultural languages (peasant and avant-garde) has become a "creole," a language in its own right, capable of developing, indeed sure to develop in ways that will involve and surprise us.

The lesson of this experiment for Western Europe, shifting uneasily in the bonds of American cultural imperialism, cannot be that tradition is best. An aesthetic tradition that has become an "option" is just antiquarian bad taste, as the decimated folk cultures of the Third World attest. The Europeans will have to make something new of bits and pieces that now include modernism itself.

A Left Intelligentsia Program

If the relationship between the American intelligentsia and the American "masses" is at all as I've been describing it, it was never likely that radical intellectuals in the United States could live the

European dream. We simply lack the base of traditional authority that has been the hidden underpinning for the influence of thinkers on European radical politics.

Of course, there is more to it than that. The American state does not exist in the sense that the national states of Europe exist, because of the fragmentation of formal political power not just through federalism but also through municipal home rule and regional administration by autonomous agencies. And the American working class seems obviously ill adapted to the role of "virgin soil" for the wielders of the "lightning of philosophy."

It seems unlikely that radical intellectuals will exercise significant power through representative democratic institutions (above the municipal level), and more unlikely that they will succeed at or even be drawn to revolutionary direct action. It seems to me that, in America at least, we would do better to take seriously the injunction of the 1960s to "organize your own people." By this I mean that *radical intellectuals should entertain the project of radicalizing the intelligentsia by splitting its soft liberal center into opposed left and right groups.*

Workplace Organizing

The American intelligentsia is numerically enormous, partly because the United States is such a big country, and partly because the educational system is much larger in relation to the economy as a whole than it is anywhere in Europe. There are many millions of intellectual workers. Within occupational subcategories, we have multitudes where European countries have coteries. (For example, there are about 5,000 law teachers in the United States.) This intellectual mass is just too big to be elite. But it is a significant social and economic force in the society as a whole, in the mode, say, of the unions or the financial sector.

The sheer numerical size, nonelite social character, and decentralized work organization of the intelligentsia favor the creation of small autonomous radical networks in workplaces and make it a potentially significant base for dissident politics. The strong tradition of voluntary groups in the United States provides a kind of human capital for the uncentered politics that follows the demise of the industrial-state order.

The first implication of this approach is that radical intellectuals should learn the skill of workplace organizing. Most of us have had experience of successful autonomous radical activity through the single-issue petition, fundraiser, or newspaper ad, putting together conferences or putting out publications for a left audience, or perhaps contributing to the issues staff of a political campaign.

What I am proposing is closer to, indeed an extension of, the strategy of forming feminist and minority networks within professional subgroups, and black or women's caucuses in professional associations. But it is still different from these forms of activity, and difficult in its own particular way. It is a matter of conjecture whether radical intellectuals could succeed at it even if they were willing to try.

Workplace organizing involves long-term, multi-issue, emotionally complex relationships, both with allies and with opponents. Single-issue organizers and networkers pull mutually sympathetic intellectuals from their different contexts for a short time, and can treat opponents as emotionally distant targets for rhetoric. In the workplace, opponents are dangerous colleagues toward whom one feels ambivalent. There is dependence as well as confrontation. Allies are more like family members, with whom you have to work things out against the background of long involuntary association and mutual critique, than like "signers" or "people who agree with our position on *x*."

For all its difficulty, workplace organizing has a particular claim on us, just because it involves the detailed transformation of everyday life situations. The mobilization it induces, even if it involves small numbers, may be deep and enduring in a way in which reform through state action may not. But beyond that possible practical advantage, it reflects the underlying radical commitment to the humanization of work.

If we already knew how to humanize work, it might be plausible to argue for applying our knowledge first and most urgently to the lives of the "masses." But we don't know how to do it—either how to organize even ourselves for self-determination, or how to determine ourselves once organized. It seems fair to ask a person who aspires to be the "brains of the people" in the project of radical change to do at least an apprenticeship in his or her own backyard before offering us enlightenment.

Office Politics Are Real Politics

A first reaction to this proposal is likely to be that the material interests of intellectuals are so far divergent from those of the oppressed and exploited groups in American society that it is utopian to expect them ever to ally with those groups. I have two responses.

First, the proposal is to try to split the intelligentsia along a left–right axis, not to convert it en masse. Ideal or cultural interests and commitments, as opposed to material ones, play a real role in the life of this group. How the material and ideal or cultural interests intersect with politics cannot be determined a priori through a class analysis that never worked and that practically no one even claims to understand anymore. The work of framing issues, interpreting situations, and organizing people *might* split the mushy center.

Second, the interests of the intelligentsia are harder to determine than traditional class analysis suggests. It is in many ways an autonomous corps with interests that diverge from those of all other groups, even while the interests of particular members are in internal conflict. If it is true that the world is moving into some kind of postindustrial age, it will become harder and harder to argue that any group of this size is a totality occupying a structural position either of alliance or of inevitable opposition vis-à-vis any other group or groups.

High tech, the decentralization of industry, the blurring of the distinction between service and manual work and of the class lines based on it, and the effacement of the membrane between state and civil society will make politics more and more diffuse and pluralist. Whatever can be said at the very abstract level of class material interests, the issues confronting cultural workers will continue to converge with those facing other workers in all sectors of the economy, so that alliances will be possible, though not in any sense inevitable.

Quite apart from the issue of material interests, the idea that organizing the intelligentsia could be a (not *the*) central activity of radical intellectuals seems to strike most radical intellectuals as elitist and self-indulgent. The intelligentsia looks parasitic and privileged by comparison with Central American refugees or the black underclass, and the workplace and "lifestyle" issues that preoccupy it look frivolous compared to Reaganomics or the nuclear freeze.

This reaction seems to me a hangover of the traditional left European understanding of the political role of the intelligentsia. For white male radicals especially, it has been easy within that framework to explain why, over the last fifteen years, we have done very little actual organizing of *any* social group (contrast the women's movement or the Jesse Jackson campaigns). We have taken the attitude either that "the times are not right" or that what we have to offer is "thought," which will find agents to put it into practice if it is theoretically sound.

When our "thought" is directed to the overall structure of late capitalism or to the problems of the groups most oppressed by late capitalism, we have felt politically correct, at least to the extent it is possible to be politically correct in a compromised class position in a time of mass quiescence. This attitude derives from the idea that a radical intelligentsia is the "theory" part of a mass movement of the left.

When we work on issues, it is important to us that they be issues that transcend intelligentsia interests, even though we find ourselves involved *only* with other intellectuals, just because working on issues is the closest we come to involvement in the political life of the country. It is important to be able to imagine that we would be playing the (European intelligentsia) role of acquiring state power to transform civil society according to a rational plan, if only the masses had the correct consciousness that would bring them into our camp.

Radical intellectuals who adopt these attitudes often seem to have split themselves into three parts: theorists of the left, co-opted participants in the workplace and family arrangements of the dominant liberal culture, and issues activists networking with other intellectuals outside the workplace and also outside formal political institutions. I am arguing that not only the personal but also the professional is political, and that we should make intelligentsia workplace struggles a central part of our political lives.

This strategy involves the risk that to the very extent that the left was successful in organizing intellectuals, it would slide into parochialism. For this reason, the strategy looks more problematic, to me as an outsider, for feminist and minority intellectuals than for white males. Feminist and minority intellectuals have more substantial connections, to the women's movement and the minority communities, than white male intellectuals have to the working class or any other group outside the intelligentsia.

I am not suggesting that we abandon any current strategy that works, but rather that we look for a new source of energy. Workplace organizing might build a left intelligentsia of a kind that has existed neither in America nor in Europe, one that would be capable of acting as a coalition partner with other organizing groups, rather than as theorist or tragic chorus. We could do more for the working class and for the various oppressed minorities of the United States if we converted a substantial fraction of the liberal center to radicalism than we will ever be able to do within the European intelligentsia model.

American Intelligentsia Issues

Organizing around workplace and lifestyle issues of the intelligentsia doesn't mean putting the choice between brie and hot goat cheese at the center of politics. We should look to the experience of the intelligentsia as a "quasiethnic group" in American society, and *see if the particular experiences that set that group apart from other groups provide the starting point of a left-wing organizing strategy.*

Like the culture of the masses, that of the intelligentsia is more independent, and less an absence of Europe or an imposition by capital, than the orthodox view allows. It has at least three traits, each with associated issues.

Humanist Politics

The intelligentsia has been strongly influenced by Freudian psychoanalytic ideas, by progressive education, and, since the 1960s, by humanistic, third-force psychology. Everyday life in left culture, in particular, is saturated with "process orientation." T-groups, touchy-feely, Esalen to EST, and a thousand university-level training programs for social workers and others in "human services" have created a vocabulary, numerous conflicting styles, a kind of psychologistic consciousness that does not yet exist in Western Europe except on the fringes of the Green movement.

This development has political meaning, dramatically reinforcing the antisectarian, freewheeling, anarchodemocratic, egalitarian, small-group-oriented, improvisational strand in American left politics. It has also made it more respectable for middle-class progressives to focus on organizing themselves and on developing internal group processes, rather than on joining or trying to create working-class organizations. The psychologistic style infuriates or just repels more-traditional American intellectuals, whether of the left or right.

The workplaces of the intelligentsia are authoritarian, hierarchical, and repressive when judged by the standards that psychological humanism sets for group life. Most of the supervisors and workers in universities, hospitals, newspapers, and the like see themselves as subscribing to a vague list of humanist values that they know might be but never have been applied in their offices. It is often puzzling that there can be such consensus, however vague, and so little practical reflection of the consensus where it seems most relevant.

This is the first set of issues for intelligentsia workplace organizing. Taking humanism seriously within a formally liberal but actually repressive workplace can split the workforce along a new axis. Many who have quite sincerely subscribed to liberal or humanist platitudes will find they don't like them at all when put into practice. Others will discover themselves as left political activists.

The next step is the formation of left minorities and the exercise of some real power in office politics, as opposed to the current situation of radical grumbling at the fringe. The slogan should be not "'68," the failed revolutionary moment, but "the '60s," a diffuse cultural rebellion with a thousand specific implications for daily life in the '90s.

Gender Politics

One of the things middle-class white male intellectuals believed most strongly in the 1950s and early 1960s was that Europeans were more sexually "advanced" than Americans. This meant more premarital and especially more casual sex; toleration of extramarital affairs; less censorship of sexually explicit books and films; skinny-dipping and nude sunbathing; more open, less tacky prostitution; and the Folies Bergères.

Europeans had a critique of American culture as uptight Protestant, but also as child-centered and Momist. American women were innocent, energetic, wholesome, but also intrusive and dominant if given half a chance. American middle-class men had renounced the fundamental male prerogatives of the café, the gang of guys, and the mistress in exchange for the gilded cage of suburbia.

That seems a very long time ago. Middle-class white male intellectuals have undergone an experience—traumatic, transcendent, boring, epochal—of sexual liberation followed by white middle-class feminist revolt that has left us confused and uneasy at home but distinctly supercilious abroad. The strongest and most successful social movement, cultural critique, and emerging political force in the United States is the women's movement. (There are brilliant feminist theorists in Western Europe, and they have begun to influence the American scene. But my impression is that feminism has barely begun to disrupt daily life there—even that of the intelligentsia—and that in this respect Western Europe is simply a primitive milieu.)

The workplaces of the intelligentsia have always been full of gender politics, played out between men and women (it used to be bosses and secretaries), men and men, and women and women. But the issues have changed as more and more women have moved into professional and managerial positions. There are the almost invisible forms of discrimination against women at the top, and also changes in the polymorphous ways we sexualize our workplaces as men and women try to operate as equals within supposedly merit-based formal hierarchies.

Gender is grained so finely into the slightest of interactions that it would be impossible, even if it were desirable, to deliberately eliminate all its effects. But I think we should accept the radical feminist insight that our culture not only inculcates but also eroticizes the submission of women to the power of men. Male and female identity are socially constituted so that sexual pleasure reinforces gender hierarchy in everyday workplace relations, no matter how much we emphasize legal and institutional and even personal "gender blindness." When eroticizing domination and submission interferes with women's exercising power as equals, we should fight it, the way we fight other politically incorrect emotions, like, say, the desire for job security at any cost.

The project of organizing the intelligentsia is also that of figuring out how people of different genders and sexual preferences can cooperate *during* and *after* the moment of undiluted, intense, antagonistic otherness in which these patterns of subordination are fully acknowledged. It is not for straight white men to theorize or direct the rage against us (rage that is in no way less valid because we identify ourselves as leftists). The point (for us) is to learn to suffer it, control our inevitable counterrage without groveling, change to the extent we can, and see what happens when the next gender issue cries out for coalition.

The hope is that post-rage, post-change coalitions will sometimes be intimations of what it would be like to have less of our being controlled in spite of ourselves by our histories as superiors and subordinates.

Race Politics

In the 1950s and early 1960s many intellectuals—white and black—believed that Western Europe was a place without deep race prejudice. That seems a long time ago. It no longer seems likely that there is or will soon be any place that is free of racism in the way we imagined Western Europe might be.

In the United States the white left is haunted by the memory of the early civil rights movement, the passionate feelings of self-discovery and of rejection when black pride and black nationalism emerged in the late 1960s, and something between unease and anguish that twenty years later the issue of race sits just out of view in every discussion of social policy, every utopian discussion, every attempt at organizing *anything*. (In Europe the best thing that could happen might be for guest workers to shake white society to its foundations.)

At the rhetorical level, the institutions in which intellectuals work have embraced affirmative action more explicitly and more insistently than any other part of the economy. But the managers and much of the white staff of those institutions also see the goal of increasing minority presence as in direct conflict with the meritocratic principles that justify their place in the larger society. Common or garden racial prejudice is formally rejected at every level, but discrimination still operates in myriad ways often invisible to whites, and institutional racism reigns supreme.

The result is hypocrisy, with lots of individual injustices to minority students, applicants for intellectual jobs, candidates for promotion, authors seeking publication, would-be institutional managers. An intelligentsia workplace-organizing strategy must focus on these issues, and some success in creating coalitions across race lines within the intelligentsia seems a fair test for any claim by white radicals to participate in coalitions with black, Hispanic, or Asian masses.

Ending

We can form coalitions through, not in spite of, the acknowledgment of a permanent condition of alienation within which there is no transcendent theory. There are only the theories that particular people, diffusely grouped according to what they experience as irreducible in themselves, are making as tools in the undefinable project of liberation and community. This white male Talk aspired to be more than Chat but less than Thought, however paradoxical such an ideal may be. The left values associated with the particular historical experience of the American intelligentsia are not so much things we know to be true that the authoritarian, sexist, and racist larger culture refuses to learn from us, as things to work on at work tomorrow.

The radical intelligentsia I have been describing is one of the endless plurality of cultural subgroups in the United States rather than an organically powerful element in the class hierarchy. Our hope lies not in philosopher-kingship nor indeed in any kind of state power, but in organizing our own millions with a view to linking up one day with other organizing millions. In the interim, we must make do with the sense of loss and sense of gain that come of putting aside the lightning of philosophy to take tea with the *bourgeois gentilhomme.*

2

A Cultural Pluralist Case for Affirmative Action in Legal Academia

This essay is about affirmative action in legal academia. It argues for a large expansion of our current commitment to cultural diversity on the ground that law schools are political institutions. For that reason, they should abide by the general democratic principle that people should be represented in institutions that have power over their lives. Further, large-scale affirmative action would improve the quality and increase the value of legal scholarship.

My goal is to develop in the specific context of law school affirmative action the conception of "race consciousness" that Gary Peller describes and advocates in a 1990 article in the *Duke Law Journal*.[1] We need to be able to talk about the political and cultural relations of the various groups that compose our society without falling into racialism, essentialism, or a concept of the "nation" tied to the idea of sovereignty. We need to conceptualize groups in a "postmodern" way,[2] recognizing their reality in our lives without losing sight of the partial, unstable, contradictory character of group existence.

I present my argument in the form of a dialogue with our society's dominant way of understanding race and merit in academia, which I call "color-blind meritocratic fundamentalism." I use Randall Kennedy's article "Racial Critiques of Legal Academia"[3] as principal representative of this point of view. Throughout, I will be responding to Kennedy's general understanding of how we should organize legal academic life in a situation of racial and cultural division, rather than to his specific attacks on works of race-conscious scholarship.

I think the articles Kennedy discusses,[4] along with others in the genre of Critical Race Theory,[5] represent the most exciting recent development in American legal scholarship. On some issues I agree with Kennedy's criticisms.[6] But overall the articles develop positions that I share, and I don't find his article a convincing refutation of them.[7] I leave it to the authors to debate him point by point. I am more interested in working out a left-wing (white ruling-class male academic) take on the underlying questions than in discussing whether his article is "fair."

I begin with color-blind meritocratic fundamentalism, a system of ideas about race, merit, and the proper organization of academic institutions. Fundamentalism is a critique of race-conscious decision making in academia. The second part of the essay presents the political and cultural cases for large-scale affirmative action. The political case is based on the idea that the intelligentsias of subordinated cultural communities should have access to the resources that are necessary for groups to exercise effective political power. The cultural case is based on the idea that a large increase in the number of minority legal scholars would improve the quality and increase the social value of legal scholarship, without being unfair to those displaced.

The third section presents a "cultural pluralist" understanding of American life, one that recognizes that there are dominant and subordinate communities competing in markets and bureaucracies. It proposes that the political and cultural good effect to be anticipated from affirmative action is the development within legal scholarship of the ideological debates that minority intelligentsias have pursued in other fields. I then take up the question whether race-conscious legal academic decision making "derogates from the individuality" of minority scholars. I conclude that we can judge scholarship without regard to culture and ideology only if we are willing to use criteria of judgment that leave out the most important aspects of legal academic accomplishment.

Color-Blind Meritocratic Fundamentalism

My attitude toward meritocracy derives from my experience as a white male ruling-class child who got good grades, gained admission to one elite institution after another, and then landed a job and eventually tenure at Harvard Law School. I belong to a group (only partly generationally defined) that since some point in childhood has felt alienated within this lived experience of working for success according to the criteria of merit that these elite institutions administer.

This alienation had and has two facets. First is a pervasive skepticism about the "standards" according to which we have achieved success. Always subject to the charge that we are simultaneously biting the hand that feeds us and soiling the nest, we just don't believe that it is real "merit" that institutions measure, anywhere in the system. Success is a function of particular knacks, some socially desirable (being "smart") and some not (sucking up)—and of nothing more grandiose. This is not rejection of the idea that some work is better than other work. It is rejection of the institutional mechanisms that currently produce such judgments, of the individuals who manage the institutions, and of the substantive outcomes.

The second facet is a sense of shame and guilt at living in unjust, segregated racial privilege, combined with a sense of loss stemming from the way we have been diminished by isolation from what the subordinated cultural communities of the United States might have contributed to our lives, intellectual, political and personal. I might add that the members of this wholly hypothetical group have not done much (but not nothing, either) about the situation.

These attitudes were held by a scattering of people within elite institutions, and we had little contact with people outside that milieu. The experience on which the reaction was and is based is limited. It's hard to know whether the attitudes are really right. It's hard to know whether there is any alternative to the existing system that would work.

During the 1960s, these attitudes fed into the much larger complex of the New Left, the Movement, and the Women's Movement. The participants came from many different sectors of society. They were male and female, white and black, upper-middle, middle, and—to a limited extent—working class. The whole thing was over before the deep differences among them were worked into anything like coherence. It remains an open question just how the antimeritocratic alienation I have described dovetails or doesn't with the attitudes of people who come from disadvantaged or nonelite backgrounds.

When political alliance and real communication between black and white and male and female radicals fell apart in the 1970s, the project of working out a critique of meritocracy split apart too. But before that happened, there was a counterattack, associated with the general reaction against 1960s militancy and specifically addressed to the various contradictory radical critiques that had gained some currency. This reaction, which I call fundamentalism, won the day. It became one of the ideological legitimators of society's retreat from messing around with established institutions.

Color-blind meritocratic fundamentalism is a set of ideas about race and merit. Like other substructures within the consciousness of a time, it is no more than one of many fragments out of which people construct their personal philosophies. It is intrinsically neither right nor left, male nor female, black nor white. Fundamentalism has a long history within American liberalism and within orthodox Marxism, as well as within the conservative tradition.

Fundamentalism as a System of Ideas

Fundamentalism consists of a set of tenets.[8] Each is a slogan with appeal of its own. They are rarely presented all together. Believers deploy them one by one as the argument may require. Some tenets are about knowledge and others about the social value of individuals and their work.

1a. Knowledge:
    i. Attributes of the product rather than of the producer determine the value of purported contributions to knowledge.
    ii. In judging the value of a product, the race, sex, class, and indeed all the other personal attributes of the producer are irrelevant (derived from i).

Kennedy identifies these tenets with "the ethos of modern science."[9] The scientific ideal is linked to an image of how intellectual work is done.

1b. The production of knowledge:
    i. We produce work by individual application of talent to inert matter.
    ii. The value of the work is a function of the quality of the individual talent that produced it rather than of the inert matter of experience out of which the individual formed it (derived from i).

Fundamentalism includes the complex of liberal attitudes toward race that Peller calls integrationism,[10] but which seems to me better called color-blindness.[11] Kennedy's article demonstrates better than any other recent document I know of how meritocracy and color-blindness can be made mutually supportive.[12] For our purposes here, the important tenets of color-blindness are as follows:

2a. "Prejudice" and "discrimination" are defined in opposition to "assessment of individuals on their merits":
    i. Merit is a matter of individual traits or products.
    ii. People are treated irrationally and unjustly—in short, they are discriminated against—when their merit is assessed according to their status rather than according to the value of their traits or products (derived from i).

2b. Racial discrimination as stereotyping:
    i. There is no reason to believe that race in any of its various socially constructed meanings is an attribute biologically linked to any particular meritorious or discreditable intellectual, psychological, or social traits of any kind.
    ii. Racial discrimination is irrational and unjust because it denies the individual what is due him or her under the society's agreed standards of merit (derived from (i).

From these two sets of tenets, the fundamentalist moves easily to propositions about the proper institutional organization of academic (and other) rewards and opportunities.

3. The institutional organization of the production of knowledge:
    a. Academic institutions should strive to maximize the production of valuable knowledge and also to reward and empower individual merit.
    b. Institutions distributing honor and opportunity should

therefore do so according to criteria blind to race, sex, class, and all other particularities of the individual except the one particularity of having produced work of value (derived from a plus 1 and 2).

Color-blind Meritocracy and Affirmative Action

Fundamentalism does not preclude adopting affirmative action programs so long as we recognize that they conflict with meritocratic allocation, and that the sacrifice of meritocratic to race-based outcomes is a social cost or loss. But, in this view, versions of affirmative action that obscure the cost by distorting standards in favor of minorities end up compounding it. They go beyond departure from merit in particular cases to endanger the integrity of the general system of unbiased judgment of value.

The political and cultural arguments for affirmative action I put forward in the next section are consistent with fundamentalism in that they openly abandon the use of color-blind criteria, rather than distorting them in order to achieve desirable results. They do not treat race as an index of merit in the sense of making it a source of honor in and of itself, nor do they presume that minority scholars are, just by virtue of their skin color, "better" scholars.[13] There remains an important area of disagreement. Fundamentalism treats a color-blind meritocratic system as the ideal. Kennedy's article, for example, concedes (even affirms) that our actual system departs very far from the ideal,[14] but urges that we should therefore redouble our commitment to purifying it:

> It is true . . . that there are many nonracial and ameritocratic considerations that frequently enter into evaluations of a scholar's work. The proper response to that reality, however, is not to scrap the meritocratic ideal. The proper response is to abjure *all* practices that exploit the trappings of meritocracy to advance interests . . . that have nothing to do with the intellectual characteristics of the subject being judged.[15]

If the concern is with racial justice, then loyalty to meritocracy suggests two paths. First, according to Kennedy, "there is nothing necessarily wrong with race-conscious affirmative action"[16] if one has a good reason for it. But the reasons he imagines include neither cultural diversity as an *intellectual* desideratum nor the recognition of the cultural and ideological relativity of the standards that faculty members apply in distributing jobs and honors: "[O]ne might fear that without a sufficient number of minority professors a school will be beset by an intolerable degree of discord or believe that an institution ought to make amends for its past wrongs or insist upon taking extraordinary measures in order to integrate all socially significant institutions in American life."[17] Second, Kennedy favors attacking the underlying social conditions, particularly the class stratification, that reduce the pool of minority applicants.[18]

The point about affirmative action seen as peacemaking, as reparations, or as integration for its own sake, and also about increasing the pool of minority applicants, is that they allow us to preserve a sharp boundary between meritocratic decision and race-based decision: "I simply do not want race-conscious decisionmaking to be naturalized into our general pattern of academic evaluation. I do not want race-conscious decisionmaking to lose its status as a deviant mode of judging people or the work they produce. I do not want race-conscious decisionmaking to be assimilated into our conception of meritocracy."[19]

The political and cultural cases for affirmative action propose to do each of these things.

The Political and Cultural Arguments for Affirmative Action

The Political Case

I favor large-scale race-based affirmative action, using quotas if they are necessary to produce results. The first basis for this view is that law school teaching positions are a small but significant part of the wealth of the United States. They are also a small but significant part of the political apparatus of the United States, by which I mean that the knowledge law teachers produce is intrinsically political and actually effective in our political system. In short, legal knowledge is ideological.[20] A second basic idea is that we should be a culturally pluralist society that deliberately structures institutions so that communities and social classes share wealth and power. The sharing of wealth and power that occur automatically, so to speak, through the melting pot, the market, and meritocracy are not enough, according to this notion. At a minimum, cultural pluralism means that we should structure the competition of racial and ethnic communities and social classes in markets and bureaucracies, and in the political system, in such a way that no community or class is systematically subordinated.[21]

From these two ideas I draw the conclusion that, completely independently of "merit" as we currently determine it,[22] there should be a substantial representation of all numerically significant minority communities on American law faculties. The analogy is to the right to vote, which we refuse to distribute on the basis of merit, and to the right of free speech, which we refuse to limit to those who deserve to speak or whose speech has merit. The value at stake is community rather than individual empowerment. In the case of affirmative action, as in those of voting and free speech, the goal is political, and *prior to* the achievement of enlightenment or the reward of "merit" as determined by existing institutions.

Race is, at present, a rough but adequate proxy for connection to a subordinated community, one that avoids institutional judgments about the cultural identity of particular candidates. I would use it for this reason only, not because race is itself an index of merit, and in spite of its culturally constructed character and the arbitrariness involved in using it as a predicter of the traits of any particular individual. My argument is thus addressed to only one of the multiple forms of group subordination, though it could be extended to gender, sexual preference, social class, and ethnicity within the "white community."[23]

The political argument includes the idea that minority communities can't compete effectively for wealth and power without intelligentsias that produce the kinds of knowledge, especially political or ideological knowledge, that will help them get what they want. To do this, they need or at least could use some number of legal academic jobs. It also includes the idea that cultural diversity and cultural development are good in themselves, even when they do not lead to increased power for subordinated communities in markets and political systems.

The political case is complicated by the fact that when law faculties distribute jobs in legal academia, they do more than distribute wealth and the power to participate in politics through the production of ideology. They also distribute power to influence who will participate in the future, because those they choose will vote on those decisions. In deciding whom to hire or promote according to color-blind criteria, law faculties make culturally and ideologically contingent judgments about which candidates are most promising or deserving, *and* about who should make these very judgments in the future. Given the ideological and cultural character of these choices, and their limited but significant political impact, white males have no more business monopolizing the process of distributing the benefits than they have monopolizing the benefits themselves.[24]

A serious obstacle to this proposal is the "pool problem."[25] The number of minority teaching candidates is limited, and the prospects for the future are clouded by the decline in the number of black college graduates. (The situation is different for each cultural community.) I would therefore limit affirmative action by imposing a floor or cutoff point in the form of a requirement of minimum actual or anticipated competence in performing the instructional function of a law professor.[26]

It would seem to me a problem (requiring tradeoffs) if the implementation of this view would be unfair to individual whites excluded from teaching jobs, or if it would lead to a decline in the quality of legal scholarship. But I believe that massive affirmative action would not be unfair to excluded whites, and that it would improve the quality of legal scholarship. It would also have, I think, a beneficial effect on the quality of life, by undermining the fetishistic, neurotic, and just plain irrational attitude toward "standards" and merit-based "entitlement" that prevails in legal academia.

Affirmative Action and the Quality of Work

The standards that law schools apply in deciding whom to hire and whom to promote function to exclude scholars from cultural communities with a history of subordination. Because we exclude them, we get contributions to legal knowledge from only a small number of people with ties to those communities. I believe that if there were a lot more such people, they would make contributions that, taken as a whole, would have a culturally specific character. Judging by my own culturally and ideologically contingent standards, I think they would produce outstanding work not otherwise available. Law schools would do better to invest resources in evoking this contribution than in the fungible white male candidates at the margin who get jobs under the existing selection systems (though quite a few who appear marginal turn out to be terrific).

I don't mean that there would be a minority "line." But there would be a variety of positions, debates, and styles of legal academic writing that everyone would identify as resulting from the rise of minority legal culture. Some of these debates, positions, and styles would be produced by whites, but would be no less a product of change in the racial makeup of the academy. Some of the new work would certainly look wrong or mediocre to me. But some would knock our socks off, in unexpected ways and in ways already presaged by Critical Race Theory.[27] I have no doubt that in terms of the social and intellectual value of scholarly output, legal academia would be better off than it is now. We have lost a lot by preventing minorities from making this contribution. We can't get it unless we give them the resources, in the form of legal academic jobs, to make it.

Second, some legal scholarship is exciting and enriching and stimulating, but not very much. People seem to produce the good stuff through neurotic, often dramatic processes, full of twists and turns and surprises. Most legal scholarship seems to be done pretty much by the numbers, and it's hard to make any sharp quality differential between articles. This stuff is useful. Writing it is hard work. But it doesn't require deep scholarship or reflect high ability. A great many people who are excluded by the "standards" from teaching law could do it as well or as mediocrely as those who do it in fact. I think we would lose little in the way of quality even if massive affirmative action failed to produce the rich harvest of new ideas and approaches that I anticipate.

The possibility of dramatically improving legal scholarship provides a second strong reason for a massive affirmative action program. It is not just that there is no tradeoff between quality and affirmative action. The existing system denies us a benefit. Even in the absence of the political justification, I would favor a new system on this ground.[28]

Affirmative Action and White Entitlements

Suppose a law faculty adopts this version of affirmative action because it hopes to improve the quality of legal academic work, as well as because it is politically more just. When the faculty chooses a minority job applicant over a white even though the present system would give the job to the white, it does so, in part, because it thinks that in the long run this approach will improve scholarship and teaching. We are treating race as a credential (as a proxy for culture and community) because we anticipate outstanding work from some of these applicants, work that we don't think we can get from the whites they replace. The reason we don't expect it from them is that we believe that work from authors with ties to subordinated communities is likely to have different excellent qualities than work from inside the dominant community.

Are the excluded whites "entitled" to prevent this improvement in scholarship? I would say they are not. Even if all the color-blind criteria of academic promise that we can think of favor a white candidate, he or she lacks something we want in some substantial number of those we will hire. He or she has less promise of doing work with the particular strengths likely to derive from connection to a subordinated cultural community.

The white male law teaching applicant whose résumé and interviews would get him the job were it not for affirmative action has indeed accomplished something, and will not be rewarded for it with the job. But if he understands in advance that the terms of the competition are that he is competing against other white males, for the limited number of slots that a politically just system makes available to people who have had his advantages, then I don't think he has any reason to complain when a job he would have gotten under a different (less just) system goes to a minority applicant. But the excluded white candidates do not have as strong a claim as assumed above.

First, those who win out in the existing system have no claim to be "the best," even according to the color-blind criteria, because the underlying systems of race and class, and the system of testing, exclude so many potential competitors from the very beginning. The competition in which our teaching applicants and tenure candidates win out is restricted, with only a tiny number of notable exceptions, to people born within a certain race-class distance of those positions. At every step, the differences in educational resources and the testing process screen out millions of people who might be able to do the job of law professor better than those who end up getting it. As against those excluded from the competition by race and class and the vagaries of the testing system, those who win out have only a very limited claim of entitlement.

Second, the "standards" that law schools apply in hiring assistant professors and promoting them to tenure are at best very rough proxies for accomplishment as we assess it after the fact. People who get good grades and have prestigious clerkships often turn out to be duds as legal scholars and teachers by the standards of those who appointed them. People with less impressive résumés often turn out to be exciting scholars and teachers. People who get tenure on the basis of an article that looks good to the tenure committee (and those of the faculty who read it) often never produce anything of comparable quality again. "Entitlements" based on these rough proxies are worthy of only limited respect. The white males who would be displaced to make way for large numbers of minority scholars would be hurt, but not in a way that would be unfair, given the importance of the goals to be achieved.[29]

Third, law school faculties apply a pedestrian, often philistine cultural standard in judging white male résumés, interviews, and presentations at the entry level, and white male teaching and tenure work at the promotion level. They administer this pedestrian, philistine standard with an unconscious but unmistakable moderate-conservative-to-moderate-liberal bias. And they serve it up with a powerful seasoning of old-boyism and arbitrary clique preference *as between white males.* I don't mean that a more pluralist academy would necessarily do better or produce more political diversity. But there is an element of laughable exaggeration in the claims often made for the meritocratic purity of existing arrangements. The people who would win out in this system were it not for affirmative action have weak claims of unfairness just because they are not so wonderful, even by comparison with other white males, that they can regard themselves as innocent victims.

There is no tradeoff between racial justice and legal academic quality. Indeed, both goals point in the same direction. There is no claim of entitlement against these goals even for candidates who are

plausibly the best by every color-blind criterion. The claims of actual candidates likely to be rejected are weakened by the exclusion
of competitors, especially competitors from the groups that would
gain by affirmative action. Their claims are further weakened by the
fact that their accomplishments are mere proxies for legal academic
merit, and by the low cultural quality and arbitrary subjectivism of
the screening system that would otherwise have delivered them the
goods.

Destabilizing Attitudes about Race and Merit

It would be a beneficial side effect of massive, politically and culturally grounded affirmative action if it upset or destabilized the
way most law teachers experience the whole issue of merit, and
especially its relationship to race. One of the least attractive traits
associated with fundamentalism is the tendency to fetishize "credentials" that are only proxies for actual achievement. Consider the
case of the faculty member in the hiring meeting who wants the
law school transcript of a candidate for a teaching job who is
thirty-five years old, has written four law review articles, and has
taught several thousand law students.

But this is just the extreme case. We are generally dependent on
the stream of pellets of meritocratic praise and blame, addicted to
the continual reward of being told that we are better, and that our
law schools are better, according to an objective merit scale, than
other teachers and other schools. And as a group we are excessively
susceptible to injury by judgments that we fall below others.

One resulting vice is resentment, intense preoccupation with the
ways in which one has been unjustly denied the praise or job or
honor that one's "merit" "entitles" one to, and with the ways in
which others have received more than their due. A second vice is
careerism or opportunism, in which an interest in climbing the ladder or maximizing one's academic capital comes to dominate at-
tachment to any set of ideas or any set of autonomous judgments
about others.

On the flip side, obsession with merit funnels emotional energy
into generating distinctions that will justify the claim that differences in people's rewards and punishments are deserved rather than
arbitrary. Sometimes we just can't admit that our standards lack

power to make the distinctions that law school roles require of us, among students or job applicants or tenure candidates. Intensely debated but meaningless small distinctions at the margin allow us to imagine that merit is ruling the day, so that no one has been wronged, when the distinctions that have real meaning are too crude to do the job.

Sometimes what we are denying is that merit is only part of the story of colleagueship. The torturing of standards until they confess that "he got what he deserved" may be a coverup for other motives. Obsessive standards-talk also has a narcissistic payoff, since it endlessly reaffirms the merit of those who make judgments of merit.[30]

Affirmative action has already somewhat destabilized these patterns. They might be further jarred by an explicitly political and culturally based increase, because everyone involved in the enterprise would be forced to recognize a degree of relativity to the idea of merit. Dissociating some hiring and promotion decisions from any particular set of credentials undermines everyone's sense that one's true being is one's academic capital.

A political move to large-scale affirmative action would say to minorities, "Here is a part of the resources. Do what you can with it." It would free whites from some of the political obligation that comes of unjust treatment of minorities. It would reduce the nagging sense that our ability to assess merit is consciously or unconsciously corrupted because we now accomplish limited power and wealth sharing through academic decisions on hiring and promotion.

It would reduce the sense that we coerce minorities who want the rewards we have to offer into "being like us." It would also increase integration, the chance for more relations with minorities in our own workplaces. But it would do this without presupposing that our "merit" joins us together in a way that is "more important than" or "independent of" cultural community. In short, it might promote integration while undermining the ideology of color-blindness.

There are obvious dangers. The proposal might increase the stereotyping of minorities as intellectually inferior. It might lead to protracted, destructive racial conflict between majority and minority groups on faculties, and within those groups. It might be impossible to design a scheme of wealth and power sharing that would be easy to administer so as to avoid endless conflict about how to define it in practice. I don't deny these dangers. I just think them worth risking, given the possible benefits.

The proposal obviously contemplates race-conscious decision making as a routine, nondeviant mode, a more or less permanent norm in distributing legal academic jobs. A "racial distinctiveness" (actually cultural distinctiveness) theory combined with race-conscious decision making is "assimilated into our conception of meritocracy,"[31] which is just what Kennedy's article urges us to avoid at all costs. The position is problematic as well as controversial because it relies on the idea of cultural subordination rather than on the more familiar fundamentalist ideas of prejudice and discrimination.[32]

The Cultural Subordination Thesis

The issue is whether there is enough cultural distinctiveness, and enough subordination and exclusion, so that we must treat representation in academia as a political question, and so that we can expect major intellectual gains from doing so.[33] The argument thus far has been largely hypothetical. Even if one accepted the value of the notions of culture and ideology, one might deny that, in the actual conditions of the United States today, cultural and ideological differences are significant. Or one might merely deny that they are large enough so that we need to structure law schools to take them into account.[34]

The cultural pluralist position to the contrary rests on a whole complex of ideas about American society. I introduce them below in highly schematic form. Together they define a variant of the "nationalist" ideology.[35]

Premises of Cultural Pluralism

Groups exist in a sense that goes beyond individuals' having similar traits. People in groups act together, working out common goals and then engaging in a cooperative process of trying to achieve them. Just as important, they engage in discussion and mutual criticism both about the goals and about what members are doing (or not doing) to achieve them. This is true of small task-oriented groups (family members getting the car packed for a trip) and also of large, diffuse ones, like "the black community" or a law faculty.

An important human reality is the experience of defining oneself as "a member of a group" in this strong sense of sharing goals and a discursive practice. Another important experience is being treated by others as a group member. One's interlocutor interprets what one says and does as derived from a shared project. We all constantly identify groups and their members, assuming that we need to in order to understand other people and predict what they will do.[36]

Communities are more than mere statistical groupings of individuals with particular traits, but less than self-organized groups. Membership presupposes interaction, but the interaction may be sporadic, routine, alienated. A community is a historically specific collection of people with a common past, and a future that will take place on the basis of what has gone before. That basis can be reinterpreted but not obliterated. We are stuck, at any given moment, in the communities we started or ended in, and that is never "just anywhere." Wherever it is, it is both more inert than a self-organized group and less demanding. The crucial idea is that communities are made up of living individuals, but they have an element of transindividual stability and particularity; to be a member is to be *situated,* and we can be situated only in one or two places at a time. Membership is limiting as well as empowering.

Communities have cultures. This means that individuals have traits that are neither genetically determined nor voluntarily chosen, but rather consciously and unconsciously taught through community life. Community life forms customs and habits, capacities to produce linguistic and other performances, and individual understandings of good and bad, true and false, worthy and unworthy. Culture is first of all a product of community. People living in different groups possess different understandings of value as well as exhibiting different capacities and behavior traits (kinship, cooking, dress). But as I am using it, culture is a characteristic of an individual as well. You can break all your ties to a community yet remain a person with that community's cultural identity.[37]

A large part of the population of the United States lives in racial and ethnic communities that have a measure of cultural distinctiveness. The distinctiveness comes in part from the origins in Africa, Asia, Europe, and Latin America of the different groups that live here. But the cultures of particular communities have been dramatically transformed by the experience of immigration, forced transportation, or annexation and by the heterogeneous cultural life of this country. Each group has put its culture of origin together with its peculiar circumstances in the United States to produce a distinct set of behaviors, attitudes, beliefs, and values.[38]

The racial and ethnic communities of the United States are in constant contact with one another. This contact is asymmetrical. There is a dominant cultural community that is less influenced by and less conscious of the subordinated groups than they are influenced by and conscious of it. As a result, it is hard to identify any aspect of the cultures of subordinated groups that might be relevant to academic production and that has not been influenced by contact with the dominant culture.

The boundaries of cultural communities are blurred by the presence of large numbers of people who can trace their family history back into a subordinated community, but who now regard themselves and are regarded by others as situated in a culturally intermediate space, or as assimilated to the dominant culture. There are millions of people for whom the "authenticity" of having always belonged to a relatively homogeneous community with an unselfconsciously shared ethos is simply impossible. Most of those likely to benefit by a program of culturally conscious distribution of academic power and opportunity come from these intermediate, multicultural positions. (The existence of this group may make it more likely that we could actually succeed in implementing cultural diversity.)

Though communities are different in some ways that are best understood through the neutral idea of culture (some groups do things one way, value one set of things; other groups do it in different ways), other differences are not like that. Americans pursue their collective and individual projects in a situation of group domination and group subordination; that is, we can compare "how well" different groups have done with regard to income, housing, health, education, local and national political power, and access to cultural resources. The groups are not so different that they define these things in radically different ways, or that some groups are just not interested in them. With respect to these common measures of equality and inequality, we all recognize that some groups are enormously better off than others.

The experiences of youth in a particular community, or on the border between communities, equip individuals with resources for competition in markets and bureaucracies. Different communities have different access to wealth and power with which to endow their members. Even if the rules of competition were neutral with respect to cultural identity, differences in resources would produce predictable differences in rewards.

In fact, the rules of competition in markets and bureaucracies are structured in ways (both formal and informal) that advantage people from dominant communities regardless of the resources they bring as individuals to the competition. Historically, the white community imposed systematic race-based discrimination, outright job and housing segregation, and rules that excluded racial minorities and women from directly exercising political power. In the current situation, particular cultural groups control or dominate some markets and bureaucracies, and these groups exercise thier inevitably enormous range of discretion in ways that favor dominant over subordinated communities. Racial and gender discrimination still direct the flow of opportunities and thereby affect the shares groups achieve.

The notion of domination and subordination is meant to indicate that we cannot understand what happens according to a model in which all people in the society have innate or individual qualities and individual preferences that they bring into a neutrally structured competitive process that correlates their rewards with their social contributions. There are patterns to the characteristics of the individuals society produces—they are identifiably members of the particular communities they grew up in, and their fortunes depend on that fact.

Differences of fortune result from themselves in a circular process. To speak of domination is to say that the group and individual exercise of power given by resources occurs in a competitive struggle in which the better-off communities manage over time to reproduce their advantage by winning enough in each game to reconstitute their stakes. Even the rules of the game are produced by the game, in the sense that power to compete is also power to modify the rules. The dominant communities are those that have the most resources and rewards, those that manage to influence the rules that define the game to their advantage, and those that through time manage to reproduce or improve their top-dog position through competitive struggle.[39]

The game is cooperative as well as competitive. In order to gain rewards, the members of the different communities have to cooperate across ethnic lines in producing goods and services. There are all kinds of influences and concrete alliances formed, and there are areas in which and moments when community identity is actually pretty much submerged in the collective aspects of tasks. Within the communities, there are divisions that are best understood in class terms, and other crosscutting divisions that represent the community's participation in national life (region, gender, religion, and so forth). Both power and resistance to power pervade the structure.[40]

Though there is a self-conscious ruling class at the top, neither the class nor the structure fully controls the outcomes and impacts of the game for the communities whose members play it. All the players are functions of the game, as well as vice versa. There is no "outside position." Communities themselves change internally and through collision with other communities, but the process has as much fate, drift, and chance mutation to it as it does mechanical necessity or self-organized group will. Communities can disperse or assimilate and then reform, and they can die out or be killed.[41]

The American racial and ethnic communities have intelligentsias, linked in overlapping patterns to a national intelligentsia and to each other. By an intelligentsia, I mean a "knowledge class" working in education, the arts, social work, the law, religion, the media, therapy, consulting, and myriad spinoffs like charitable foundations, or for-profit research ventures. Intelligentsia members perform multiple functions beyond their formal job descriptions. In self-organizing groups or individually, some of them work at defining their community's identity (its cultural distinctiveness) or lack thereof, its interests in competition and cooperation with other communities, and its possible strategies.[42]

The national, racial, and ethnic intelligentsias are internally divided along ideological lines. One national ideological axis is radical-liberal-moderate-conservative-rightist. Another is traditional-modern-postmodern. Another is science–social science–humanities–

arts. There is also a wide range of ideological debates within particular intelligentsias, for example about their relationship to the national community.

An ideology in the sense in which I am using it is a set of contested ideas that provides a "partisan" interpretation (descriptive and normative) of a field of social conflict.[43] The social conflict could be between capital and labor, farmers and banks, men and women, gay and straight, North and South, native-born and foreign-born, export industries and import industries, or whatever. The concepts that describe and justify the positions of the conflicting groups can be drawn from almost anywhere, from philosophy to economics to religion to biology. Ideologies reflect and at the same time influence social conflict.[44]

Ideologists choose their ideas, in the sense that there is no consensus either in their favor or against them. Many people may think a particular system is objectively right and many others that it is objectively wrong, or it may be seen as posing a question that one can resolve only by a leap of faith. The most basic criticism of ideologists is that they choose thier ideas to fit thier partisan allegiance, and therefore lack allegiance to "truth." In the conception of ideology I am using, it must always be recognized that people sometimes distort their intellectual work to serve causes or interests they adhere to. At the same time we have to recognize that where there is social conflict, and contested interpretations of that conflict, there is no intellectual space outside ideology. Intelligentsia virtue consists not in maintaining "objectivity" or "neutrality," which is impossible once there is ideological division, but in attempting to empower an audience to judge for itself.

It follows that being an ideologist doesn't mean being closed-minded, uninterested in questioning fundamental assumptions, or blind to evidence that contradicts those assumptions. In this sense of the term, one is in the position of the ideologist just by virtue of having, at any given moment, made choices between contested views that influence (and are influenced by) the intellectual work one does. "Moderates" are ideologists because when they call themselves that they implicitly appeal to a controversial critique of "ideologues." (This is the ideology of moderation.)

Members of minority intelligentsias are linked to their cultural communities in various ways, and divided from them as well, usually by social class, income, intelligentsia interests, and by connections to the national intelligentsia and culture that are different from those of the "masses." A basic ideological conflict is over how to describe and evaluate the courses of conduct that intelligentsia members adopt in this situation. There are ideologies of assimilation and of authenticity, of group accommodation and of group resistance, of individual self-realization and of collective obligation, and so forth.

The existence of ethnic intelligentsias, their size, and the power they produce for communities all depend on access to resources, as does their ability to contribute to national intellectual/political life. One index of a community's cultural subordination is dependence on others to produce knowledge in areas where it would seem, at least superficially, that community interests will be affected by what that knowledge is. Another is the inability of its intelligentsia to influence the national intelligentsia, and indirectly the American mass culture audience, on issues of importance to the community.[45]

The foregoing definition of cultural subordination is patently ideological. The conceptual scheme proposed is only one of many available to describe and judge the status of an intelligentsia, and within each scheme there is a well-developed critique of its rivals.

What Might Be Gained through Large-Scale Affirmative Action

In light of the above, I would deny the existence of a "black point of view" or a "black voice" in any essentialist (or racialist) sense.[46] But that denial doesn't answer the particular questions that are relevant to the political and cultural arguments for large-scale affirmative action. The first of these is whether minority communities would get, from a much larger minority legal intelligentsia, a scholarly output that would better serve their diverse political, social, and economic interests than what they get from an overwhelmingly white legal intelligentsia. The second is whether the legal academic community as a whole would get a more valuable corpus of scholarship.

I see two likely changes in this regard. A much larger minority intelligentsia should produce more scholarship about the legal issues that have impact on minority communities. The subject matter of scholarship is determined at present by the unregulated "interest" of academics. What we decide to write about just "flows naturally" from our backgrounds, education, and individual peculiarities. It is obvious that some significant proportion of minority intellectuals would be led in this way to write about minority legal issues.[47]

The precedent for this is the creation of modern civil rights law by black lawyers who devised the litigation strategy of the National Association for the Advancement of Colored People. It would be farfetched to argue that the race of these lawyers was irrelevant to their choice of subject matter, or that the black civil rights cause would have evolved in the same way had all the lawyers involved been white.[48]

Along with more scholarship on minority issues, there should be more scholarship on the implications for minorities of *any* issue currently under debate. In other words, Hispanic scholars working on the purest of corporate law questions within the most unquestionably Anglo scholarly paradigm are still, I think, more likely than white scholars to devote, over the long run, some time to thinking about the implications of law in their chosen technical area for the Hispanic communities.[49]

The second anticipated change is crucial to my argument. Along with a quantitative change in focus, it seems likely that an increase in minority scholarship would change the framework of ideological conflict within which issues concerning not only race but also other matters are discussed. I do not mean by this that there is a black (or other minority) ideology. The point is rather that there are historic, already established *debates* within the minority intelligentsias that are obviously relevant to law but have been largely absent from legal scholarship.

In the black intellectual community, debates that have only begun to get played out and transformed in law include those between nationalists and integrationists,[50] between progressives and conservatives,[51] between those who see current racism as a more or less important determinant of current black social conditions,[52] and between black feminists and traditionalists.[53] The nationalist versus integrationist and gender debates are now for the first time beginning to get a hearing as a result of the presence of more minorities in the legal academy.[54] There are similar debates in the other minority communities.[55]

The Cultural Case in the Context of Cultural Subordination

It comes down to a question of value. I have come (belatedly) to
the view that American culture and politics are rendered radically
more intelligible when viewed through the lens that intellectuals of
color have constructed over the years. There is more in this general
literature than any one person can assimilate. But there is nowhere
near as much legal scholarship as there ought to be. Scholars with
ties to subordinated communities are uniquely situated in respect
to these ideological resources, and more likely than white scholars
to mobilize them to contribute to our understanding of law-in-
society.

They are uniquely situated because, in Randall Kennedy's words,
"even taking into account class, gender, and other divisions," there
does indeed remain "an irreducible link of commonality in the experience of people of color: rich or poor, male or female, learned
or ignorant, *all* people of color are to some degree 'outsiders' in a
society that is intensely color-conscious and in which the hegemony of whites is overwhelming."[56] The ideological literature of subordinated communities comes out of this experience, in all its vari-
ants, and is addressed to it. The flowering in legal scholarship of this
literature combined with these experiences is just not something
we can plausibly expect from white scholars.

Again, the resources are not Truths to which only people of
color have access (though, who knows, such truths may exist), but
debates involving all the complexity of incompatible conceptual
frameworks and flatly contradictory conclusions. They relate the internal dialectics of subordinated communities, and the dialectic of
their interaction with the United States at large. They are open to
multiple interpretations, including specifically white interpretations.
For this reason, a substantial increase in the number of minority
scholars should also improve white scholarship.

An increase in scholarship that takes seriously the issues that have
been raised by the black intelligentsia would have relevance to the
debates in legal scholarship about gender, sexual orientation, and
class. Indeed, I find it hard to think about, say, the separatist or
culturalist strand in modern feminism without relating it to the debate about racial identity with which it is intertwined. The historical influence of black liberation thought on all other forms of late

twentieth-century American theory about subordinated groups has been enormous. But the influence has been indirect in legal thought, in part because of the small size of minority legal intelligentsias. Wherever groups are in question, whether in corporate or family law, or in the law of federalism or local government law, the historic minority debates and their contemporary extensions should have an impact on sophisticated mainstream thinking.

The issue is not whether there should be a cultural bias in judging actual work. When we have the work before us, there is no reason not to consult it and decide for ourselves, individually, who has produced knowledge of value to us. In judging value to us, the cultural status of the producer is irrelevant, and so is the "merit" of the producer. In and of themselves they neither add nor subtract value, though knowing the author's status and accomplishment can change our understanding of a work and allow us to find value in it that we would otherwise have missed. This knowledge can also mislead us. There is no way to eliminate this risk, since, as I will argue in the next section, we can understand and assess the work only as a text situated in *some* presupposed cultural and ideological context, and assess it only from our own particular cultural and ideological situation.

There is nothing that *precludes* white scholars from making the contributions anticipated from scholars of color. An outsider may learn about a culture and its debates and produce work about or even "within" them that is "better" than anything an insider has produced. There are advantages as well as disadvantages to outsider status, and everyone in a multicultural society is simultaneously inside and outside. And there is nothing to guarantee that minority scholars will choose to or be able to make those contributions. They may squander their resources or decide to do work that is indistinguishable in subject matter and approach from that of white scholars. But their track record, with and without affirmative action, has been good enough, easily, even as tokens, to sustain a prediction of excellence to come.

The Political Case in the Context of Cultural Subordination

Through scholarship focusing on their own concerns and through ideological debate played out in the legal arena, minority communities (through their intelligentsias) develop themselves internally, assimilate for their own purposes the resources of the culture at large, and build power for the competitive struggle with other groups. The power to create this kind of knowledge is political power. Therefore, it should be shared by all groups within the community affected.

This argument has two levels. First, both the choice and the application of academic standards have strikingly contingent cultural and ideological dimensions. Law faculties distribute political resources (jobs) through a process that is political in fact, if not in name. One group (white males of the dominant culture) largely monopolizes this distribution process and, perhaps not so surprisingly, also largely monopolizes the benefits (jobs). This outcome is politically illegitimate. Second, anybody who disagrees with what I have just said, and maintains instead that standards are and should be apolitical, holds a position that is itself ideological. Law faculties shouldn't make the ideological choice between color-blind meritocracy and some form of race-conscious power-sharing without a substantial participation of minorities in the decision.

Cultural and Ideological Dimensions of Academic Standards

There are different questions we ask when assessing an academic work. There is the question of truth or falsity, understood to be a question susceptible of answers that when argued out will produce a broad consensus. Then there are questions of "originality" and questions of "interest" or "value."

My experience has been that work in law (like, I assume, some work in physics) is sometimes wrong or untrue in a quite strong sense. I am convinced that when the error is pointed out just about everyone will agree that it was an error. I don't think the kinds of cultural differences that can plausibly be asserted to characterize American society have much impact on these judgments. This is *sometimes* true as well of questions of originality, interest, and value.

Judgments of originality are obviously more contested. And judgments about whether the problem addressed was "interesting" or "valuable" seem to be strongly influenced by the politics of academic life.[57] Different people in a field often have very different ideas about which true, original work is interesting. Though the judges have a strong sense that they know what they mean by interest, and that they are not making "merely" subjective judgments, they also concede that the standard is difficult to apply.

More important for our purposes, they will generally concede that interest or value can be judged only by reference to a particular research tradition or scholarly paradigm, usually one among many that might have won dominance in the field.[58] Yet conclusions at the level of what is valuable or interesting are very often dispositive in deciding which of two articles is better.

Once we acknowledge the possible existence of different research traditions, or collective scholarly projects, we have to acknowledge that the white male occupants of faculty positions have more than the power to decide which performances are better. They have also had the power to create the traditions or projects within which they will make these judgments. It seems obvious that these traditions or projects are culturally and ideologically specific products.

The projects themselves, as well as the judgments of originality, interest, and value they ground (not the narrow judgments of truth and falsity) would almost certainly change if people of excluded cultures and excluded ideologies were allocated power and opportunity to create research traditions and scholarly projects of their own, or to participate in those ongoing. If this were done, there would be a gradual reevaluation of existing legal scholarship. Some currently low-ranked work would gain esteem, and some high-ranked work would lose it. There are no metacriteria of merit that determine which among culturally and ideologically specific research traditions or scholarly paradigms is "better" or "truer." Judgments of merit are inevitably culturally and ideologically contingent because they are inevitably paradigm-dependent.

The choice of standards of originality, interest, and value in judging academic work has profound consequences for what a society knows about itself and its values, and for who the members of society *are* in consequence of their existence within the particular known universe that the knowledge-licensers have promoted. Who they are in turn reacts back through their powers and weaknesses onto the knowledge-licensing process that has created its own author.[59]

At a much more mundane level, the choice of standards controls the choice of personnel in the enterprise of knowledge production, which in turn affects the relative power of the cultural communities that compete in civil society. Excluded communities compete in the legislative process, for example, on the basis of social science data assembled in research projects whose funding and direction is under the control of the dominant community. They compete for favorable rulings from courts on the basis of economic theories about the relative importance of distributional equity and efficiency that are unmistakably tied to the white conservative and white moderate research agendas of law and economics scholars.

The fundamentalist has to deal with the claim that choices to allocate scholarly opportunity are grounded in power rather than in merit, and function to reproduce the very distribution of power they reflect. The power is that of white, mainly male academics, mainly of "moderate" ideology, to impose their standards. They hold, and have held for many generations, the positions to which society has allocated authority to distribute this kind of opportunity. And they have distributed it to themselves.

As with the cultural case, there is nothing to guarantee that a larger minority legal intelligentsia would use the resources of law schools in ways that I would find politically constructive. More jobs might just widen the gap between scholars of color and their communities, and the hiring process might select those least likely, for class and ideological reasons, to pursue the project of empowerment. If that happened, those for whom empowerment is the goal would have to think of something else.

Who Gets to Decide Whether or Not to Share Power?

The decision-making process is decentralized, and largely depoliticized, in the sense of not understood as political. The main decision-makers are faculty members of law schools. My (ideological) position is that the depoliticization is bad, the decentralization good. If politicization would lead to centralization within the state sector, then these positions conflict. But assume for the moment that they are not in conflict—that faculties so inclined could go a long way toward power-sharing with subordinated cultural communities (and social classes) without losing their autonomy through conflict with other political institutions (such as state legislatures) committed to color-blind fundamentalism.

Faculties decide personnel questions by voting, usually on the basis of one-tenured-person-one-vote. In the process, individual faculty members decide between color-blind fundamentalism and the vague available alternatives. Much more important, given the political weakness of advocates of alternatives, they decide how to interpret fundamentalism in the face of its internal gaps, conflicts, and ambiguities.

These choices are incomprehensible unless put in the context of conflicting ideologies about the past and present of race in the United States. The question is whether law faculties as presently constituted are the proper people to make these ideological decisions. Our selection processes, combined with our historic selection *practice,* fail to guarantee adequately that the whole community will be represented in these decisions. That is, they are democratically inadequate. Some measure of democracy is required in decision making that will affect the very being of the community.

At this point the argument does a kind of backflip. Suppose that the fundamentalist responds to the claim of inclusion, based on the political nature of knowledge production, that the premise is wrong. Knowledge is true or false, not left or right. The goal is to produce as much of it as possible, without regard to the politics of the producers. This goal is inherently apolitical or suprapolitical.

The second-level argument is that the question whether these decisions are necessarily ideological is itself ideological. Even if you think knowledge production can be, is, and ought to be nonpolitical, you still have to decide whether that view is one you should be authorized to implement institutionally without having to argue and contend with people who disagree.

Color-blind meritocratic fundamentalism is itself an ideology. The very concepts of race, culture, merit, and knowledge are intensely contested both within and between groups.[60] As the tone and passion of Kennedy's article show on every page, it is a matter of commitment, a choice, to be a fundamentalist. He rightly presents it as a fighting faith. The question whether knowledge production is political is itself political. Is the community's process for resolving the contest—its political process, in short—a good one?

The current procedure is inadequate because it involves neither the normal democratic procedure of majority vote nor any of the more complex procedures that often seem adequate to guarantee representation of all interests. Recognition of the political character of the decisions being made need mean neither merger into the central state apparatuses nor local "home rule" through elections. But it does mean that the licensers have to do *something* to bring about accountability for their choices between and within the competing ideologies. That something should be affirmative action sufficiently extensive that minorities have enough representation on faculties to be players in the decision about whether to adopt race-conscious decision making.[61]

Do Race-Based Criteria of Scholarly Judgment "Derogate Individuality"?

Randall Kennedy claims that race-conscious decision making "derogates from individuality." This argument is typical of fundamentalist thinking as it might apply to a culturally and politically based affirmative action program. (As noted above, Kennedy is sympathetic to affirmative action, though on other grounds.)[62] Kennedy's article makes the familiar argument that racial categorization is dangerous per se, because it can be and and is used for racist purposes.[63] I recognize that this is a danger, but I think its degree has to be assessed case by case. In most situations, it is easy to distinguish between racist and antiracist use of racial categories. Facially neutral categories can accomplish almost anything a confirmed racist would want. Whether we do better on balance by using race explicitly in institutional decision making, or by finding other ways to achieve racial objectives, isn't a question to which we will ever find a decisive empirical answer. I advocate pervasive use of race-conscious decision making because we can't deal with the problem of subordination without confronting it directly, we can't fully achieve the value of cultural pluralism without self-consciously designing our institutions with that in mind.

Kennedy's contrary position is not just a different empirical-intuitive assessment of the probabilities of "misuse" or "socially destructive" application.[64] Rather, it is tied to the general fundamentalist conception of prejudice and discrimination as subspecies of the evil of stereotyping. And the intense fundamentalist preoccupation with stereotyping is, in turn, closely tied to what strikes me as the fetishizing of "individual merit."

Kennedy devotes a few paragraphs to bad consequences of racial classification,[65] but the single most important theme of his article as a whole is that "racial generalizations, whether positive or negative, derogate from the individuality of persons insofar as their unique characteristics are submerged in the image of the group to which they are deemed to belong."[66] "Derogation from individuality" occurs whenever there is a failure to distinguish between the "will" of the individual and his or her merely "social," "accidental," "ascribed," or "inherited" characteristics. And it occurs equally whenever we fail to distinguish the act of "will" from the materials, likewise merely given, on which the individual works:

> [N]either one's racial status nor the experience one suffers as a result of that status is capable of translating itself into art, a point applicable as well to scholarship, the 'art' of academicians. An experience is simply inert—something that happened. That something only becomes knowable in a public way through an act of will: interpretation.[67]

Kennedy's article is a brief against allowing "race-conscious decisionmaking to be assimilated into our conception of meritocracy,"[68] because that would be unfair to "the individual," whether white or black, who is denied recognition of his or her "merit" (in the sense of accomplishment, attainment, achievement).* This argument de-

---

*The following quotations show, I think, that Randall Kennedy's article is very strongly preoccupied with the "derogation of individuality," "act of will," "ascribed versus achieved," and "given materials versus willed addition" issues:

"[E]ven if the scholarship at issue was narrowly concerned with the inner experience of a single racial group, it would still be improper to presume expertise merely on the basis of a scholar's membership in a given group. One's racial (gender, religious, regional) identity is no substitute for the disciplined study essential to achieving expertise. Although one is born with certain physical characteristics to which society attaches various labels, one is not born with knowledge we expect of experts; that characteristic is attained and not merely inherited." Randall Kennedy, "Racial Critiques of Legal Academia," 102 *Harv. L. Rev.* 1745 (1989).

And again: "My central objection to the claim of racial distinctiveness [is] . . . that it *stereotypes* scholars. By stereotyping, I mean the process whereby the particularity of an individual's characteristics [is] denied by reference to the perceived characteristics of the racial group with which the individual is associated . . . But . . . 'any stereotype results in a partial blindness to the actual qualities of individuals, and consequently is a persistent and prolific breeding ground for irrational treatment of them'" (id. at 1786–87, quoting Lusky, "The Stereotype: Hard Core of Racism," 13 *Buffalo L. Rev.* 450, 451 [1964]). "There are many types of classification that negate individual identity, achievement, and dignity. But racial classification has come to be viewed as paradigmatically offensive to individuality" (id. at 1794).

pends on our ability to separate people from their context: "As I define the term, 'merit' stands for achieved honor by some standard that is indifferent to the social identity of a given author."[69] Judgments that are colored by "social identity" are "ameritocratic." Social identity gets in the way when we allow our judgment to be distorted by the skin color or ethnic experience of the person or work in question, and also when we allow personal relationships to influence us.

Kennedy's initial list of ameritocratic motives in scholarly citation includes: "to display one's knowledge of a given literature, to show deference to those in a position to harm or help one's career, and to advance the careers of friends or *ideological* allies."[70] He then adds racial favoritism.[71] A second list begins with "academic nepotism by using citations to promote friends."[72] Then, along with racial favoritism, he denounces "*all* practices that exploit the trappings of meritocracy to advance interests—friendship, the reputation of one's

---

And again: "Rather, the point is that distance or nearness to a given subject—'outsiderness' or 'insiderness'—are simply social conditions; they provide opportunities that intellectuals are free to use or squander, but they do not in themselves determine the intellectual quality of scholarly productions—*that* depends on what a particular scholar makes of his or her materials, regardless of his or her social position" (id. at 1795).

According to Kennedy, application of Delgado's idea of racial standing "would be bad for all scholars because status-based criteria for intellectual standing are anti-intellectual in that they subordinate ideas and craft to racial status. After all, to be told that one lacks 'standing' is to be told that no matter what one's message—no matter how true or urgent or beautiful—it will be ignored or discounted because of *who* one is" (id. at 1796).

"[S]cholars should keep racial generalizations in their place, including those that are largely accurate. Scholars should do so by evaluating other scholars as individuals, without prejudgment, no matter what their hue. Scholars should . . . inculcate . . . a skeptical attitude toward all labels and categories that obscure appreciation of the unique features of specific persons and their work" (id. at 1796–97). For more, see id. at 1798 n.240. In passing, the article emphatically applies the same individualist idea to virtue and art as to merit: "Participation in struggles against racial tyranny or any other sort of oppression is largely a matter of choice, an assertion of will. That is why we honor those who participate in such struggles" (id. at 1800). Quoting Ellison: "[W]e select neither our parents, our race nor our nation . . . But we *do* become writers out of an act of will, out of an act of choice" (id. at 1804 n.265). Back to the theme, again quoting Ellison: "What moves a writer . . . is less meaningful than what he makes of it" (id. at 1804). Kennedy again: "A badge of merit should not be pinned onto someone simply because she exists in a state she had no hand in creating. Merit should be limited to describing something that a person *adds* to their received conditions" (id. at 1805 n.271).

school, career ambitions, *ideological affiliations*—that have nothing to do with the intellectual characteristics of the subject being judged."[73]

From the point of view of the political and cultural cases for affirmative action, there are three problems with the "derogation from individuality" argument. First, it repeatedly confuses the scholarly judgment of a particular work with the judgment of a candidate for a job or promotion. It is uncontroversial that when we are assessing a particular article, we don't give it a higher quality ranking because it has a black author than we would if it had a white author. But Kennedy often seems to interpret the "racial critiques" as though that were their position. I don't read them that way. The question is whether, in assessing candidates, we should "presume" that we will get a different and ultimately more valuable body of scholarly work if we allocate resources in a race-conscious way.[74]

Second, the cultural and ideological aspects of my achievements (accomplishments, attainments) aren't separable, for purposes of the

---

"The strategy of elevating racial status to an intellectual credential undermines the conception of intellectual merit as a mark of *achieved* distinction by confusing the relationship between racial background and scholarly expertise; the former is a social condition in which one is born, while the latter is something an individual attains. Confusing accidental attributes and achieved distinctions in turn derogates the process by which all individuals, simultaneously limited and aided by the conditions they inherit, personally contribute to human culture.

"As I use the word, 'merit' is an honorific term that identifies a quality of accomplishment that has been achieved; it does not refer to inherited characteristics such as race or gender" (id. at 1805–06).

"All he [Isiah Thomas] rightly argues is . . . that observers not be so overwhelmed with his God-given attributes that they fail to appreciate what he, on his own, adds to them . . ." (id. at 1806 n.272).

Part I of Kennedy's article discusses the "cultural context" of the racial critiques. There is a nod to the idea that this context requires an understanding of the "relationship between knowledge and power" (id. at 1749), but the overwhelming emphasis is on negative stereotyping of black intellectuals by whites. The notion of "derogation" is central. See id. at 1751 ("derogatory comments") and n.25 ("derogation of Negro capacity").

"[A]lthough the overt forms of racial domination described thus far were enormously destructive, *covert* color bars have been, in a certain sense, even more insidious. After all, judgments based on expressly racist criteria make no pretense about evaluating the merit of the individual's work. Far more cruel are racially prejudiced judgments that are rationalized in terms of meritocratic standards. Recognizing that American history is seeded with examples of intellectuals of color whose accomplishments were ignored or undervalued because of race is absolutely crucial for understanding the bone-deep resentment and distrust that finds expression in the racial critique literature" (id. at 1752–53).

judgment of others, from the effects of my "individuality" or my "will." So there's nothing wrong, nothing "derogatory," in judging my work or my promise in a way that is race-conscious and sensitive to my ideological commitments. (Of course, the judgment may be incorrect, and it may be prejudiced.) Third, the judgment process, whose integrity Kennedy's article wants above all to preserve, is always already corrupted by the ideological and cultural factors he wants to exclude. We can avoid this corruption only if we deliberately impoverish and trivialize judgment by excluding the very aspects of individuals and their works that legal academics should care most about.

Culture, Ideology, and Individuality

Culture

The category of culture fits neither the color-blind meritocratic view, emphasizing individual freedom to succeed or fail under universally agreed standards, nor the racialist view that biology has the power to determine people as meritorious or meritless. Its significance for fundamentalism is that membership in a culture looks somewhat like a status attribute of the individual rather than like something "earned" or "achieved." Culture is reproduced through child rearing and through life in a habitually closed discursive system.

It is also true that people can "change cultures" or "assimilate" to a culture other than their own. People are often "bicultural" or even "tricultural." As with class, there seem to be no inherent limits on what a person can achieve in an adopted culture. On the other hand, assimilation is hard work, a talent in itself. At moments of cultural crisis, or as a matter of course, depending on the culture's self-understanding, the assimilated person's "authenticity" may be questioned, and the mere existence of this possibility makes for a distinctive relationship to the community in question.

Introducing the notion of culture blurs the distinction between judging on the basis of "mere" status, assumed to have no connection with capacities or other qualities of individuals, and judging on "achievement of the individual," assumed to be independent of status. Culture is both deeply ingrained (not changeable at will, even if changeable over the long run) and strongly differentiating;

my ability to produce artifacts with meaning is therefore tied to my status.

This concept of culture makes the notion of "inert" experience transformed into something of value by the "individual" seem pretty crude. The individual is "made" by a whole body of experiences, shaped into a particular cultural being. When he or she sets out to produce an artifact out of a particular experience, what gets made is a product of all these other experiences that are collective, group, consciously and unconsciously cultural experiences. These collective things influence everything from the way the particular "raw material" is experienced to the way it is translated into whatever artifactual medium the "individual" chooses.

Culture is an attribute of an individual that is "inherited" (though not biological), both in the sense of "coming from the past" and in the sense of being, in any particular case, partially ineradicable through individual will. And it is an attribute that produces a heavy collective influence on all the performances and capacities of the individual. The fundamentalist cannot level against cultural claims the charge of "irrelevance" or "irrationality" that is enough to dismiss claims based on race per se.[75]

At the same time, there is the experience of freedom within culture (indeed, where else could one experience it, since there is no extracultural space), and the experience of individual accomplishment. A given culture may be more or less committed to the "cultural fluidity, intellectual freedom, and individual autonomy"[76] Kennedy's article defends. People self-consciously make their own selection from among the positions or attitudes available within a culture, and they choose positions and attitudes *toward* the very culture that constitutes their being. A person's action can change the culture that defines the possibilities of action. Recognizing culture doesn't *annihilate* the individual. But recognizing it does blur the boundary between self and social context, and problematizes the assertion that a capacity or an artifact can be divided up into one part that is the inert matter and another part that is reflective of "will," "accomplishment," or "achievement."

Ideology

Once you choose an ideology, you have "rejected one path in favor of another," and what you see and do as you travel that path will be different from what you would have seen and done going the other way. Ideology is commitment. It is the decision to work on this line of inquiry rather than that one, to assume away these issues rather than those, in a situation in which you cannot say that there was no other course available. You may be able to say that given your good faith belief in the rightness of your path, you obviously had no choice. But if other people believed equally in good faith that your path was wrong, and theirs right, then your choice was ideological. Once you've made, explicitly or implicitly, choices of this kind, there are kinds of work you don't find yourself doing and kinds of problems you find yourself just ignoring.

My view is that it just isn't possible to do legal scholarship without making choices of this kind, consciously or unconsciously. (This view is part of my ideology.) Within legal scholarship, we are fighting out basic questions about how society is organized. More specifically, we are fighting about the lives of the ethnic minorities and majorities of the country. The descriptive and prescriptive categories we use (such as balancing, rights, efficiency, domination) are sharply contested among us, as are underlying conceptions of American social reality itself.[77]

One's ideology is more a matter of choice than one's cultural identity, but it poses similar difficulties for the fundamentalist understanding of individual merit. When you choose one among the possible ideological paths, you lose, as you travel along it, access to the data and the perspective you might have had along another possible path. Of course, it is not as though the view from another ideological vantage point is just unimaginable. And it is always possible to go back and start again or to set off through the underbrush. But whenever you stop and decide to write something, you do it from a particular position on the ideological map. You are enlightened but also limited, "situated" in ideological space much as you are situated in a community and in a cultural identity. There is no no-position position.

Further, ideologies are collective projects created over time. Individuals discover them, in the sense of coming upon them, but do not invent them, any more than an individual can invent a culture. Once you discover an ideology, you explore it, grapple with its great figures or its everyday clichés, assimilate to it little by little or undergo conversion. You adapt it to your purposes and perhaps try to change it, even radically, but it has a transindividual continuity. Someone else will reinterpret your reinterpretation.

Finally, the "you" who pursues preideological purposes is never in a purely instrumental relation to the ideology that consciously or unconsciously provides your framework and conceptual vocabulary. The frame remakes you through and through even as "you" "use" "it." Kennedy's article treats ideological affiliation as just another bias, like friendship or the desire to advance one's career.[78] But the "slant" that each person's ideological formation gives his or her work and his or her judgments of other people's work is neither an idiosyncratic individual matter, irrelevant in the same way that hair or eye or skin color is irrelevant, nor a distortion that one could purge if one tried hard enough.

Individuality

Individuality, against this background, is a problematic as well as an indispensable idea. There are many possible interpretations, but two seem to me to emerge tempered rather than consumed by critical fire. Both start from the notion that culture and ideology provide a vocabulary from which "individuals" pick and choose, constrained by their situation in time and space but with plenty available, even in the most apparently "disadvantaged" position, from which to produce their "selves."

In the first interpretation, individuality is something we read into behavior, from the most mundane to the most exalted, behavior that may seem at first glance nothing more than a jumble of familiar elements culled from the stockpiles of culture, ideology, and psychology. Everyone has a race, a sex, a class, a culture, ideological presuppositions, even a more or less immutable neurotic style. But no one is only these things, because each person's production of self at any given moment, in any given law review article, is a particular selection and combination from an inexhaustible universe of possibilities. "Individuality" is an effect produced on, an experience of, "readers," brought about by the juxtaposition of elements in a way that is neither logically compelled nor arbitrary, but recognizably designed to say something to someone.

In this way of looking at it, my individuality is something you have access to only through my behavior, my tone of voice, or my tome on hardy perennials. I exist, even for myself, only embedded in materials—some of my choosing, some not—materials produced by others for purposes other than those I now pursue.

In the second interpretation of individuality, we try to get at the producer of these shows, to sneak behind the curtain and confront the Wizard of Oz. But there is an infinite regress. Who is the wizard producing the modest humbug who produced the Wizard? The condition of meeting up with another "individual," in this second view, is accepting that he or she will just appear on your wave length, in moments of intersubjective zap. There is no assurance that he or she will be there, in contact, at the next moment, or that when he or she reappears it will be as "the same person." There is no way to fix the other through understanding (through an image of what he or she is really like, or a theory of his or her personality, or whatever). Both the other and the self are unitary in the moment but multiple over time—intelligible in the moment but contradictory taken all together. The individual, in this view, is what is not embedded, and therefore what is ineffable, unjudgeable, ungraspable with the apparatus of thought.

I subscribe to both views (they do not seem to me incompatible), and so am happy to be called an "individualist."[79] But neither view allows the operation of meritocratic judgment of a person or a work, without regard to cultural and ideological context, that is so important in fundamentalism.

"Individuality" Cannot Be Distinguished from Culture and Ideology

In deciding to hire or promote, it is not unfair to judge the individual on the basis of the social characteristic of connection to a cultural community, because the individual cannot be separated from his or her culture in the way that Kennedy's article requires. The "individual" simply doesn't exist in that way. It is quite reasonable, and I have no cause to complain, if you expect different things of me, predict different things of me, and make different interpretations and hence different evaluative judgments of what I say, because you know something of my cultural context.

It doesn't derogate from my individuality that you "do this to me." There just isn't work I do or a me you can evaluate, or about whom you can make reasonable predictions, that isn't embedded in culture. All I can do in response is to reserve the right to argue when I feel that the stereotypes you apply distort your perceptions of my meaning or my capacity.

Second, I wouldn't *want* my legal scholarship to be evaluated in a color-blind way. Because we do our scholarly work in a context of culturally specific meanings, we are limited as individuals in what we can do and express, even in what we can be understood to say. But we are also empowered to do things that are intelligible only because we do them in the particular context. Because I know that Randy Kennedy's article is written by a black American intellectual in 1989, I get much more out of it than I could if I had to guess at who had written it and when and where.

In an earlier article, "On Cussing out White Liberals,"[80] Kennedy described a style of black protest and critiqued it. "Racial Critiques of Legal Academia" has much the same agenda. I read both articles as written in the cussing-out-black-militants genre, in which a progressive integrationist black author takes black radicals to task. I suspect that I don't pick up on all the subtleties, but because I have a notion that this genre exists, the article has a whole level of coherence for me that it would not otherwise have.[81]

An important rhetorical move in cussing is to begin with denunciations of white racism adequate to refute in advance the accusation of Uncle Tomism. Then comes the central pitch: the militants are using unsubstantiated accusations of white racist discrimination and white cultural bias as lame excuses for their own and the minority community's failure to live up to neutral standards of excellence. All the hot but in the end contentless talk about racial identity is just posturing.

Writers in this genre typically charge that black militant posturing diverts attention from the real problems of minority performance and lays a spurious claim to special treatment from white institutions, a claim that white liberals are all too willing to accept. That acceptance is condescending, because the liberals won't openly apply to what the militants say the same standards of sensible discourse that they apply among themselves or to their white adversaries. This phenomenon supposedly reflects both white liberal wimpiness and an underlying white racist belief that sloppy militant rhetoric is the best that can be expected from black (and Hispanic and Asian) folk.

Kennedy's article falls into the trickiest subspecies of this genre, the one that is concerned with the "academic study of academia." The basic move in this subgenre is to apply the standards the militants are criticizing to the militants' own critique. Neutral standards of scholarly excellence show that the attack on neutral standards of scholarly excellence lacks scholarly excellence. This type of argument can cut to the quick because of the history of racial stereotyping of minorities as intellectually inferior, and because mainstream post-1960s political thought dismisses radical minority intellectuals as hysterical second-raters or racists.

I don't think it derogatory to assess Kennedy's article as a performance in this specific genre. The article is more interesting, and better in some ways and worse in others, when read as coming from a racial (cultural) and ideological position. The "individual" who wrote it is more accessible when we understand the literary materials he was working with. The danger is that we will confuse the "voice" of the genre with the actual author, whose individuality, as I suggested above, is ungraspable. If we confused the person with the genre in this case, it would be difficult to understand how Kennedy could have written the following:

> In the forties, fifties and early sixties, against the backdrop of laws that used racial distinctions to exclude Negroes from opportunities available to white citizens, it seemed that racial subjugation could be overcome by mandating the application of race-blind law. In retrospect, however, it appears that the concept of race-blindness was simply a proxy for the fundamental demand that racial subjugation be eradicated. This demand, which matured over time in the face of myriad sorts of opposition, focused upon the *condition* of racial subjugation; its target was not only procedures that overtly excluded Negroes on the basis of race, but also the self-perpetuating dynamics of subordination that had survived the demise of American apartheid. The opponents of affirmative action have stripped the historical context from the demand of race-blind law. They have fashioned this demand into a new totem and insist on deference to it no matter what its effects upon the very group the fourteenth amendment was created to protect.[82]

Because you know that I am a white American intellectual writing in the 1990s, there are a million things I can say in this article without saying them, because you will infer them from this cultural

context. And there are a million things you will read in that I
didn't mean to be there. I see the interdependence, the inseparabil-
ity, of my individuality and my context as inevitable and also as
something to be embraced. Likewise my simultaneous limitation
and empowerment by the fact of working in a context. My individuality is not "derogated" when I am judged and when I communicate in a context, though there is bitter with the sweet. The
same is true of ideology.[83]

Rational Meritocratic Judgment Cannot Be Culturally and Ideologically Neutral

The flip side is that there is no evaluation aimed at getting at what
I value in my own work that won't be contingent on your cultural
identity. What I am trying to achieve in my work is a contribution
to a cultural situation in which I am implicated, culturally specific.
This is equally true of the people whose judgment I most value. If
I can't be judged outside of my context, they can't judge me outside of their context. No matter how favorable the judgment, I
can't take it as "objective." But I can criticize critiques and reject
their condemnation as "distorted." I don't have to claim or to
abandon either universality or context-dependence. I can switch
back and forth between the two perspectives, though without any
"metalevel" assurance that I'm ever getting it right. All of the above
applies to my ideological as well as to my cultural context.

There are a million misunderstandings, based on racial, ideological, national, and temporal stereotypes, to which Randall Kennedy
and I are subject because you read us in this context. And because
you know what you know of the context, there are good readings
of our texts that you may discern against our will. There is nothing
we can do about this, except argue on our own behalf.

The argument may involve racism. I see racism as more than
inaccurate stereotyping. It is "neurotic" in the same sense that the
fetishizing of merit is. It is insisting on the stereotype's truth because you want or need it to be true, in the absence of evidence, or
in the face of evidence that the group or a particular member is
completely different from what you expected. The racist, whether
white or black, won't let you be other than what he or she wants
you to be, and that is something bad. But if you accept that you

have a cultural identity, the attack on it can't be dismissed as "just" irrational, in the way it could if all cultural communities were the same, or if the differences between them made no difference.

It might be true that the racist is making a correct negative judgment about something that really is a part of you but that there is little or nothing you can do about. It might be true because cultural communities are different and you have characteristics that are derived from your cultural community. The hatred you encounter is wrong or crazy, as hatred. But there might be, somewhere mixed in with it, a valid negative judgment on your group identity. If you don't think that's so, then even after you have rejected and condemned the crazy hatred dimension, you have to defend the communal aspect of your being on the "merits."

Against this background, it seems legitimate and useful for Richard Delgado to attempt an explicitly race-conscious assessment of the white liberal constitutional law scholarship of the 1970s and 1980s.[84] "Scholars should . . . evaluat[e] other scholars as individuals, without prejudgment, no matter what their hue," as Kennedy suggests,[85] in the sense of avoiding stereotyping like the plague. But Kennedy urges us (somewhat ambiguously) to "keep racial generalizations in their place, including those that are largely accurate."[86]

I don't agree with this if it means that we can't try to figure out whether, for example, a distaste for the "reparations" argument for affirmative action is a characteristic trait of a particular white liberal mode of constitutional law analysis. And I see nothing wrong with trying to connect such a trait to the unconscious motives of white liberal scholars as a culturally and ideologically distinct group, or with condemning it as a "defect." It is not, for me, a question of the legitimacy of a type of analysis, but of the plausibility of a particular interpretation.[87]

In short, it is legitimate for Delgado to argue for a "linkage of White scholars' racial background to the qualities in their work that he perceives as shortcomings," so long as he makes his case.[88] Kennedy's article poses a false alternative:

> [T]he point is that distance or nearness to a given subject—"outsiderness" or "insiderness"—are simply social conditions; they provide opportunities that intellectuals are free to use or squander, but they do not in themselves determine the intellectual quality of scholarly productions—*that* depends on what a particu-

lar scholar makes of his or her materials, regardless of his or her social position.[89]

Cultural and ideological situations are neither "simply social conditions" (in the sense of "inert matter") nor attributes that "determine . . . intellectual quality." They are betwixt and between. They are "formative" rather than "inert" or "determining." And this is the premise of Kennedy's own article, the first section of which is "The Cultural Context of Racial Critiques."

In that section Kennedy argues that the racial critiques "share an intellectual kinship with several well-known and influential intellectual traditions."[90] We learn that we can't "understand" the racial critiques except in the context of "the ongoing effort by intellectuals of color to control the public image of minority groups."[91] In the sections titled "The Racial Exclusion Claim as a Form of Politics," and "The Politics of Publicity," Kennedy assesses the arguments of Bell, Delgado, and Matsuda as *the arguments of scholars of color.* Their claims have an "*outer* facet addressed principally to whites and an *inner* facet addressed principally to minorities."[92]

He then proceeds to analyze the bad motives (guilt-tripping white liberals and cheerleading for minorities)[93] behind their arguments in a way that seems indistinguishable from what Delgado did with the white liberal constitutional law scholars.[94] Kennedy's attribution of motives is an inference from their texts, but also from his knowledge that they are scholars of color writing in the radical intellectual tradition that he has identified, and pursuing a particular political (ideological) project.

Imagine that Kennedy's article shows up in the file of Professor Bell, Matsuda, or Delgado when one of them is being considered for a lateral appointment. The article would certainly be read as an assessment of the "merit" of their scholarship, but hardly as applying a "standard that is indifferent to the social identity of a given author."[95] Wouldn't it, using Kennedy's criterion, "derogate from [their] individuality . . . insofar as their unique characteristics are submerged in the image of the group to which they are deemed to belong"?[96] Indeed, one might argue that the article "stereotypes" them as "militants of color" in order to cuss them out for the sins of the Black Panthers and the black sociology movement of the 1960s.[97]

Of course, it is not unimaginable that any of the racial critique articles could have been written by a white. In that case, it seems likely that Kennedy's article would have leveled many of the same criticisms against the white author, but omitted some and added others. Kennedy's article asserts that "some observers do not have much confidence in the abilities, or perhaps even the capacities, of minority intellectuals . . . they lack the sense that those with whom they disagree are their intellectual equals."[98] If Bell, Matsuda, or Delgado were white, Kennedy might critique the "merit" of their discussions of minority scholarship through the observation that "[s]ometimes observers display their lowered expectations . . . by more generously praising work by minorities than they would praise similar work by whites."[99]

My point is not to censure Kennedy's article for "race-conscious" assessment of merit. It is rather that if one wants to take work like theirs seriously, as he does, it just is not possible to make the rigid separation he proposes between the authors' merely accidental or inherited aspects and their "will" or "achievement" as "individuals." Kennedy is wrong to claim that the cultural background (race) and ideological affiliations of an author "have nothing to do with the intellectual characteristics of the subject being judged."[100]

Since it is legal scholarship and law teaching that are in question, culture and ideology (mediated through intellectual paradigms and research projects) permeate the subject being judged. Legal knowledge is *about* how our culturally diverse and ideologically divided society should be organized. We can achieve color-blind neutrality and ideological neutrality only if we refuse to assess these aspects. Kennedy's article proposes (his own practice to the contrary notwithwithstanding) to judge the work without considering its subject and purpose. This is an evasion of politics.[101]

Taking Color-Blindness Seriously

Many law faculties adopt in practice (though not in theory) a rule that if you publish some number of articles on clearly legal topics in well regarded law reviews, you will get tenure. Period. No one will try to decide whether they think the articles are any good.

A judgment of this kind is not outside culture and ideology, because what counts as "legal," which law reviews are "well regarded," and the criteria by which those reviews judge articles submitted for publication are all culturally and ideologically contingent. But it is perfectly true that when members of the faculty accept the standard, they can apply it without animadversion to culture or ideology. They can grant tenure to anyone who meets the standard, even if all the articles would be culturally strange and ideologically abhorrent to them if they read them.

Another tack is to distinguish "craft" or "technique" from substance, conceding the cultural and ideological contingency of the latter but maintaining neutral standards for the former. The distinction is problematic because different cultures and ideologies and paradigms have different conceptions of craft. It is problematic because different paradigms may be at different levels of technical development at a given moment. But the deeper objection is that judging on this basis a work that aspires to substantive importance is arbitrary if the judges are themselves interested in rewarding valuable substance (as well as in virtues of execution). The result is to hire people who are substantively empty or evil because they are "competent," and to refuse to hire people who have profound insights because they lack something valuable but less important.

Yet another approach is to recognize that there are "genres" of legal scholarship, and to hire or promote "the best" within each. The obvious objections here are that "outsider" judgments about what is good within a genre are likely to vary dramatically according to the ideological commitments and genre loyalties of the judger. And once you have ranked works within various genres, there is the question of allocating the "slots" among them. If you think right-wing law and economics work is the most valuable now being done in legal academia, your neutral "intragenre" criteria won't help you choose between a third-rate econ-jock and a much higher-ranked centrist "doctrinal" candidate. Ultimately some quite patently ideological or cultural criterion of appropriate pluralism will have to come into play, or the outcome will be random.

But what of the scholar of color who rejects this patently ideological version of standards, and himself or herself demands to be judged on a color-blind basis?[102] If this demand is addressed to a law faculty that is deciding on hiring or promotion, it is misaddressed. The faculty will decide by vote, on the basis of each faculty member's understanding of the appropriate criteria. I wouldn't see myself as bound to vote against a candidate I would otherwise favor because the candidate wanted to be judged color-blind.

Candidates who think they have had the benefit of an illegitimate preference can refuse the job, or take it and use their power as voting members to influence their colleagues to abandon the error of their ways. I don't see a faculty member as obliged to abandon his or her position in the ideological dispute about culturally conscious decision even if the candidate views the criterion as "insulting" or as "derogating from individuality."[103]

But now suppose I am addressed as an individual, rather than as someone voting on hiring or promotion. The demand is simply for my judgment: Is this person of color "the best law teacher" in the school, or "the best scholar," or is this particular article "the best in the field"? Suppose further that this scholar does his or her utmost to write as a member not of an ethnic culture but of the "cosmopolitan" culture to which Kennedy refers approvingly.[104] It might be possible to answer without cultural identity's playing any role at all. A white or a black scholar might so overwhelmingly dominate that it just wouldn't be plausible that anyone else could be "the best."

In this sense, law teaching and scholarship have an irreducible resemblance to a game with highly determinate rules. The resemblance is not in the rules, but in the possibility of a person's being so good that any particular observer will judge without hesitation.[105] This possibility also exists at the bottom end. But such cases are rare.

In the usual case, it will be possible to answer "without regard to race" only if we pose the question narrowly enough. The article is within a particular genre. Suppose the author has either deliberately or just naturally written it in such a way that no reader would be likely to advert to the question of the author's race in reading it. A white reader is likely to assume that the author is white. But suppose the reader is reading lots of articles and knows that some of them are by blacks. The reader can rank the articles color-blind.

If I am the reader, I will have an ideological judgment about the genre. The genre is the product of a joint scholarly endeavor in paradigm creation. It has a cultural history. The vast majority of recognizable genres, moreover, have a specifically white, ideologically moderate or conservative history. Their culture and ideology are built into their rules, their habitual literary and intellectual devices. If I am asked to compare an article in such a genre with one that has a different cultural and ideological history, my comparison will be based on my own cultural and ideological situation. I can rank the black author of an antitrust article in the interest-balancing-cum-institutional-competence genre against other authors in the same genre without race's having any effect on the judgment. But in the crossgenre comparison, I will understand and rank his on her article as the product of a white, ideologically moderate group identity.

When I am told after the fact that the author was black, my reaction will be that the author is an excellent performer in the cultural mode of the dominant community. This is a far cry from "the best, period." In other words, I do not regard the genres of the "cosmopolitan" culture as universal vessels into which each of us is free to pour his or her individual content. They are vessels but they are also molds, each with a history as part of the project of domination and subordination, *as well as* a history as part of the project of transcendence and enlightenment.

Now suppose the question is about teaching. I judge teachers according to the values I myself subscribe to as a teacher. My view is that law teaching is inescapably an intelligentsia activity of cultural and ideological development in a situation of contest, of domination and subordination. But I also fully recognize and embrace the craft dimension of law. I can rank teachers color-blind according to their skill in getting students to understand the meanings and relationships among themselves of an easement, a covenant and an equitable servitude. But a teacher whose course teaches only this kind of determinate content and cognitive skill is pursuing a culturally derived, ideologically charged agenda, teaching a philosophy of law by omission. The teacher who goes beyond this cognitive minimum is moving neither toward nor away from "neutrality," but toward some *different,* more explicit but no less ideological, philosophy of law.

Whatever the solution, from the purely cognitive to the explicitly culturally-conscious and political, the teacher's relation to the students has a symbolic dimension: the teacher is black or white, a purported "neutral, black letter man" or a touchy-feely liberal. Every teacher does something with these contingent attributes in the classroom, consciously or unconsciously. His or her individuality does not exist in a way that can be distinguished from them. Well, you will say, he or she could teach from behind a screen. Then the choice to use a particular voice would be a choice to situate himself or herself in the American cultural context. But he or she could write on a word processor that would flash his or her words onto the screen. Right. But the words themselves would communicate not only an individual but an individual's choices among the multiple ways of expression that characterize a society divided the way ours is. And so forth.

And what would be gained by teaching from behind a screen with a word processor flashing one's words before the students? The teachers who chose this method could be ranked color-blind a lot more plausibly than those who chose the "normal" method. But in comparing them with those who taught as culturally and ideologically situated individuals, openly deploying and developing those aspects of their identity, we would find ourselves judging the cultural and ideological context of the choice. Unless the fundamentalists made everyone teach their way, they could never be sure they were "the best, period," and not just "the best white" or "the best black."

In order to achieve Kennedy's ideal meritocratic academy, we have to imagine that both the bitter and the sweet of cultural and ideological differences are eliminated or reduced to such an extent that it no longer seems important to take them into account in structuring hiring and promotion. So long as they exist, there will be an element of cultural and ideological contingency to judgments of merit, or an element of arbitrariness in substituting "objective" but nonsubstantive criteria. I see the differences and the process of self-consciously negotiating to take the element of contingency into account as valuable in themselves. So the fundamentalist utopia seems to me impoverished. We could have color-blind meritocracy only in a society less desirable than ours would be, if we could preserve class, cultural, community, and ideological differences but consciously mitigate their bad effects.

Conclusion

If there is a conceptual theme to this essay, it is that of "positionality," or "situatedness." The individual in his or her culture, the individual as a practitioner of an ideology, the individual in relation to his or her own neurotic structures is always somewhere, has always just been somewhere else, and is empowered and limited by being in that spot on the way from some other spot. Communities are like that too, though in a complicated way. One of the things that define a community's position—its situation, and the specific possibilities that go with it—is its history of collective accomplishment. Another is its history of crimes against humanity. It seems unlikely that there are communities without such histories.

The crime of slavery is deep in the past of white America. But ever since slavery, in each succeeding decade after the Emancipation Proclamation, we have added new crimes until it sometimes seems that the weight of commission and omission lies so heavily on nonwhite America that there just isn't anything that anyone can do about it. All anyone can hope is to be out of the way of the whirlwind, the big one and all the little ones played out in day-to-day life.

The bad history also creates opportunities that other communities don't have, or have in different ways. It would be quite something to build a multicultural society on the basis of what has happened here, where we have neither a consensual foundation in history nor a myth of human benevolence to make it all seem natural. An American multicultural society will arise out of guilt, anger, mistrust, cynicism, bitter conflict, and a great deal of confusion and contradiction, if it arises at all, and would be, to my mind, the more wonderful for it.

The specific proposal put forth above, for a kind of cultural proportional representation in the exercise of ideological power through legal academia, would be a very small step in that direction. As is true of any very specific proposal that can be implemented right now by small numbers of people holding local power, it is a drop in the bucket. But the minute we imagine it as a government policy applied in a consistent way across the whole range of situations to which it is arguably applicable, it loses most of its appeal. First, none of us local powerholders could do much to bring it about, and, second, taking the proposal seriously as state policy might lead to all kinds of disastrous unintended side-effects.

This has been a proposal for drops in the bucket, not for the reorganization of state power. If it made a trivial contribution at vast social cost, we could abandon it as we adopted it, faculty by faculty, decision by decision. If it worked, the "kerplunk" of drops falling in nearly empty buckets might cause others to prick up their ears. And in any case legal academics can, and so should, exercise their power to govern themselves in accord with the ideals of democracy and intellectual integrity—ideals that white supremacy compromises all around us.

3

The Stakes of Law, or
Hale and Foucault!

started law school in 1967 with a sense that the "system" had a lot of injustice in it, meaning that the distribution of wealth and income and power and access to knowledge seemed unfairly skewed along class and race lines. I thought law was important in the skewing process and in efforts to make distribution fairer, but I had no clear idea how or why. This essay describes what I think I have found out in the intervening years about this elemental question.

In the 1920s and 1930s, the legal realist institutional economists, and most particularly Robert Hale, worked out an analysis of the role of law in the distribution of income between social classes.[1] That analysis retains its power today. The basic idea is that the rules of property, contract, and tort law (along with the criminal law rules that reinforce them in some cases) are "rules of the game of economic struggle." As such, they differentially and asymmetrically empower groups bargaining over the fruits of cooperation in production.

In the 1970s, Michel Foucault and his collaborators developed an analysis of "power/knowledge" that has much in common with that of the realists.[2] Foucault gives law an important place in his general social theory, but his version of law is, unfortunately, prerealist. At the same time Foucault offers an indispensable antidote to the premodern understanding of the "individual" or the "subject" that infuses realist thinking about the economy.

This essay is more a rude appropriation of text-fragments of Hale and Foucault than a study of their thought. The motive of the appropriation is to get help in developing a method for analyzing the role of law in the reproduction of social injustice in late capitalist societies. The resulting pastiche of positive insights from the pragmatist/legal realist/institutional economics school and from postmodernism and poststructuralism may make up in practical usefulness—for example, in the study of class, race, and gender aspects of low-income housing markets—what it lacks in purity of origin. But in this essay I do no more than begin to explore compatibilities and incompatibilities of the two schools.

The focus here doesn't mean that I think the only important thing about law is its distributive effect. Legal rules function to distribute, but they also "resolve disputes" in ways that people find more or less fair or just (this is where ideals like altruism and individualism come in). Legal discourse is the language for stating the legal rules that function distributively, but it has many other uses and effects (this is where ideas like legitimation, rationalization, apology and utopia come in).

The Importance of Legal Rules in Determining the Distribution of Income between Social Classes

> The market value of a property or of a service is merely a measure of the strength of the bargaining power of the person who owns the one or renders the other, under the particular legal rights with which the law endows him, and the legal restrictions which it places on others.[3]

A crucial factor in the distribution of income between social classes is bargaining between capital and labor over wages. Labor and capital cooperate (and battle) in the production process, so that the output is a joint product. Nothing tells us a priori how the value of the joint product will be divided. If we analogize bargaining to a game played under rules, the outcome of the game is the distribution of the benefits of cooperation. Each rule of the game, even if stated in a way that "applies to all players," can be analyzed for its impact on the chances of all players. For example, the rules of basketball could be changed so as to increase or decrease the advantages of tall players over short ones, fast ones over slow ones, and so forth. Lowering the height of the hoop would affect, in complex ways, the relative "ability" of each player.

Bargaining over joint products differs from many games in that the outcome is an agreement. An important goal of the realists was to show that it was unreal to treat the agreement as an instance of "freedom," if what we mean by that is "doing or getting what you want." They preferred to characterize the outcome as the product of "coercion," by which they meant that neither party got what it wanted (the whole joint product) and each had the experience of being "forced" to settle for less.

This recharacterization was important in part because it punctured the conservative economic rhetoric of the time. That rhetoric justified the existing capitalist system on the ground that it was based on freedom (the free market, free labor, freedom of contract, consumer sovereignty) by contrast to socialism, which supposedly replaced all these freedoms with their opposite, namely state coercion. According to the realists, capitalism was as coercive in its way as socialism.[4]

The realist analysis was equally hostile to the Marxism of the time, which offered a model in which the "absolute impoverishment" of the working class meant that capital was "free" (within the constraints of competition among capitalists), but the working class was coerced into "accepting" an exploitative wage rate. In that model, there is no bargaining at all, since one side has no bargaining power. In the realist model, each side is constrained, each can inflict harm on the other in some ways but not in others, each has limited alternatives to cooperation, and capitalists are as much coerced as workers.

The realists' coercion analysis contained a substantive insight as well, an insight into the role of legal rules. The state uses force to ensure obedience to the rules of the game of bargaining over a joint product. To the extent that these rules affect the outcome, forcing the parties to settle for x rather than y percent of the joint product, the state is implicated in the outcome. It is an author of the distribution even though that distribution appears to be determined solely by the "voluntary" agreement of the parties.[5]

Looked at in this way, late nineteenth- and early twentieth-century judges influenced the distribution of income between workers and owners when they decided whether or not a secondary boycott (union refuses to deal with employer X to induce him to stop dealing with employer Y, with whom the union has a dispute) was legal or illegal. When Congress much later outlawed secondary boycotts, it changed the balance of power between labor and capital. And when judges today decide in doubtful cases whether a particular tactic falls into that category, they are deciding the distributive consequences of the statute.

This example is an easy one, because it is intuitively plausible that there was an open legal question at the end of the nineteenth century about the legality of secondary boycotts, and we are now used to thinking of legislation in the labor/management area as at least partly distributively motivated. It seems plausible to see this as a situation in which the contribution of the judges and the legislature was to deal with a new situation and then work out the implications of the solution (the National Labor Relations Act ban on secondary boycotts).

The problem with this way of looking at it is that it distracts attention from the fact that legislators and judges are responsible for the framework of ground rules within which labor conflict is conducted, including such basic rules as that corporations can "own" factories, that no one "owns" the ocean, that you have no legal obligation to help a starving stranger, that workers can sell their labor and must refrain from taking its product home with them when they have agreed that it will belong to their employer.

Most of the time these ground rules of the system are just assumed, as are the hundreds and hundreds of other articulated rules that it takes to decide what it *means* to "own a factory." But someone had to decide whether the recognition of employee rights to self-organization in the National Labor Relations Act did or did not imply a right of union organizers to go onto employers' premises against their will. In other words, they had to decide whether the property rights of the employer, which most laypeople assume must include as a matter of course a right to exclude trespassers (just like the right of a residential homeowner to exclude trespassers) would or would not trump the right to organize. When the judges decided that under some circumstances the organizer can enter the plant against the employer's will, they potentially altered the distribution of income between the parties.

In the realist analysis, there are two particularly important general categories of rules affecting bargaining strength. The first and more obvious contains the rules governing the conduct of the parties during bargaining. The second is the set of rules that structure the alternatives to remaining in the bargaining situation.[6]

In the first category are the rules governing strikes, lockouts, picketing, blacklisting, dismissal for union activity, sabotage, boycotts, and so forth. These include both general tort law rules and the rules governing "labor torts" (torts that occur only in labor situations or that have been defined differently in those situations than in situations not involving labor and management). The category also includes the rules about which contracts will be enforced (for example, the rule invalidating individual worker-employer contracts that attempt to supersede a collective bargaining agreement), about remedies for breach of contract (say, limiting the remedy for an unfair labor practice to back pay and an injunction against future violation), and about compulsory contractual terms (say, the incorporation of the Fair Labor Standards Act into collective bargaining agreements).

The second category includes both the rules that influence the availability and desirability of alternative employment and those that influence the possibility and desirability of abandoning employment altogether and taking up either self-sufficiency or self-employment.

Rules Structuring Bargaining Conduct

The legal rules in the first category appear to most observers to be of no more than marginal interest, because it seems obvious that in the negotiation of the division of the joint products of labor the parties' shares are determined by such things as (1) their marginal productivity, meaning that how much they get is proportional to their contribution; (2) the scarcity of what they have to offer, so that they can "hold up" others, who need what they have to offer and can't get it elsewhere; (3) their strategic position, say, in providing a service that's a small part of the total cost but is absolutely indispensable to the whole operation, so it makes sense to avoid large-scale disruption by giving in to what seem disproportionate demands; (4) their bargaining resources, that is, wealth that allows them to hold out for a long time rather than caving in; (5) allies to help out in the struggle; (6) bargaining skill; (7) crazy intense commitment that makes some people willing to do things that the other party regards as irrational (Nixon's theory in bombing Hanoi).

The realist analysis does not deny that all these factors are profoundly significant. Indeed, the analysis takes them as a starting point.

The point is that each has significance in practice only within the framework of legal rules, and the rules affect each factor's "value" to the parties. If you can't strike at all (public employees), the size of the strike fund is irrelevant. If legal rules impose strict requirements on how much training you must give substitute workers before they can take over strikers' jobs, you have less bargaining power than if you can deploy them immediately. If the employer can discharge you for engaging in union activities (supervisory personnel, such as university professors), you won't be able to cooperate with allies with the same effectiveness as you would if you were protected by law from such conduct. And so forth.

The obvious ways in which legal rules structure the bargain, which mostly have to do with acts of aggression by one party against the other, such as strikes and blacklisting, are only the tip of the iceberg. The whole list of factors that we include in bargaining power is subtly constituted by the legal background. The word *constituted* signals that there wouldn't be a balance of bargaining power in the way we customarily refer to it without a set of ground rules defining what you can and cannot do to the people you are cooperating with in production when the moment comes when you are fighting over the product.

We can imagine enormous variation in the definition of the ground rules. In almost any type of situation, we can imagine modifying them so far in one direction or another that the outcome of struggles in that type of situation will also be dramatically modified. In this sense, law is at least partially responsible for the outcome of every distributive conflict between classes.[7]

The first way to grasp this is with a "partial equilibrium" analysis, in which we imagine a bargaining relationship in which all the listed factors are relevant, but all are constant. The parties bargain repeatedly and come up with more or less the same outcome every time. Then imagine changing just one of the relevant background legal rules, say, the rule that an employer can spend money to inform workers of why it opposes their joining a union. Changing the legal rule should, other things being equal, marginally shift bargaining power from employers to workers.

Now imagine changing a very large number of the background rules, all in favor of one of the parties. It is easy to imagine an additive process by which each rule change modifies the bargaining outcome marginally until it has shifted substantially toward one side at the expense of the other. The outcome is still in one sense determined by the list of factors above (marginal productivity and so forth), but because they play out within a different framework they yield a different outcome.

The Significance of Hale's Analysis

Hale's analysis of the impact of law on distribution has two quite different kinds of significance. First, it suggests a method of analysis of particular legal rules in order to determine their effect on bargaining power and thereby on the distribution of income between whatever groups are concerned. It seems to me truly extraordinary how little of this kind of analysis gets done by legal academics. But, of course, those who propose legislation, and legislators and their staffs, do it every day.

It is obvious that one can do a distributive analysis of *any* set of possible solutions to a legal problem, and do it from the point of view of whatever interest one cares about. It is equally obvious that the answer may be that there is little distributive difference between the alternative rules under discussion. Even rules that seem radically different from the point of view of justice between particular parties may turn out to have little or no impact on any significant question of justice between social groups. But it is no objection to the method that it sometimes reaches this conclusion; indeed it is a strength of the method.

The second significance of Hale's analysis is in a quite different domain: that of the social theory of law. The analysis suggests a *theory about the distribution of wealth, income, power, and knowledge in capitalist society.* That theory is that law, or rather the legal ground rules that structure bargains between competitive/cooperative groups, plays a larger "causal" role in distribution than it is allotted in either conventional Marxist or conventional liberal accounts.

In conventional Marxist accounts, law plays a minor role because distribution is determined by the "relations of production." There are a capitalist class and a proletariat, defined by their ownership or nonownership of the means of production. Although these relationships to capital and land have a legal form, that form is merely reflective of an underlying set of material conditions. Once the basic structure is in place—numerous proletarians bargaining with capitalists from a position of destitution—the capitalists expropriate the whole joint product except for what is necessary to reproduce the working class. In this model, the kinds of variations in the rules about bargaining that I discussed above have no significance whatsoever.

In the liberal model, law plays a major role in the form of "the rule of law," a defining element in the liberal conception of a good society. But the content of the background of legal rules is seen to flow either as a matter of logic from regime-defining first principles (rights of bodily security, private property, freedom of contract) or from the will of the people, or from both together in some complex combination. The distributive issue is present, but understood as a matter of legislative intervention (for example, progressive taxation, labor legislation) to achieve distributive objectives by superimposition on an essentially apolitical private law background.

The mere possibility of doing a distributive analysis of changes in the legal rules does not, of course, establish that they play a larger role than they are generally accorded in these theories, and such an assertion is interesting precisely because it is controversial. I will argue it briefly later on, but it seems a good idea to get a fuller version of the analytic method on the table first.

A basic reason for the invisibility of the distributional consequences of law is that we don't think of ground rules of permission as ground rules at all, by contrast with ground rules of prohibition. This is Wesley Hohfeld's insight: the legal order permits as well as prohibits, in the simple-minded sense that it *could* prohibit, but judges and legislators reject demands from those injured that the injurers be restrained.[8] For example, in most jurisdictions a home-owner or developer can block the light and air of neighboring buildings with impunity, even though doing so reduces real estate values dramatically and deeply annoys the victims. This is not a "gap" in the law, but a conscious decision that it is better to let builders have their way, and make victims buy them out if they care that much about their view.

Permissions to injure play an enormously important role in economic life, since all competition is legalized injury, as is the strike, the lockout, picketing, the consumer boycott, and the leveraged buyout. Think also of our refusal to impose liability in many cases of nonnegligent injury. The invisibility of legal ground rules comes from the fact that when lawmakers do nothing, they appear to have nothing to do with the outcome. But when one thinks that many other forms of injury are prohibited, it becomes clear that inaction is a policy, and that the law is responsible for the outcome, at least in the abstract sense that the law "could have made it otherwise."

Within this category of legal permissions, perhaps the most invisible is the decision not to impose a duty to act on a person who is capable of preventing another's loss or injury or misfortune. Cases in which lawmakers do require action include: obligations of parents to children, teachers to students, contractual partners to one another in some but not all imaginable cases; hospital emergency rooms are required to take in patients even if they have no money; restaurants are required to act up to various standards in food preparation. It is clear that lawmakers *could* require almost anything. When they rerquire nothing, it looks as though the law is uninvolved in the situation, though the legal decision not to impose a duty is in another sense the cause of the outcome when one person is allowed to ignore another's plight.[9]

The Hohfeldian insistence on the legal character of permissions allows us to distinguish the realist analysis of distribution from the familiar notion that law has *become* distributively central, but only as a result of the increasing ordering role of courts and legislatures. It is a long-running cliché that statutes have "proliferated" and that we face a litigation "explosion." In the realist sense, these developments do not increase the distributive importance of law, but only bring to visibility what was there all along.

Before the regulation of workplace safety, the employer's legal permission to operate with no other threatened sanctions for dangerous conditions than the possibility of worker job actions, or tort suits for injuries, structured the distribution of welfare just as fully as does a legal prohibition through the Occupational Safety and Health Administration. The law has no greater impact on wages after enactment of a comparable worth statute than it has when it permits employers to set wages according to "supply and demand."

When lawmakers change lots and lots of background rules in a short time, it looks as though the law itself is playing a larger role than before. When many of those changes shift us from permitting to prohibiting or compensating harm, law is more intrusive, in the sense that injurers more often have to deal with regulators. But the question of intrusiveness is different from that of causal responsibility. Once there is a legal system, the choice of any particular set of background rules is a choice of a set of distributive outcomes, whether achieved through many rules or only a few.

Circular Causation and Unstable Equilibrium

We can go beyond the partial equilibrium framework and recognize that other things are never equal in reality. The various factors that affect bargaining power are changing all the time for all parties, and the changes are interrelated or mutually interactive. This is the phenomenon of circular causation, or the feedback effect. Sometimes the effects are cumulative, and the system is consequently in unstable equilibrium.[10]

In a situation of circular causation and unstable equilibrium, a small change in one factor initiates a small change in another factor, which "feeds back" or reinforces the first change. This initiates a second change in the second factor, another reaction back, and so forth, until the system restabilizes at a new level that is much further from the starting point than would seem plausible if we looked at the first small change in isolation. For example, a set of plant-specific factors that allow a union to win a single union election by a very small margin might increase union resources for organizing enough to win another election by a small margin, providing yet more organizing resources and starting a "snowball."

By contrast, a change that looks as though it would substantially increase the union share, if other things remained equal, may bring about a countervailing change in another factor that nullifies the first impact. For example, an increase in the willingness of unions to support each other in secondary boycotts might produce a reaction of public opinion against unions inconveniencing the public that would cancel out the increased leverage from specfic boycotts.

The Instability of the Legal Framework

The context of legal rules within which these shifting factors are deployed is itself constantly shifting, not in the sense of our experiment with a deliberate "change" in a preexisting rule, but in the sense of evolution of the existing set of legal rules and materials as new situations arise. It is easy to see that a new bargaining situation, resulting from a change in one of the factors, may provoke new bargaining tactics whose legality or illegality is unclear. For example, can a large union pension fund, on whose viability depend the retirement incomes of the union members, engage in aggressive buying and selling of the stock of an employer with whom the union has a dispute? The question won't arise unless and until unions acquire pension funds large enough so that the tactic has a chance of success.

It is less obvious but no less important that new tactics whose legality is unclear are constantly invented by smart people looking for ways to modify the balance of power without a change in the intractable, large, general determinants of strength. Legal innovation is built into the system: the parties deliberately confront the courts with the necessity to make new law, because the parties are intensely aware of the significance of the legal background and try to manipulate it. As union pension funds grew, someone had to come up with the idea of the "corporate campaign." It didn't "invent itself," so to speak.

Finally, the lawmaking process itself is dependent on the balance of forces in the "private" sphere of economic conflict and cooperation. Hale wrote almost nothing on how law is made by legislators, let alone by judges, except to insist that they all make policy choices willy-nilly. He wrote throughout his life as a member of a ruling elite addressing other members of the elite on the subjects, first, of how their actions as rulers worked or operated in determining the distribution of income and, second, how they ought to exercise their responsibilities given the description of the world he had developed.

What he has to teach us is that the legal ground rules of economic struggle constitute the economic bargaining power of the combatants. But he was aware that the ground rules are themselves at least in part the product of the conflicts they condition. The process of circular causation works between the private economic system and the public lawmaking system as well as within the economy.[11]

Thus an increase in labor's economic power may translate into an increase in legislative power, which may then feed back into further economic gains. Or the increase in economic power may set off a counteracting reduction in legislative power, so that the system restabilizes itself rather than moving through a series of cumulative changes. This is much less obvious but just as true for the judicial process as it is for the legislative.

Crisis

One kind of "crisis" in the relationship between workers and owners occurs when the parties believe that the outcome of a particular bargaining session will initiate a series of changes that will cumulate and bring about much larger changes in rapid succession. The parties believe the system is in unstable equilibrium, at a "tipping" point or "threshold" beyond which the bargaining situation may be "transformed" rather than modified additively or incrementally. One side may end up, when the situation restablizes, with a much larger and the other side with a much smaller share of the joint product.

In this situation it will seem worthwhile for the parties to mobilize all their resources to control this outcome, whereas within a stable equilibrium situation neither party would have seen the small change as meaning anything at all. Once the parties are mobilized, the outcome may hinge on a very small difference in the comparative force of the parties, as in the classic "for want of a nail . . . the kingdom was lost." Their comparative force is determined by the total set of all factors contributing to bargaining power, and it makes no sense to attribute the margin of victory to any of these, where they are combined indiscriminately into the force that produces the final result. When you win by one vote, everyone's vote determines the outcome.

In this sort of crisis, very small changes in the legal system may have dramatic long-term effects. Where there are many union organizing campaigns going on, and many of them produce close elections won by management, a relatively small change in the rules governing the elections might almost immediately dramatically increase the number of successful union organizing drives, and ultimately significantly modify the distribution of income between workers and owners and between union and nonunion workers.

In a crisis, the parties are particularly likely to devote resources to throwing the established rules into legal doubt, to inventing new tactics whose legal treatment presents a case of first impression, and to mobilizing legislative resources. The basic claims about the legal rules governing bargaining between capital and labor are therefore twofold:

1. If you went about systematically changing the rules of bargaining behavior that affect an outcome, you could dramatically change that outcome, so that law is a major "cause" of the existing distribution, even if we restrict our focus to situations of stable equilibrium.
2. In situations of unstable equilibrium, small changes in apparently insignificant legal rules can make the difference between victory and defeat for one side or the other, and thereby affect subsequent distributions much more dramatically than seems at first sight compatible with the minor character of the rules and the changes. A rule is sometimes the "nail" for want of which a kingdom is lost.

Sometimes a rule may be plausibly regarded as causal even though the participants never focused on it as something that might have been changed to the advantage of one side or another. But often a crisis evokes behavior that is not easily or unselfconsciously disposed of by the rule, or that spurs people to look for reinterpretation of what seemed clear rules. Then people are aware that lots is at stake.

Rules Structuring Alternatives to the Bargaining Situation

Hale described the second category of legal rules, those structuring the parties' alternatives to remaining in the bargaining situation, as follows:

> If the non-owner works for anyone, it is for the purpose of warding off the threat of at least one owner of money to withhold that money from him (with the help of the law). Suppose, now, the worker were to refuse to yield to the coercion of any employer, but were to choose instead to remain under the legal duty to abstain from the use of any of the money which anyone owns. He must eat. While there is no law against eating in the abstract, there is a law which forbids him to eat any of the food which actually exists in the community—and that law is the law of property. It can be lifted as to any specific food at the discretion of its owner, but if the owners unanimously refuse to lift the prohibition, the non-owner will starve unless he can himself produce food. And there is every likelihood that the owners will be unanimous in refusing, if he has no money. There is no law to compel them to part with their food for nothing. Unless, then, the non-owner can produce his own food, the law compels him to starve if he has no wages, and compels him to go without wages unless he obeys the behests of some employer. It is the law that coerces him into wage-work under penalty of starvation— unless he can produce food. Can he? Here again there is no law to prevent the production of food in the abstract; but in every settled country there is a law which forbids him to cultivate any particular piece of ground unless he happens to be an owner. This again is the law of property. And this again will not be likely to be lifted unless he already has money. That way of escape from the law-made dilemma of starvation or obedience is closed to him. It may seem that one way of escape has been overlooked— the acquisition of money in other ways than by wage-work. Can he not "make money" by selling goods? But here again, things cannot be produced in quantities sufficient to keep him alive, except with the use of elaborate mechanical equipment. To use any such equipment is unlawful, except on the owner's terms. These terms usually include an implied abandonment of any claim of title to the products. In short, if he be not a property owner, the law which forbids him to produce with any of the existing

equipment, and the law which forbids him to eat any of the existing food, will be lifted *only* in case he works for an employer. It is the law of property which coerces people into working for factory owners—though, as we shall see shortly, the workers can as a rule exert sufficient countercoercion to limit materially the governing power of the owners.[12]

At first glance, this second version of Hale's assertion of the centrality of law to distribution seems to say no more than that if we had a different system than capitalism, or a system not based on private property, we would have a different distribution of income. Since what we mean by capitalism or by private property is a particular legal regime, then law, in the form of that regime choice, is responsible for the distribution of income that we actually get.

The point Hale emphasized repeatedly was that this particular property regime allows something close to unlimited accumulation of property at one extreme, and something close to absolute destitution at the other. Property rights may be formally the same for all citizens, but given the unequal distribution of "factor endowments" or actual property,

> the law endows some with rights that are more advantageous than those with which it endows others.
>
> It is with these unequal rights that men bargain and exert pressure on one another. These rights give birth to the unequal fruits of bargaining . . . With different rules as to the assignment of property rights, particularly by way of inheritance or government grant, we could have just as strict a protection of each person's property rights, and just as little governmental interference with freedom of contract, but a very different pattern of economic relationships.[13]

In Hale's initial very global analysis, it seems obvious that having "capitalism" or "private property" just plain "means" that a worker can't compel anyone to give him any money, because he doesn't "own" that money. So he has to "bribe" someone to release money to him by offering to work for him in exchange. It also seems an obvious consequence of the initial regime choice for capitalism or private property that if he can't occupy free land or get free access to capital to go into business on his own, the worker will starve.

This seems uncontroversial but also not very interesting, or only historically interesting. To see the modern power of Hale's insight, we have to follow him in abandoning the on/off all-or-nothing understanding of capitalism and private property. What we have in fact is a "mixed" capitalist system in which, first, nothing like the whole economy is organized in terms of wage labor and the confrontation between worker and capitalist, and, second, property rights are neither "absolute" nor self-defining.

In our system there are well-established alternatives to wage labor, and each has a legal structure that affects how available and desirable it is. Examples include welfare; criminal activity; independent petty commerce, from the corner store to the street vendor; the status of franchisee; independent professional activity, from the therapist, to the real estate broker working on commission, to the "consultant"; and providing household services in a marriage, or equivalent form, in exchange for support.

Moreover, as we have seen already, the mere choice of a regime doesn't settle the thousands of questions that will arise about the ground rules in particular situations. We have private property, but the courts have held that a factory owner must permit various kinds of access to union organizers. Just as legal choices about bargaining conduct and the content of agreements structure the parties' deployment of power in negotiations, so legal choices about the alternatives to bargaining structure the desirability of the alternatives. Increasing welfare payments reduces the incentive to take unskilled, dead-end, service jobs. Pervasive licensing of petty commerce (say, driving a taxi), designed perhaps both to guarantee quality and to restrict competition, reduces the bargaining power of wage workers.

Whereas it is generally fairly easy to predict the distributional effect of a change in the rules of bargaining, it is often hard to figure out how improving alternatives affects the parties' power. When marriage and the role of wife-homemaker is a widely available alternative to unskilled labor, the effect may be to make women demand more from their employers to "keep them in the labor market." Or it may be that many women come to see wage labor as temporary or incidental to other obligations and activities, so that they invest less time and energy in securing good terms and conditions for themselves than they would if they saw themselves as committed to the labor market for life. Making divorce easy may increase the bargaining power of women at work by making marriage more desirable, or it may reduce their power by reducing the security available outside the labor market. However it works out in particular cases, it seems clear that we can extend the partial equilibrium analysis of rule changes to the alternatives to bargaining. In other words, we can imagine the impact of legal rules on bargaining power by imagining small rule changes that make the alternatives more or less desirable, with the indirect effect of making workers more or less willing to settle for what the employer is offering. And we can do the same with the more general analysis that emphasizes the interdependence and changeability of all the factors making up bargaining power. A change in welfare eligibility rules might set off a cumulative series of changes in the low-income job market that would react back on the size of the welfare rolls, cause a crisis, legislative reform, and so on.

To sum up: when people think about what determined the outcome of a conflict over distribution, they tend to ignore the role of law in setting the background conditions of the conflict. As a final example, why was Reagan able to break the Professional Air Traffic Controllers (PATCO) strike of 1981? The factors we think of first are his choice of a public relations strategy, the "power of the presidency," the effect on that power of a recent massive electoral victory, the choice of a set of demands by the union, the union's strategic mistakes in dealing with the other airline unions, the availability of substitutes, their role in the production process, and the overall state of the economy.

If we think of law as having played a significant role, we might focus on the fact that the whole strike was illegal, because federal employees have no right to strike. Because the strike was illegal, it was enjoined, and some union officials and members went to jail. This may have determined the outcome (although it may also have built striker morale). Then there is the fact that because a public employee strike is not protected under the NLRA, the government can fire all the strikers and permanently replace them. This too may have determined the outcome, even though under the NLRA a private employer can hire temporary replacements for legal strikers, and the fact that the employer doesn't formally "fire" the strikers may make very little difference.

But of course the employer can hire substitute workers only because she or he is "legally privileged" to do so. Suppose a law forbids this practice, so that the employer negotiates from a closed plant. The choice between that hypothetical legal ground rule and the one actually in force plausibly "caused" the outcome of the PATCO strike, in the simple sense that the union might have won the strike under the alternative regime.

Most of the time, the role of legal rules in labor-capital conflict over distributive shares is even less visible than it was in the PATCO strike. There are few occasions on which the police are called in or a party goes to court alleging that the other side is breaking a rule. Law-abidingness is usually a relatively small issue. Usually neither side argues to the legislature or the courts that they should make changes in the ground rules or that they are unclear in important ways. Yet in the legal realist sense, law plays a very large role, because it is easy to imagine changes in legal rules governing the conduct of the parties that would have brought about a different outcome.

Extending the Realist Analysis to Racial and Gender Conflict

The realists developed this analysis as liberal advocates in the late nineteenth- and early twentieth-century conflicts between labor and capital, but they soon applied it to distribution between capitalists. Here the crucial legal rules are those defining the property rights of businesses against competitors. Antitrust statutes are so vague that the judges have had the major role in deciding the issues they merely allude to. Unfair competition law has been largely judge made, and has impacts just as great as antitrust. These bodies of law are important determinants of the level of concentration and the degree of vertical integration—that is, the dimensions of business enterprise in the United States.

The basic point applies to distributive issues wherever they arise. I will illustrate it in the contexts of conflict between blacks and whites and between men and women, but I do not at all mean to suggest that these are the only or even the most important non-class distributive conflicts. Nor will I try to give a complete picture of the distributive impact of law in these areas.

The realist analysis faded from progressive political consciousness in the 1950s, with the apparent settlement of the labor issue during the New Deal and the tendency to deny the significance of class conflict during a period of economic growth, imperial expansion, and cold war against an enemy preaching orthodox Marxism. The civil rights and women's movements seem to have reinvented the realist focus on the centrality of law rather than adapting it.

Distributive Conflict between Blacks and Whites

The focus of the civil rights movement and of the liberal political community on the maldistribution of power and welfare between blacks and whites led in the 1960s and 1970s to a search for causes. The realist analysis was not obviously relevant, because the realists were interested in class conflict within a liberal legal order composed of formally equal rights bearers. Their implicit contrast was with a feudal society in which law heavily regulated all distributive outcomes by assigning distinct legal statuses to members of different social classes. The realist goal was to show that the political enfranchisement and private economic liberty of the working class (the granting to white workers of legal rights—to vote, hold office, sell labor, acquire and dispose of property—equal to those of employers) did not eliminate but merely changed the manner of the law's influence over distribution.

By contrast, an obvious cause of racial maldistribution was the inferior legal status of blacks. It was hard to deny that *de jure* segregation in primary elections, schools, and public accommodations, and explicit invidious racial categorizing in numerous other areas of law, had massive economic effects. Moreover, the civil rights movement and its allies in the media were gradually able to represent both segregation and the violence necessary to maintain it as inconsistent with the equal civil and political rights that most of the society identified with "the American Way." So law was initially salient in the race context not as apparently neutral background rules, but as nonneutral foreground rules.

Law was also obviously important in situations in which formally equal legal rights of blacks and whites were unequally enforced, as in the cases of voting rights and protection against racially motivated violence. With time, de facto housing and job segregation led to the demand for legal reform by withdrawing a permission—to engage in private racial discrimination—that had once seemed just an implication of a larger, neutral, natural, prelegal universal privilege to refuse to enter transactions except when one wanted to.

In short, there was a progressive increase in our consciousness of law's implication in racial maldistribution as the civil rights movement and liberal reformers conceived legislative and judicial actions to change the legal ground rules in ways favorable to blacks. By the late 1960s, there was arguably more consciousness of the ways law structures racial inequality than of the ways it structures class inequality.

This consciousness of law as active even when it had been the same for many years, of law as active when it merely "permitted" (racial discrimination by public officials or by private parties), and of law as active when it merely failed to grant meaningful remedies for acknowledged legal wrongs (voting rights) was focused on racially discriminatory intentions of public and private actors. A second massive influence of law on racial distribution is through the disparate impacts of the application of facially neutral laws, some of which are directly motivated by racism (such as the poll tax and literacy test for voting). In employment discrimination cases, the courts began to throw out work rules that had a disparate racial impact and couldn't be given a business justification.

Our thinking tends to stop short of applying the same analysis to the enforcement of the apparently neutral economic ground rules that structure any poor population's relations with a rich one. In other words, we don't tend to think of the poverty of blacks overall as caused by law any more than we think of the poverty of the working class as caused by law. Yet the outcome of economic conflicts between black workers and white employers, like those between white workers and white employers, has been conditioned dramatically by the permissive rules about capital mobility that authorized the deindustrialization of the northern and midwestern cities where black men held many skilled and unskilled industrial jobs.

Blacks were particularly vulnerable to deindustrialization because they were skilled and unskilled workers rather than white-collar workers, managers, or entrepreneurs. And their job and income status was in turn a consequence of the "disparate impact" on freed slaves of the background regime of legal rules that structured their participation in the economy after emancipation.

I am speaking now not of the formally unequal rules of civil status or the implicit rules of racially discriminatory enforcement, but of our particular legal regime of property and freedom of contract. This regime structured black agriculture in the South in one way, so as to maximize the poverty and dependence of farm labor and to minimize the chances of black farm entrepreneurs, when it might have structured it in the opposite way, with different outcomes.

Distributive Conflict between Men and Women

Distributive issues arise in every context in which men and women have conflicting or competitive goals. The power of men as a group and the power of women as a group are constituted through the legal system, just as is the case with labor and capital or black and white.

For example, that most women *could* be raped or beaten by most men is an important physical datum. Its actual effect on the balance of power between men and women depends on how often rape and battery actually occur, and on the way men and women see society as viewing it when it occurs. That effect is modified by the legal remedies available to women in these cases, to the extent that legal remedies deter men from raping and battering through punishment and convey a social message of disapproval.

But the legal rules are substantively limited, as when they impose particular evidentiary requirements in rape or legalize marital rape. They may impose on the wife who kills a battering husband in his sleep the "neutral" requirement that action in self-defense be in response to an "immediate" threat of bodily harm. And protective rules are dramatically limited in their impact by the decision to make available only a given quantum of resources for enforcement, with the consequence that rape and marital battery are sufficiently common that the possibility of their occurring is part of the background of all relations between the sexes.

The impact of battery, threats of battery, and, in the absence of threats, women's calculations of its likelihood are easy to see when we are talking about relations between violent men and their partners. But the point goes deeper. The continually present reality of the practices of rape and battery constitutes the bargaining context for men and women who see their relationships as nonviolent, or even of an exemplary consensual, equal kind, because it defines the possibilities of male behavior in a particular way, within a particular structure.

Men may not often rape or threaten rape in disputes over housework, but men who categorically renounce rape do so as part of a complex bargain with women that affects who does how much housework. It seems plausible that they get more cooperation, in return for not raping, than they would if the idea that all men are potential rapists was simply not part of our culture. Since we can imagine a legal program that would radically reduce the incidence of rape, the impact of rape on the relative bargaining power of nonviolent men and women is a function of the legal system.

This is only the beginning of the story. The relative bargaining power of men and women when they confront one another from gendered positions is affected by hundreds of discrete legal rules. For example, the following legal choices structure women's bargaining power within marriage: the legalization of contraception and abortion, limited protection against domestic abuse, no-fault divorce, a presumption of custody in the mother, some enforcement of child support rules, and alimony without a finding of fault in the husband.

Rules governing the alternatives to wife-homemaker status also influence bargaining. We have to take into account the availability and amount of AFDC, limited legal protection against sex discrimination and sexual harassment in employment, and facially neutral rules structuring women's participation in the governance of unions that represent them in collective bargaining. Taken one by one and together, these legal rules put wives in a better bargaining position vis-à-vis their husbands than they would be in under a set of imaginable alternatives. And they leave them in a worse bargaining position than they would be in if the rules were modified in their favor. (We shouldn't make facile assumptions about how "well off" women as a group have been under different legal regimes. We are talking about bargaining power in specific situations rather than about overall social welfare, and each rule is likely to have a different impact according to the race and class of the people it affects.)

Some Objections to the Claim of Pervasiveness of Distributive Impact

When we want to explain why something happened, we look at the options that seemed open to the actors at the time of the conflict, rather than at stable factors that were present before and are expected to be present after. We don't explain the outcome of a strike by looking to the absence of superhuman powers in the strikers, though such powers would have changed the outcome. We assume the legal ground rules are stable, and that what "counts" is the ability of actors to work within them, "bend" them, or get good intepretations "at the margin." Law as ground rules therefore seems uninteresting as a focus of explanation.

Yet even if we remedy this blindness by looking hard at the ground rules, and begin to trace the ways in which they structure bargaining, it does not follow that we will reach the conclusion that law is an important cause of distributions we consider unjust. There are limits to the plausibility of legal explanations of distribution that might lead us to award the causal palm to other factors in the situation.

Limits on the Ability of the Legal System to Affect Behavior

Law constitutes bargaining power in the sense that the content of background rules conditions the outcome of conflict. I make this point by showing that changing the legal rules would (or at least might) change the bargaining outcome. But what of the response that the legal system and the state apparatus in general, including police, prosecutors, judges, hearing officers, and so on just don't have the capacity to enforce legal rules in the way that would be necessary if we were to make such changes?

We shouldn't assume that the remedial availability of the legal system is just fixed, so that if a given law is unenforced it is unenforceable. We may be dealing with a covert legal permission, which would often be highly controversial if formalized. Thus the remedies for a worker discharged for union activity are not adequate to assure a realistic person contemplating getting involved in organizing that her employer will have to leave her alone. This looks like one of those situations in which the law is not a factor because it is ineffective. But the legal system could dramatically increase enforcement efforts if those who define the ground rules decided that would be a good idea.

Maybe it wouldn't work. We operate with a weak federal government, inept and unprofessional state government, and local institutions that have shown over and over that they are terrible at affecting behavior, whether it be through local sanitation codes, the collection of taxes, competence testing of school teachers, or whatever. The law in books is different from the law in action, according to this view, because there is a lot *less* law in action than law in books.

To the extent the legal system just can't get a deterrent handle on an aspect of social reality, its role in distributional issues is less than it appears to be. But it is easy, when focusing on noncompliance, to underestimate how much difference admittedly ineffectual enforcement makes by comparison with no enforcement at all, or with legalization. The National Labor Relations Board is ineffective at protecting workers from being discharged for exercising their right to organize, but if there were no protection at all there would be a lot more discharges. We shouldn't believe claims about the limits of legal ordering in any particular context until we've tried massive enforcement, and kept it up long enough to change people's expectations of future enforcement.

Still, the argument for the pervasive causal significance of law in distribution is meant to be more than the tautology that because the legal system *could imaginably* make anything happen, it is causally responsible for everything that does happen. Limits on the effectiveness of law, whether we attribute them to the "nature of bureaucracy" or to "human nature," are limits on the claim that law is causally central.

Social Norms Rather than Legal Rules Are Responsible for Distribution

Another critique of Hale's position goes like this: The legal system deals with extreme cases, and with only a few of those. Most people go through their lives without ever invoking them one way or another. Most men aren't rapists. Most employees never go out on strike. Very few blacks are lynched. Most people pass their whole lives with little or no direct contact with the legal system. So the legal rules governing these behaviors can't possibly be as important in constituting bargaining power as Hale claims they are.

It is clear that background rules *may* be important even if *never* invoked. The prohibition against murder would have the greatest, not the smallest, impact on everyone's bargaining power vis-à-vis everyone else if the rules against it were successful in completely eliminating murder. So the mere frequency of invocation doesn't mean much.

Another version of the objection is that the behavior controlled by law should be understood as the violation of widely internalized social norms. If the restraint on rape or union busting or lynching is that people are socialized to have internal inhibitions against them, then law is a mere tidying-up operation. Law is important, because "there has to be some mechanism of social control to deal with deviance," but not "constitutive."

First, the legal system draws lines in thousands of situations in which there are no deep-seated internalized norms that are the same across the culture, shared by the disputing parties, about what behavior is clearly wrong or crazy. Workers and employers don't assess the legitimacy of tactics in labor disputes from a position of agreement about what, in the absence of legal rules, it would be fair to do to each other. Neither do couples living together, or whites and blacks working out the difference between kidding and racial harassment in bureaucracies like the Federal Bureau of Investigation.

I think it would be possible to make "revolutionary" changes in the distribution of income, wealth, power, and knowledge between social groups by changing *only* ground rules (without using, say, the tax system), and *only* ground rules governing areas in which there is normative conflict rather than deeply internalized consensus.

Second, the legal system creates as well as reflects consensus (this is true both of legislation and of adjudication). Its institutional mechanism "legitimates," in the sense of exercising normative force on the citizenry. Even when we are dealing with *very* deep-seated norms, like that against intentional killing of another person, the legal system can be an important vehicle of change, as is shown by the example of the evolution of the battered woman's right to kill in self-defense.

Although legal ground rules are more important to distribution than liberal or Marxist accounts have usually recognized, there are often nondistributive reasons for a rule that would prevent us from changing it in order to modify a particular outcome. When that is the case, it is implausible to hold that rule responsible for the distribution in question. The law forbids murder as an aggressive tactic in labor disputes. But it wouldn't be sensible to figure out what the distribution of income would be if murder were legalized in collective bargaining, and then attribute to law the difference between that distribution and what occurs in fact.[14]

The Importance of Judicial as Opposed to Legislative Lawmaking

Probably the most important objection to the claim that law is pervasively important in distribution is that law is simply the medium for popular consensus worked out within a set of democratic procedures. When this is the case, we can plausibly disregard it in analysis, when we are trying to explain a given distribution, in favor of the forces that shape consensus.

For example, if we want to explain the shift in bargaining power between labor and capital during the New Deal, it would seem odd to focus on law as a significant causal factor, as opposed to focusing on Roosevelt's presidential and congressional victories. Although it is true that the NLRA affected distribution, it did so as an instrument of the will of a political majority. To the extent that the NLRA still structures distribution, it still does so as an instrument.

This view is complex, as well as intuitively plausible and familiar, and I think quite misleading. My line of critique is legal realist. It is that there is an (often implicit) untenable assumption behind the notion that it is consensus rather than legal institutions that is responsible for distributive outcomes. That assumption is that there is a sharp distinction between legislation (lawmaking) and adjudication (law application), with legislation allocated to democratically elected bodies, and adjudication (including enforcement of the Constitution) to courts. We can therefore dismiss the distributive impact of background rules by referring it to the combination of consensus in legislative lawmaking (subject to constitutional constraints) and judicial adherence to the constraints implicit in the role of adjudicator.

The case for the distributive significance of law turns out to be linked to the realist critique of adjudication. It makes sense for the social theory of law to attribute distributive importance to the background rules just because the above assumptions are wrong. The background rules are largely the responsibility of judges who have made and continue to make and unmake them without seeing, and without other political actors' seeing, that what they are engaged in is independent decision-making about distribution. From the social theoretical point of view, the background rules are causally significant just because they are made in large part by a group acting politically, but using a technique of rationalization that denies the political component and thereby justifies limited democratic control of their work.

This is not the place to argue the case that adjudication should be understood as a mystified political activity, or to examine the distributional consequences of doing politics in this rather than in some other way. My purpose here is only to show the link between Hale's analysis of the distributive role of background rules and the more familiar part of the realist project.[15] Here are three qualifying remarks.

First, no one involved in academic legal theory believes anything quite so simple as the primal argument that judges apply rather than make law. Indeed, one might say that academic jurisprudence is mainly concerned in showing that there is some attenuated, highly sophisticated judge/legislator distinction that legitimates our form of judicial lawmaking and preserves judges from responsibility for distributive justice in society, without falling into the vulgar error of formalism.

On the other side, the attack on the judge/legislator distinction by the realists and their successors didn't, and didn't need to, deny that much judicial activity is "just" rule-following, or that, for all its sacred-cow status, the rule of law, in the basic sense of judicial independence, is a very good thing, even if judges exercise their independence in a political culture that mystifies their political role and thereby, as a matter of fact, reinforces social injustice of various kinds.

Second, the stakes in the discussion of the judicial role are high because judicial activity has a very large place in the total legal picture. Judges seem to be involved in constant making and remaking of the background rules for distributive conflict. This is most obvious in the case of constitutional law, and particularly the law-making activity of the U. S. Supreme Court. Indeed, for several decades we have thought of the Supreme Court as perhaps the single most important institution influencing the structure of distributional conflicts between whites and blacks and between men and women.

The role of the courts in interpreting broad statutes like the Reconstruction Civil Rights Acts, the Sherman and Clayton antitrust statutes, the NLRA, modern voting rights laws, and antidiscrimination statutes governing employment and housing is also obviously important. But one of Hale's most basic points was that the very visibility of the role of the courts in these "exceptional" cases tends to obscure the power over distribution they exercise in the course of their "normal," common or garden activity of resolving what look like purely private civil disputes.

For example, it never occurred to me until I went to law school that the basic ground rules defining property, tort, and contract had no other textual authority behind them than judicial decision. I knew perfectly well that we have a "common law" rather than a "code" system. But I hadn't really absorbed the idea that this meant there was no other basis for the enforcement of contracts than cases, citing earlier cases, citing earlier cases . . . And it hadn't occurred to me to understand the body of statutory law as a set of ad hoc changes in a presumptively complete preexisting judge-made system "valid" except where modified.

What this means is that judges, not the legislature, typically decide in the first instance whether a new technology or a new resource is property or not, whether a new contract clause is enforceable, and so on. In other words, in cases in which it is obvious to everyone that there is a gap, a conflict, or an ambiguity in the system, the judges resolve it.

But it also means that it is up to the judges to decide when to change the rules of the complete preexisting system even in the absence of a gap, conflict, or ambiguity. Again, I knew that judges overrule cases, but I had not absorbed the importance of the fact that the rules about when to overrule are judge-made rules. The judges see themselves as empowered to overrule any rule in the whole system if there are "good legal reasons" for doing so, and good legal reasons include both the notion that the rule was wrong or unjust from the beginning, and the idea that though it may once have been good, changing circumstances have now made it bad.

Against this background, it should be clearer why so much depends on the notion that judges have a well-defined role in settling disputes "according to law." If, but only if, that is the case, we can concede that judges play a major role in setting ground rules and could change the distribution of income dramatically by changing those rules, but still deny that either the judges or the ground rules are "really" that important. To change outcomes, we might imagine, judges would have to violate the well-defined procedures that they are supposed to follow in interpreting constitutions and statutes and common law precedents. It's not very interesting to say that judge-made rules play a major role, if what we mean by judges is people following these procedures, and these procedures determine their rule making.

Third, the social theoretical assertion of the distributive importance of the ground rules of economic struggle is as valid for code as for common law systems. True, in code countries adjudication is far less salient as lawmaking than it is in the United States. It may actually be true (though I doubt it) that legislatures play a larger and judges a smaller role in determining the actual content of law. It is certainly true that judges do not play the countermajoritarian role that they do here.

But the crucial similarity is that civilian legal culture presupposes a radical difference between the general law of property and contracts, understood as neutral background rules, or as rules derived from regime-defining abstractions, and special legislation (for example, labor law), understood as distributively motivated. Legal ideologists legitimate distributional outcomes by depoliticizing them, just as they do in the United States. The difference is merely that a sovereign legislature has formally enacted the neutral background, and academic theorists and authorities produce the legitimating discourse, rather than leaving these functions to the judges.[16]

Hale and Foucault!

It is instructive to compare Hale's approach with Michel Foucault's. Both start from the more or less categorical rejection of two great traditions: that of classical liberalism, which tended to restate the outcomes of social conflict as voluntary agreements; and that of orthodox Marxism, which tended to restate these same outcomes as the unilateral exercise of the power of capital over labor. Both writers choose power over liberty as a central concept (and in this extend the Marxist tradition), but both reject an understanding of power as unilateral imposition, emphasizing its situational, bilateral, and indeterminate character (and in this extend the liberal tradition).

For Hale, the point is that bargaining power is exercised within an institutional context all of whose elements influence the outcome, but none of which can be said to organize and determine it according to a single logic. "Law" is an element of the context, constitutive of bargaining power, and influential on the outcome, not as a single bloc that directs, but rather as an almost indefinitely long list of *particular legal rules,* each of which has a part in the strategic calculations of the parties.[17]

Owners coerce workers, deploying their legal right to withhold money unless they are offered labor; but workers also coerce owners, deploying their legal right to withhold labor, unless offered money in return. When the bargaining begins, labor threatens to strike, picket, and boycott, within the parameters set by the legal system, while capital threatens to lock out, blacklist, and permanently replace, likewise within legal parameters. "Bargaining power" is a complex, odd concept, ultimately a black box referring to all the factors that allowed each party to get so much but no more, *within that particular context.*

The notion of "power" that Foucault expounds in his (poststructuralist) discussion of "method" in *The History of Sexuality* has many of the same qualities as Hale's (pragmatist, legal realist, institutionalist) "bargaining power." (Foucault and Hale also share an aversion to the paragraph break):

> By power, I do not mean 'Power' as a group of institutions and mechanisms that ensure the subservience of the citizens of a given state. By power, I do not mean, either, a mode of subjugation which, in contrast to violence, has the form of the rule. Finally, I do not have in mind a general system of domination exerted by one group over another, a system whose effects, through successive derivations, pervade the entire social body . . . It seems to me that power must be understood in the first instance as the multiplicity of force relations immanent in the sphere in which they operate and which constitute their own organization; as the

process which, through ceaseless struggles and confrontations, transforms, strengthens, or reverses them . . . [Power] is the moving substrate of force relations which, by virtue of their inequality, constantly engender states of power, but the latter are always local and unstable. The omnipresence of power: not because it has the privilege of consolidating everything under its invincible unity, but because it is produced from one moment to the next, at every point, or rather in every relation from one point to another. Power is everywhere; not because it embraces everything, but because it comes from everywhere . . .

. . . [P]ower is exercised from innumerable points, in the interplay of nonegalitarian and mobile relations . . .

—Power comes from below; that is, there is no binary and all-encompassing opposition between rulers and ruled at the root of power relations, and serving as a general matrix—no such duality extending from the top down and reacting on more and more limited groups to the very depths of the social body. One must suppose rather that manifold relationships of force that take shape and come into play in the machinery of production, in families, limited groups, and institutions, are the basis for wide-ranging cleavages that run through the social body as a whole . . .

. . . [N]either the caste which governs, nor the groups which control the state apparatus, nor those who make the most important economic decisions direct the entire network of power that functions in a society (and makes it function) . . .

—Where there is power, there is resistance, and yet, or rather consequently, this resistance is never in a position of exteriority in relation to power. Should it be said that one is always "inside" power, there is no "escaping" it, there is no absolute outside where it is concerned, because one is subject to the law in any case? Or that, history being the ruse of reason, power is the ruse of history, always emerging the winner? This would be to misunderstand the strictly relational character of power relationships. Their existence depends on a multiplicity of points of resistance: these play the role of adversary, target, support, or handle in power relations. These points of resistance are present everywhere in the power network. Hence there is no single locus of great Refusal, no soul of revolt, source of all rebellions, or pure law of the revolutionary. Instead there is a plurality of resistances, each of them a special case . . .[18]

Along with the similarities, there are great differences between the approaches of Hale and Foucault. I think Foucault is inferior to

Hale in his presentation of the role of law,[19] but superior to him in his understanding of the pervasive constituting role of power in the "social body."

Foucault's totalizing scheme (he quite evidently has one) does not include the market, but rather brackets it. On one side, there is the state, the Law-and-Sovereign nexus. On the other, there are institutions—the army, the prison, the church, the mental hospital, the medical hospital, the boarding school, the family—and professions. Foucault criticizes a particular vision of the relationship between these bookends, a vision he sees as shared by liberalism and Marxism. This vision is that citizens either hand over power to the sovereign state, which then uses law to order society, with the issue being the prevention of abuse of state authority (liberalism), or have power expropriated from them by the ruling class (Marxism).

The first problem with this transactional analysis of power is that it overestimates the significance of ordering by the state (or the capitalist class) and underestimates the autonomy of actors in the institutional/professional sector, who do a great deal of "disciplinary" ordering under broad grants of legal authority. They pursue their own agendas of "control, surveillance, prohibition, and constraint."[20] At the same time, private actors endlessly resist not just state ordering but all the other kinds of ordering as well.

Second, the Law-and-Sovereign theory overestimates the autonomy of the private actors who delegate power to the state, because it leaves out of account the processes not just of control but also of "subject-creation" that are located in the liminal institutions. In the institutions, professionals of all kinds are busy developing and deploying the "power/knowledge" that creates the particular effect or experience of individual subjectivity characteristic of our societies. For example, Foucault traces our modern understanding of "human" sexuality, an aspect of individuality, to the exercise of pastoral (confessional) power, to the practice of surveillance of boarding school students, and so forth.[21] The "modern soul" is "the effect and instrument of a political anatomy,"[22] and likewise the "delinquent."[23]

Foucault's understanding of power might have led him to explore economic life, including institutions like the factory and the firm, and the role of law in the outcomes of economic conflict. He believed that disciplinary power was a "fundamental instrument in the constitution of industrial capitalism."[24] In "The Subject and Power" he proposes a scheme of dimensions for the study of power that treats the economic as strictly parallel to the specialized institutional domains that mainly interested him. Moreover, he presents laws and legal institutions as elements in power situations without sharply distinguishing them from other elements, such as professional knowledge and disciplinary authority.[25]

But this passage, the closest (so far as I know) that he got to Hale's analysis, is truly exceptional in Foucault's work. He almost never focuses on the exercise of power in a bargaining situation in which the bargainers are cooperators in producing a joint product. *Negotiation in the shadow of the law* is just not part of his project. Neither are strikes, legislative reform movements, the transformation of the material conditions of working-class life, the vulgar category of the distribution of income. When he focuses on the family, it is on the control of infantile sexuality, say, rather than the division of housework through a process that includes recrimination, slacking, and explosive anger, all against the background of legal rules as well as the background of disciplines.

Foucault takes, over and over again, the first step across this gap by listing the factory or the workshop as one of the disciplinary institutions.[26] In *Discipline and Punish* he takes a second step, explicitly linking the development of disciplinary power/knowledge to the accumlation of capital and the modern transformation of the techniques of production: "the two processes—the accumulation of men and the accumulation of capital—cannot be separated; it would not have been possible to solve the problem of the accumulation of men without the growth of an apparatus of production capable of both sustaining them and using them; conversely, the techniques that made the cumulative multiplicity of men useful accelerated the accumulation of capital," and technological change as well.[27]

The third step *should be* to incorporate worker activity and resistance into the story of the factory, and the personal/political battle between men and women into the story of domestic production. Foucault repeatedly insists that there is no power without resistance, never a one-way imposition from above.[28] The outcome of these confrontations is both the distribution of income and wealth between classes through bargaining, and the concrete forms of disciplinary power/knowledge in the presence of resistance. The two kinds of outcomes are related: the distributional outcome affects the forms of power/knowledge, and vice versa.

To understand both, we need to bring law back in. We need to bring it back in as rules and enforcement institutions that condition the struggle, in the mode of Hale. Foucault doesn't do this, perhaps because the factory and marriage play compromised roles in his theory: they are unquestionably "like" the other disciplinary institutions, but at the same time operate under a legal/ideological regime that sharply distinguishes them.

The objects of discipline in the prison, the mental hospital, the barracks, and the school do not yet have, have never had, or have forfeited "normal" contractual capacity and many other rights as well. Workers and wives are supposed to be "free," in the sense of enjoying the "universal" rights of the citizen in a liberal state.

Foucault might have responded that this is a liberal distinction without a difference, that the appearance of bargaining and negotiation, of limits on mutual coercion in the style of Hale, is an illusion; the reality is discipline. There would have been an analogy to Marx's account of worker powerlessness in the first volume of *Capital*. And sometimes this seems to be just what he is doing. The problem is that his critique of legalist mystification of relations of domination applies equally to all disciplinary institutions. He doesn't take seriously the liberal claim that the factory and the suburban bungalow are different from the mental hospital or the barracks.

> The disciplines should be regarded as a sort of counter-law. They have the precise role of introducing insuperable asymmetries and excluding reciprocities. First, because discipline creates between individuals a "private" link, which is a relation of constraint entirely different from contractual obligation; the acceptance of a discipline may be underwritten by contract; the way in which it is imposed, the mechanisms it brings into play, the nonreversible subordination of one group of people by another, the "surplus" power that is always fixed on the same side, the inequality of position of the different "partners" in relation to the common regulation, all these distinguish the disciplinary link from the contractual, and make it possible to distort the contractual link systematically from the moment it has as its content a mechanism

of discipline. We know, for example, how many real procedures undermine the legal fiction of the work contract: workshop discipline is not the least important.[29]

Foucault's goal is to refute a liberal legalist mystification, along the lines that because the worker-employer relation is contractual it is "free." Fair enough. But the value of Hale is to show that we can recognize the coercive element without ending the analysis there. Every contractual situation involves a different set of *legal* parameters, there is coercion from both sides, and the possible outcomes are various. Foucault is content to stop as soon as he has debunked the liberal myth, rather than proceeding to develop his own insight that there is worker and feminine agency in modern societies, and conflict and bargaining, and many kinds of distributions. But then he would have had to produce something that seems unnecessary in a discussion of prisons, barracks, schools, and asylums: an analysis of the *intersection of disciplinary with market power.*

In "Two Lectures" one sees how Foucault's attitude toward the market (or toward the general phenomenon of bargaining over joint products) fits with a particular attitude toward law. To begin with, he claims that "the essential function of the discourse and techniques of law has been to efface the domination intrinsic to power," so that "law is the instrument of this domination—which scarcely needs saying." Foucault aims to show "the extent to which, and the forms in which, law (not simply the rules but the whole complex of apparatuses, institutions and regulations responsible for their application) transmits and puts in motion relations that are not relations of sovereignty, but of domination."[30]

But then it turns out that in order to avoid overestimation of the role of the Law-and-Sovereign complex, the study of power "should not concern itself with the regulated and legitimate forms of power in their central locations . . . On the contrary it should be concerned with power at its extremities, in its ultimate destinations, with those points where it becomes capillary, that is, in its more regional and local forms and institutions."[31] These are "extreme points of its exercise, where it is always less legal in character." [32]

The end point, in "Two Lectures," is Foucault's insistence on a radical discontinuity between legal power and disciplinary power, through which, he asserts, the real ordering of the society is produced piecemeal in its heterogeneous professionally dominated institutions.

> But in the seventeenth and eighteenth centuries, we have the production of an important phenomenon, the emergence, or rather the invention, of a new mechanism of power possessed of highly specific procedural techniques, completely novel instruments, quite different apparatuses, and which is also, I believe, absolutely incompatible with the relations of sovereignty . . . This type of power is in every aspect the antithesis of that mechanism of [legal] power which the theory of sovereignty described or sought to transcribe . . . The discourse of discipline has nothing in common with that of law, rule, or sovereign will.[33]

They are "two absolutely heterogeneous types of discourse."[34]

The relation between the two domains is that "the theory of sovereignty, and the organisation of a legal code centred upon it, have allowed a system of law to be superimposed upon the mechanisms of discipline in such a way as to conceal its actual procedures, the element of domination inherent in its techniques, and to guarantee to everyone, by virtue of the sovereignty of the State, the exercise of his proper sovereign rights."[35] In order for the "effective exercise of [disciplinary] power to be disguised, a theory of sovereignty was required to make an appearance at the level of the legal apparatus, and to re-emerge in its codes."[36]

I don't find Foucault's assertion of "absolute heterogeneity" between legal and disciplinary discourse convincing,* nor his very tight connection between law and sovereignty, nor his call to fight disciplinary power through "a new form of law, one which must

---

*Foucault's radical dichotomy rests on a typically European but utterly misconceived picture of the legal system as a domain governed by rules (as opposed to standards), by individualist (as opposed to altruist) definitions of legal rights, and by deductive (as opposed to "policy-oriented") reasoning. A basic legal realist insight was that this picture is an ideological misrepresentation, no less false for being supremely plausible to both legal and lay publics. See generally Duncan Kennedy, "Form and Substance in Private Law Adjudication," 89 *Harv. L. Rev.* 1689 (1976); idem, Duncan Kennedy, "Comment on Rudolph Wietholter's 'Materialization and Proceduralization of Modern Law' and 'Proceduralization of the Category of Law,'" in *Critical Legal Thought: An American-German Debate* (C. Joerges and D. Trubeck eds. 1989). If one understands law as contradictory in all the areas in which Foucault thinks it is coherent, his model of conflict between legal and discipinary power falls apart. The disciplinary is always already an element in legal power.

indeed be anti-disciplinarian, but at the same time liberated from the principle of sovereignty."[37] But the first point I want to develop here is that Foucault's totalizing scheme brackets, along with the market, a whole area of legality—namely, the private law rule system that constitutes bargaining situations—that is crucial to understanding economic (as opposed to disciplinary or sovereign) power. The second point is that Foucault's typical formulation of the role of legal rules in domination effaces legal institutions as loci of power/knowledge in their own right.

As to the first point, Oliver Wendell Holmes criticized the great English positivist John Austin on the ground that he approached law as a "criminalist," meaning that he was obsessively focused on the fact that the sovereign orders or prohibits acts on pain of a sanction. Holmes was much more preoccupied with law as a structure (rules of the game) within which people pursue objectives.[38] In this perspective, which became that of the realists, law is important not because it orders in the sense of telling people what to do and not to do, but because "what the courts will do in fact" is an aspect in everyone's calculation of what they can get and get away with *in their relationships with other people.*

This is the perspective of the student of private as opposed to criminal law, whose main preoccupation is with how courts and legislatures, by defining and administering contract, tort, and property rules, influence the vast range of conduct that criminal law neither compels nor forbids. For example, the ordering of the workplace through collective bargaining agreements is neither compelled nor forbidden by the criminal law. To regard the sovereign as responsible for a particular agreement, in the sense in which we can say that the sovereign is responsible for attempts to stamp out witchcraft or consensual homosexual intercourse, seems absurd. Yet the whole point of the realist analysis is that the apparently nondirective background rules of contract, property, and tort do powerfully *influence* the social order that emerges from bargaining, even though they neither compel nor forbid that ordering.

Foucault is unmistakably a "criminalist" in his understanding of law, though his goal is to show that law so understood is far less important than European social theorists of the left and right have tended to think. What he is worried about is the misconception that the sovereign is the crucial ordering agent in the society, using commands and prohibitions to bring about desired patterns of behavior.

> The analysis, made in terms of power, must not assume that the sovereignty of the state, the form of the law, or the over-all unity of a domination are given at the outset; rather, these are only the terminal forms power takes . . . It seems to me that power must be understood in the first instance as the multiplicity of force relations immanent in the sphere in which they operate . . . and lastly, as the strategies in which they take effect, whose general design or institutional crystallization is embodied in the state apparatus, in the formulation of the law, in the various social hegemonies. Power's conditions of possibility . . . must not be sought in a central point, in a unique source of sovereignty from which secondary and descendent forms would emanate; it is the moving substrate of force relations . . .
>
> It is in this sphere of force relations that we must try to analyze the mechanisms of power. In this way we will escape from the system of Law-and-Sovereign which has captivated political thought for such a long time. And if it is true that Machiavelli was among the few—and this no doubt was the scandal of his "cynicism"—who conceived the power of the Prince in terms of force relationships, perhaps we need to go one step further, do without the Prince, and decipher power mechanisms on the basis of a strategy that is immanent in force relationships.[39]

What is problematic here is that Foucault's critique of the fetishizing of sovereignty has led him to picture law as "only the terminal form" or "crystallization" of processes of power that take place at a distance from legal institutions. This understanding is no doubt superior to the animation of the legal form as something at once rational, authoritative, and all-powerful. But it ignores Hale's insight: that the play of forces that gets crystallized or formulated in a bargain or settlement between parties, or in a legislative compromise, is itself conditioned through and through by a preexisting legal context.

Suppose we want to understand the play of forces between labor and capital or husband and wife as always involving both power and counterpower, power and resistance; and suppose we conceptualize resistance as the "adversary, target, support, or handle in power relations." Then we should see state officials administering legal rules as the instruments of the combatants, and the anticipated outcomes of litigation as part of the context or field within which workers, owners, husbands, and wives pursue their strategies. There may be no new crystallization or "terminal form," but that doesn't mean that law played no role. If there *is* a new formulation of law, say, the NLRA or a change in marital rape rules, it will be the end result of the play of power relations. But an earlier crystallization, defining, for example, picketing as a crime, was one of the conditions of that play.

If there is a tendency in the intellectual surround to reduce all social order to the working out of the will of the sovereign, it may be an intelligent first move in analyzing, say, the distribution of power between married couples, to "do without the Prince, and decipher power mechanisms on the basis of a strategy that is immanent in force relationships." This frees you from the fictions and pious hopes that judges and legislators deploy in explaining legal rules that have little impact on practice.

But it is only a first step. The formal description of the marital relationship, say, as one in which neither party has legal power to compel any performance other than the provision of support, may give us no clue as to the typical constellations of forces within relationships in the real world. But that doesn't mean we should ignore the various ways in which the legal context of marital relations affects the bargaining power of the parties. The law of divorce says nothing about who gets to choose a city for a two career family, and yet it may exert a not-so-subtle influence on that choice by empowering one partner to make threats that the other cannot ignore.

My second point is that the images of crystallization and formulation make it seem that the processes of lawmaking that intervene at the end of a social struggle are not only removed but also different in kind from the processes of power in the rest of society. They register and then administer outcomes (while "concealing" and "disguising" them at the level of discourse)[40] rather than transforming them. The same view is implicit in Foucault's presentation of the relationship between legal and disciplinary power through phrases like "law is, in a general way, the instrument of this domination,"[41] or "[t]he system of right, the domain of the law, are permanent agents of these relations of domination, these polymorphous techniques of subjugation."[42]

Foucault doesn't seem to see lawmaking (or judging) as a

"praxis" in its own right. Because it is a praxis in its own right, it adds or subtracts something. This happens in part through the deployment of power inside lawmaking institutions. We need to bring Foucault's methodology into the courthouse, so to speak, rather than checking it before we go through the metal-detector.

Foucault's purpose in speaking of "formulation," "crystallization," "instruments," and "agents" of solutions worked out elsewhere is to combat the notion that the content of law flows in a necessary way from the combination of regime-defining abstract premises and technical legal reasoning. But in rejecting this notion (easier to do in the United States than in Europe) there is no need to go to the opposite extreme of reducing law to a reflection.

The problematic aspects of Foucault's treatment of law may flow from his complex relationship to Marxism. On the one hand, he critiques (deliciously) its pretensions to scientificity[43] and the indeterminacy of totalizing "class interest" analysis.[44] On the other, he seems to have thought that we have a theory of "exploitation," meaning Marxism, that has more or less solved the problem of understanding the economy. In "Intellectuals and Power" he says, "We know with reasonable certainty who exploits others, who receives the profits, which people are involved, and we know how these funds are reinvested. But as for power . . ."[45] Perhaps we should see him as trying to undo the Marxist project by completing it rather than by taking on its legal/economic core.

Completing the project by doing for institutional life what Marx did for the economy—revealing that in institutions, as in the market, results that look like mere consequences of human nature in a condition of freedom are socially constructed with a vengeance, that is, coerced. Law and legal discourse play superstructural and mystificatory roles in Foucault's disciplinary society analogous to their roles in Marx's political economy.[46] But undoing the project as well, because the disciplinary society that underlies modern capitalism may have had its most nearly perfect expression under communism. "Is it surprising that prisons resemble factories, schools, barracks, hospitals, which all resemble prisons?"[47] is a question addressed to the East as well as the West.

Foucault is also undoing the Marxist project by making an end run around it: given the plurality of centers of disciplinary power, there is and can be no total system logic (though there are overarching tendencies—such as the development of that kind of power); neither the People (through the democratic state) nor the capitalist class is or could be in charge; the economy certainly doesn't drive the society; "freedom" and "human nature" (species being) as commonly defined by Marxists (and liberals) are incoherent notions. "The man described for us, whom we are invited to free, is already in himself the effect of a subjection much more profound than himself."[48] "[I]t is not that the beautiful totality of the individual is amputated, repressed, altered by our social order, it is rather that the individual is carefully fabricated in it, according to a whole technique of forces and bodies."[49]

But even if Foucault is wrong, and the state is no more the executive committee of the disciplinary than of the capitalist class, his understanding of power relations makes it possible to move beyond Hale once we decide to take law seriously.

I mentioned above that Hale seems to me deficient in that he never tried to apply his theory of the impact of law on bargaining power to the legislative or judicial processes. A second important flaw is his single-minded focus on worker-owner and consumer-producer conflict, to the total neglect of the other "wide ranging cleavages that run through the social body as a whole," to use Foucault's phrase. A third is that he writes throughout using the economist's (even the institutional economist's) assumption that the actors who fight, bargain and cooperate exist independently of those activities as "subjects" (that is, as autonomous, individual beings) with goals that are just a given of the analysis.

Foucault's approach has two great strengths. The first is that he sees the play of force as pervading all aspects of social relations, including particularly institutions like the prison, the hospital, and the family, and the domain of sexual activity. The second is that he sees the distribution of power as one of the factors that determines the evolution of human knowledge in one direction rather than another. Power deployed across the whole range of social life shapes the consciousness of people who at any given moment in history pursue what appear to them to be their "freely chosen" or just their "natural" "human" goals through the strategic deployment of that very same power. In short, Foucault adds yet another system of circular causation and stable or unstable equilibrium to those sketched above.

Law is one of the things that constitute the bargaining power of people across the whole domain of private and public life. One of the things this power produces is a distribution of income, understood as a distribution of whatever people value that is scarce. But another product of the deployment of power in unequal relations is knowledge, meaning particular understandings of the world and how it works.

Knowledge conditions the valuation process, indeed creates valuing subjects, as well as the particular values of valuing subjects. The knowledges produced by those empowered in earlier processes of private bargaining and lawmaking alter future bargaining, future lawmaking, and future knowledge production. Thus individuals and groups organized along crosscutting lines of cleavage are themselves reconstituted through exercises of power that seem merely instrumental to preexisting goals. Then they bargain again from the new starting point.

I will close by suggesting two local studies that might combine realist with poststructuralist methodology. I argued above that the complex of legal rules governing marriage constitutes the bargaining power of men and women in the particular context of unhappiness. But men and women get to understand themselves as such partly through anticipating, living in, thinking about leaving, and sometimes actually leaving marriages. Men are (among other things) people who can be husbands, and women are (among other things) people who can be wives.

The rules make it "sensible" for women to trade services for security and for men to renounce violence in exchange for care, and this much the Hale perspective helps us to understand. But the face becomes the mask; particular male and female subjects are the products of as well as the actors in the bargaining drama. To understand how this happens we need Foucault's perspective.

The complex of legal institutions, including legal education, law firms, courts, and administrative agencies, is less universally experienced than marriage, but it may well be important in the constitution of the modern subject in an analogous way. The themes of this institutional complex are "rightness" and coercion. People in these institutions *have to,* in order to act within them, learn to "be" right, in the sense of offering transpersonal justifications of their actions.

Having the ability to produce an argument from legal necessity to justify coercion is a prototypical way of being a person in our society. By this I mean that it is one of the models for all the other kinds of rightness, in the "human" but also in the natural sciences, in the professions, in bureaucracies, and in informal peer networks. To the extent Foucault helps us understand legal necessity as an effect of disciplinary power, we are better able to deploy Hale's analysis of the effects of this effect, the mystified background rules for cooperative/competitive struggle.

4

Sexual Abuse, Sexy Dressing, and the Eroticization of Domination

This essay brings together two topics that may seem antipodal: male sexual abuse of women and sexy dressing. Sexual abuse is a serious, indeed a terrifying thing, and we often dismiss fashion, sexy or not, as trivial, no matter how much of our time it occupies. But the topics are nonetheless linked, in two opposed discourses. One of these I will call the "conventional view," by which I mean the discourse of mainstream or traditional American culture about sexuality and sex. In this view, female sexy dress is linked to abuse because it sometimes causes it. The other discourse I will refer to as "radical feminism," meaning to distinguish it from liberal, socialist, cultural, and postmodern feminisms. In this discourse, sexual abuse is a constitutive factor in the regime of patriarchy that is reflected and reproduced in fashion. Abuse causes sexy dress, rather than vice versa.

Although I respond in this essay both to the conventional and to the radical feminist views, I don't see myself as neutral between them. Rather, as a straight white male middle-class radical trying to come to terms with the sexual culture that has formed my own

This essay is dedicated to the memory of Mary Joe Frug.

identity, I see the conventional view as a foil, and the radical feminist view as a promise but also as a threat.[1] It promises understanding, routes to change, and a possible political alliance toward transcending our gender regime. The threat is to the possibility of self-respect as a straight man.

Both promise and threat derive from the power of the radical feminist analysis of the eroticization of domination. This is the notion that the regime of patriarchy constructs male and female sexuality so that both men and women are turned on by experiences and images of male domination of women. I accept these radical feminist claims: Abuse plays a central rather than peripheral role in our mode of sexuality. Sexuality plays a central rather than peripheral role in male domination. "Merely personal" phenomena like sex and dress are forms of political participation in the regime of patriarchy. The question then is whether it is possible for straight men and women to be sexual, to experience pleasure within the regime, without collaborating in oppression.

I approach this question circuitously. In the first section below I define sexual abuse and describe the legal regime that restricts and also tolerates it. In the second section I present a tentative analysis of the way sexual abuse law functions in the distribution of power and welfare between men and women. Next I take up the role of sexual abuse in the regulation of female behavior, and in the constitution of male and female identities.

These sections make two points. First, there is at least an apparent conflict of interests between men and women with regard to the legal prevention of sexual abuse. Men, and particularly men who do not abuse women, are affected in many ways by the social refusal to do more against it. It seems plausible that men count many of these effects as benefits. A serious effort to reduce abuse must address in one way or another the male interest in its perpetuation. Second, much sexual abuse is "disciplinary," in the sense that it functions to enforce patriarchal social norms. These norms cover a spectrum from the very specific (norms about sexy dressing) to the "characterological" (norms about what a man or a woman "should be like" rather than about particular behaviors).

The third section also introduces (appropriates) the radical feminist analysis of how the formation of character through the sexualization of male domination functions to support the overall regime of patriarchy. It sketches a critique of that position based on an analogy to the Neomarxist critique of orthodox Marxism for over-stating the internal coherence and homogenizing power of capital-ism. It then suggests the possibility of "pleasure/resistance" in the belly of the beast.

In the fourth section I argue that women's dress practices are the site of conflicts within the regime, rather than simply a reflection of it. Several loosely defined subcultures contest the conventional view of sexy dress—that it is a form of female misbehavior that explains and indeed justifies abuse. These include not only the feminist community, with its own version of what is wrong with the prac-tice and with the conventional response to it, but also a pop sub-culture of sexy dress with a quite different interpretation, and other ideological tendencies as well. Women, who have no choice but to dress somehow within this system of contending normativities, and their male and female audience, act neither as mere tools of patriar-chy nor as the autonomous subjects of liberal theory.

The fifth section is about the sexual significance of fashion, and specifically the complex of meanings associated with female dress that deviates in the direction of sexiness from the norm for the setting in which it is worn. A semiotic analysis of dress as the pro-duction of socially meaningful signs supports the feminist analysis that sees sexy costumes as loaded with allusions to abuse, and as a factor in eroticizing male domination of women. But the same analysis suggests the possibility of pleasure/resistance through sexy dress, and particularly the possibility of eroticizing female sexual autonomy.

Finally I return to an earlier theme, arguing that the reality of male abuse of women burdens or discourages the activities of fan-tasy, play, invention, and experiment through which we have what-ever hope we have of evolving or transcending our current modes of male and female sexuality. For this reason, men have at least a potential erotic interest in fighting against it.

As this summary has already made clear, my view is powerfully conditioned by my straight white middle-class male social position. It seems to me unnecessary to explain or apologize for my inability to write from elsewhere than where I am. But my willingness, in-deed my desire, to write about this topic from this position owes a lot to the emergence in the 1980s of what I will call pro-sex feminist postmodernism, typified for me by the work of Jane Gallop, Judith Butler, and Mary Joe Frug.[2] Like theirs, my approach is heavily influenced by structuralism[3] and poststructuralism,[4] but I do not think of myself as a feminist any more than I think of myself as a black nationalist.[5]

Most of what I have to say is about straight white middle class male existence on the terrain of sexuality. This focus engages the "perpetrator perspective," in the hope of changing it, rather than the "victim perspective."[6] It takes heterosexuality, race, and class as provisionally given systems of meanings and charges, rather than problematizing them ruthlessly throughout. And it presupposes the system of male dominance, treating it as something to be reformed or disrupted, rather than trying to see from outside it or beyond it. It is certainly open to question whether there is much if anything of value to be said within these limitations.

In the first half of this essay I speculate about the gains and losses to different classes of men and women that flow from the toleration of abuse, from the norms that abuse enforces, and from the particular social construction of male and female sexuality in which abuse is implicated. It seems risky to talk about this subject in this language—the language of cost/benefit analysis, or law and economics.[7]

That language is distancing, objectifying, flattening, alienating. It makes it sound as though all the different people with all their different costs and benefits were the same, and as though intense suffering and evil pleasure could be "aggregated" into undifferentiated masses of "utility and disutility" with "weights" to be compared. It makes it sound as though abuse were a practice with no inherent moral character, and therefore something that I might want either to condemn or to endorse, from a neutral technocratic position, according to how the numbers turn out.

It adds to the danger that sexual abuse is an eroticized topic. Many men and women, including many with strong commitments to feminism, experience some images or fantasy scenarios involving abuse, including sexual domination and rape, as sexually arousing, even though they also disapprove or fear these things, and have no conscious desire to abuse or be abused in real life. One reason for talking about the subject only in a language of horror is that such a language is a kind of antidote to the frightening salacious power of the images the subject evokes. Ironically, the ostensibly neutral language of cost/benefit analysis suggests voyeurism.

The virtue of cost/benefit analysis is that it forces us to focus on the aspect of abuse that is denied by the language of horror—that is, on the conflicts of interests between men and women, and among men and women, that are submerged when we are reacting viscerally. These conflicts can't be willed away, and they have a deep effect on social policy, on what various institutions end up doing after they have engaged in more or less heartfelt denunciations.

If men and women benefit in various describable ways from abuse, it is important to say so, because the vulgar male interest in abuse is likely to get translated into action through male control of the legislative, judicial, and administrative processes. If men have other, often unrecognized, nonmoral, material, erotic, or aesthetic interests in reducing or ending abuse, then it is important to say so. These interests, more fully recognized, might influence this same ruling male class. The goal is not to do a neutral aggregation, but to frame an argument.

There is another, more complex and problematic reason for me to use this language. I can say, and feel, that the only morally plausible attitude toward male sexual abuse of women is to be against it because it is sickening. But this way of putting it already contains a lie, because I haven't (that I remember) experienced sexual abuse. So when I say it is a horrible thing, I mean horrible as represented by people I believe. If I am going to talk about it, I am going to have to represent it too, and not from experience. It seems important to avoid any rhetoric designed to get me out of my actual, morally compromising situation of being a member of the group—all men—that benefits, in some ways, to some degree, from abuse. Cost/benefit analysis provides a clearly gendered, male-developed, male-identified language, of which I am a more-or-less native speaker. I appreciate its possibilities of power, elegance, and (distanced) insight, even if many other women and men don't. It is more "authentic," for me, than the voice of role-reversed male sensitivity—the voice of total empathy with women as victims. This is so even though I am constituted in ways I don't like, and think are dangerous, by this very language ("it" speaks "me"), and wish it were a different, better vehicle.

Sexual Abuse Law

This section explains what I mean by sexual abuse, sexual abuse law, and the "tolerated residuum" of abuse. My definition of abuse is quite narrow, limited to conduct that most men and women in our society view as clearly wrong or immoral. This leaves out all the cases in which the morality of the conduct is contested, and particularly those in which many or most men think there is nothing wrong, while many or most women think something is very wrong indeed. I think the conventional male definition of, say, sexual harassment or date rape is much too limited, and that much socially accepted male behavior is abusive. But my purpose is to argue that even with respect to the undisputed cases, there is a deep conflict of interests between men and women.

Defining Sexual Abuse

I will be dealing with two main types of male aggression against women. The first involves men using force, threats of force, non-physical frightening or degrading behavior (such as sexual insults), and threats of such behavior (the raised eyebrow that says, "Watch out or you'll get it") against women. The second involves men taking advantage of female "incapacity," including drug- or alcohol-induced stupor, the helplessness of female children, and the emotional vulnerability that sometimes affects female beneficiaries in fiduciary relationships.

The behavior is sexual abuse, as defined here, when (1) it is understood to be something that "men do to women" at least in part "because they are women," (2) most people in our society currently condemn it, and (3) there are, at least some of the time, legal restraints on it. I don't mean to suggest that women never do these things to men, or that they are not done by men to men or by women to women. But I am going to talk about the behaviors, their legal treatment, and the consequences only in the context of men abusing women.

The practices I will be talking about occur in a variety of settings and include the following: (1) domestic—wife (or partner) murder, domestic battery, marital (or partner) rape, and father/daughter incest; (2) professional—sexual victimization of female patients, clients, parishioners, and students by male doctors, psychiatrists, lawyers, clergymen and teachers (from day care through graduate school); (3) workplace—quid pro quo and hostile environment sexual harassment in the workplace of the type that gives rise to liability under federal or state law, and the murder, rape, physical abuse, or sexual enslavement of female prostitutes and other sex workers by male johns, policemen, pimps, and other sex entrepreneurs; (4) "street"—sexually motivated male killing of female strangers, stranger rape, and male street harassment of women, with or without offensive contact; (5) "acquaintance"—date rape and frat-boy gang rapes.

The notion that "men do these things to women" at least some of the time "because they are women" is complex. The starting point is a flat assertion of fact: there are many particular cases in which observers interpret abusive behavior as motivated by something more than "gender-blind" desire for money or power, "gender-blind" rage, or the like. The two most familiar gendered interpretations are that the man's sexual desires, in some direct or indirect, "normal" or "perverse," conscious or unconscious form were involved; and that the man's understanding of appropriate female role behavior, whether with regard to obedience or deference or nurturing or sex, was involved. Most interpretations involve both elements.

The sexual abuser chooses among possible victims on the basis of gender, but not necessarily blindly within the category of women. He may go after his daughter, or women in high heels, or meek women, or women with supervisory job power over him. Whatever the particulars, our common understanding is that gender, in some one of its infinitely complex (socially constructed) manifestations, is involved.

Moreover, the cases fall into a set of familiar categories, or scripts, that is limited at any moment in time but always open to expansion or elaboration. Some of these scripts are those for the male serial killer of women, the wife beater who rapes his wife each time he beats her, the workplace sexual harasser who decorates his office with pictures from men's magazines and asks all or many or particular women who visit his office to comment, and the subway fondler.

One of the ways we attribute a sexual motivation to the behavior is by interpreting it as a kind of communication using the code provided by the script. By killing women in a particular way, the serial killer seems to be telling us something about why he did it, about his view of women or of a particular kind of woman (his typical victim), relying on our understanding of the *conventional* meaning the society attaches to the actions of the players of his and her parts in the script.

As with any sign system, it is always possible that his "real" intentions were quite different from those conventionally attributed to his character—the workplace sexual harasser may care only about getting a raise by intimidating his female boss. He would have used a different script if the supervisor had been a man, but he would still have done something to get the raise. And it is possible to use the language "wrong," to do things that communicate just the opposite of one's true intentions, as in the case of the genuinely "insensitive" harasser who was "just trying to be friends" and is mortified when he discovers that he has given offense.

Adding the notion of a script to that of intention does three things. It allows us to focus on particular patterns of behavior that have important social meanings and effects without having to worry in each case about the often-unknowable inner state of the abuser. It also allows us to talk about typical women's responses to abuse. Because the scripts are part of the social knowledge of everyone in the society, it is possible for women to think and act in advance with the idea of avoiding them if possible. And there are, for every script in which the abuser interacts with the victim rather than, say, shooting her in the back without warning, various different scripted female responses among which a woman *may* be able to choose.

Finally, it is hard to understand the legal regimes governing these various kinds of abuse unless one sees them as responses to a limited but variable set of patterns of interaction. The case law on sexual harassment, date rape, and the tort of intentional infliction of emotional harm makes up an elaborate, quite self-conscious collective reflection on these social patterns. The detailed civil and criminal law subrules within each category respond to familiar variations in both the male and female parts within the basic scripts (for example, can it be harassment if the only acts alleged are requests for dates? what happens when the battered wife kills her husband in his sleep? is it rape if the man makes only verbal threats and the woman does not resist in any way?).

The Legal Treatment of Sexual Abuse

This section describes the impact of two aspects of legal reality on sexual abuse. First, primary rules define what behavior by men will give rise to liability. Second, a whole complex of procedural rules and informal practices guides decisions about things like how much to invest in enforcement, and the exercise of discretion both by public officials and by lawyers. As a result of this second layer of decision making, there may be a big difference between the "law in books," meaning the legal rules about the conduct we are concerned with, and the "law in action," meaning the impact of the system as a whole on that conduct.

I am not going to talk at all about the impact of legal discourse—that is, what judges, lawyers, and other legal speakers and writers say about why they do what they do on sexual abuse. My concern is with the rules developed in case law or with what the Massachusetts' Abuse Prevention Act[8] says about how police officers must handle domestic violence calls, but not with legislative debates or the New Jersey Supreme Court's reflections on battered women's syndrome.

The legal discourse that describes, explains, justifies, and questions the legal system, and in so doing elaborately represents our whole society, is an important part of the general discourse of authority in our society. What judges say about what sexual harassment is, and about what is wrong with it, shapes attitudes, just as judicial opinions in the early antisegregation cases shaped attitudes. But my perspective here is Holmesian,[9] focused on law as a system of incentives rather than on law as a source of values.

Formal Rules Governing Abuse

The most important thing about the formal legal definition of abuse is that it represents a complex compromise of conflicting interests, as well as a moral condemnation of behavior of which people disapprove. There are many actions that most people would regard as clear instances of sexual abuse, and as clearly wrong, that are simply not illegal. They are *damnum absque injuria,* injury without the commission of a legal wrong. Some obvious examples are marital rape in jurisdictions where the law has not been reformed, rape accomplished without resistance through credible verbal threats of future harm, and single instances of sexual harassment that do not create a "hostile environment."

But in fact these relatively well-known examples are only a small part of the picture. Male co-workers can make a woman worker's life miserable, within one of the familiar scripts of sexual abuse, without conduct that falls within the Equal Employment Opportunity Commission guidelines,[10] which require that the abuse have some overt sexual content. Thus *everyone* may know that her male subordinates are abusing a woman boss because she is a "stuck-up bitch," and *everyone* may agree that the subordinates would not see identical behavior from a male boss as provocative. If they avoid the particular script that involves overt sexual aggression, the illegal script, they can "get away with it."

On the street, it is easy for a gang of construction workers to embarrass or terrify a passing woman without committing the torts of assault or intentional infliction of emotional harm as currently defined. The hardier the victim, the less likely she is to have collectable damages, even if she could establish liability in the abstract.

To measure *damnum absque injuria* at home, imagine the nonexistent tort of domestic sexual harassment, which we could construct in a way closely parallel to the tort of workplace sexual harassment. It would include demands for sex backed by threats of divorce or separation (quid pro quo) and the creation of a hostile domestic environment through unwanted sexual advances, unwanted exposure to degrading sexual materials, insults, or jokes, or both. The cause of action might be available to all women in domestic situations, or only to women for whom, or for whose children, divorce or separation would be likely to have serious adverse consequences.

This exercise does not demonstrate that we should change the law to include all cases of abuse that are currently *damnum absque injuria,* although I favor major changes in that direction for the reasons developed in the following pages. In many particular cases, it is easy to explain the limits on liability, and in some cases they may be justified, given competing goals, such as preserving the administrative integrity of the legal system, conserving resources for use to combat other wrongs, and so on. "Privacy" and "autonomy" are often urged as competing interests justifying legal toleration of conduct we regard as unquestionably immoral and wrong, and this approach *sometimes* seems plausible to me. But it is a fantasy to believe that the formal legal rules now in force forbid even a small part of what most people would regard as clearly unjustifiable sexual abuse. For various reasons, some good, some bad, they just don't do that.

The Administration of the Formal Rules

It seems unnecessary to do more than outline the reasons why a woman who has suffered an unquestionable legal wrong under the formal rules governing abusive conduct might not be able to achieve any type of legal redress.[11] First, there are the reasons that apply to all legal claims, not just those of sexual abuse. These include rules of procedure and evidence, including rules about the burden of proof. Taken together, they mean that often a victim of sexual abuse just can't prove it in court.

Then there is the obstacle that the legal system delivers neither free, nor speedy, nor efficient, nor humane justice. A civil suit may take six years to get to trial. There can be no suit at all unless you can afford a lawyer or unless your case falls into the limited category that are profitable on a contingency fee basis. On the criminal side, police and prosecutors pursue only a small fraction of the credible allegations they receive.

For reasons that are by now familiar, the civil and criminal justice systems are particularly ineffective in dealing with sexual abuse cases. The problems that exist for any claimant are intensified by social ambivalence about the issues raised by abuse. The existence of highly charged, familiar scripts in which women either deserve or invent it, along with the profound power imbalance between men and women, make proof particularly problematic. There is also likely to be a sharp conflict in understanding between the victims and the relatively "traditional" male personnel in all parts of the legal system.

Toleration of Abuse and Its Consequences

The combination of the limits of the formal law and the actual workings of the legal system has the result that men can and do commit large numbers of sexual abuses of women without any official sanction. Although most people would probably regard the conduct as clearly wrong and injurious, there is no punishment and no redress. True, it seems likely that there would be abuse within any conceivable legal system, and clear that even in the complete absence of legal sanctions there would be significant social control of this kind of behavior through other mechanisms. But it also seems reasonable to suppose that the legal system affects the practices of abuse, reducing their incidence (probably) and channeling them into particular forms (secret forms, for example), without coming close to abolishing them.

The crucial point is that *some* abuse, what I will call the "tolerated residuum," is plausibly attributed to contestable social decisions about what abuse is and how important it is to prevent it. The law defines murder quite clearly, and the "system" devotes substantial resources to catching and punishing perpetrators. It defines rape much less clearly and sometimes devotes fewer resources to it than to less important crimes.

At the extreme, the legal system's role in the abuse of prostitutes by johns, pimps, and police seems to be more than mere toleration. The system generates the conditions for the abuses that it tolerates by criminalizing prostitution without trying to abolish it. Legalization might make it easier for prostitutes to use the legal system against rape, battery, and sexual enslavement. Legalization might also lead to a great increase in the amount of the activity and to a proliferation of its forms, including forms little better than what we have now. But it remains that the abuse of prostitutes is a direct consequence of the particular balance the society has chosen, rather than of "human nature" or the "limits of social control."

The rest of this essay considers the consequences of setting up the legal system to condemn sexual abuse of women by men in the abstract but at the same time operating the system so that many, many instances of clearly wrongful abuse are tolerated. It explores two ways in which the tolerated residuum is a factor in men's and women's lives. First, men and women gain and lose from the practices of abuse, *whether or not* they themselves are actually abusers or victims. These gains and losses are more far-reaching than is usually implied in the rhetoric either of those who minimize abuse or of those who are mainly trying to identify and condemn it.

Second, partial prevention and partial toleration create a particular set of incentives for potential abusers and potential victims, and for everyone else in the society. These induce behavior different from what would occur either in a society that drastically deterred abuse or in one that legalized it across the board. Men's and women's reactions to the particular line we've chosen to draw between sanction and toleration have extensive indirect consequences for everything from the details of day-to-day behavior to the formation of male and female identities.[12]

The Conflict of Interest between Men and Women with Respect to Preventing Sexual Abuse

There is a real, persistent conflict of interest between men and women with respect to the tolerated residuum. According to the "conventional," culturally general view, the problem of abuse implicates only or mainly the relatively narrow categories of men who abuse and women who suffer abuse. My critique of this view is, first, that most women, whether or not they are actually victimized, have something to gain from eliminating the tolerated residuum; and second, that men who are not victimizers have something to lose.

The Pathology/Competence Analysis

A common popular assessment of sexual abuse is that it is "pathological" behavior. In the words of Senator Orrin Hatch, the abuser "is not normal." The basic idea is that men by nature are either normal or abnormal, with the latter group perhaps subject to "cure" through therapy or religious experience. Sexual abuse is deviance. That there are deviants is just a fact of nature. Their conduct is defined exactly by the fact that it is not what normal people do. It has no implications for the lives of normal people except for those who are victims. In this view, most of us, most of the time, live in a universe in which legal rules about sexual abuse are irrelevant because the relations between men and women, however screwed up they may be on this or that dimension, are basically pacific and friendly.

According to this understanding, the main conflict of interests in this area is that between the abusers and the abused, and in that conflict there is no question that society should and does side with the victims. Deterring men from abusing and compensating women financially resolves the conflict in favor of actual and potential victims and against men who abuse, at some marginal cost to taxpayers.

If one accepts this view, it at first appears that there should be little objection to a massive increase in societal efforts to end abuse. The more broadly the legal system defines it and the more effectively the system responds to violations, the better off women will be, since they will be less victimized to begin with, and better compensated when they are. The only losers are a pathological subclass of men.

But there are other elements in the popular assessment that complicate the situation. Although clear cases of abuse are wrong and pathological, it is also important to the conventional view that they are exceptional, indeed much rarer than one would think from the limited empirical evidence. Rarity is important, I suspect, for two reasons. Unless cases are rare, it is hard to sustain the notion that they are "abnormal" and pathological. And unless cases are rare, it is hard to sustain the view that they play no significant structural role in the relations between "normal" men and women.

The claim of rarity gets its plausibility in part from the social construction of a balance between accusations of abuse that are validated and accusations that are rejected. The notion that abuse is common and structurally important *seems* to be refuted each time a particular incident gets interpreted in terms of one of the scripts that shift the focus from the alleged abuser to the woman involved.

In the popular view, it is always a real possibility that what is represented by the woman as abuse was invented, either because the woman is crazy or because she is trying to ruin the man. Other cases of abuse are provoked, in this view, by women whose sexual nature leads them to tempt or tease in ways that cause "normal" men to react with predictable violence of one kind or another. These women "deserve it," in the popular view, or at least don't deserve much sympathy, and what happens to them can't be taken as an indication of a general social problem.

Finally, some women know how to "take care of" or "handle" themselves, and some don't. Competent women, in the familiar stereotypical view, know how to deal with abuse at three levels. First, they minimize its probability by avoiding the behaviors that are particularly likely to provoke it, including especially acting "like a victim" and behaving in a way that will "attract attention." Second, they know how to respond in the early part of a potential abuse script so as to shift the course of events in another direction. They know how to pass things off as jokes, but to communicate firmly and clearly what their boundaries are and when a man is "out of line."

Third, when abuse is under way they know how to react directly or indirectly to save themselves from serious harm. They walk out on the abusive husband, scream loudly enough to scare away a rapist, yell at the office harasser before he is fully committed to his course, and in appropriate cases invoke the assistance of informal networks of superiors, friends, neighbors, and relatives, as well the formal mechanisms of the law.

The conventional view concedes that no amount of knowing how to handle oneself is a complete safeguard. The pathology of some men is deep enough that precautions won't stop them. Nonetheless, in this view, a considerable amount of abuse is "explained" by the incompetence (rather than the malevolence or craziness) of the victim. It doesn't really "count," because the victim could have avoided it if she had known how to take care of herself. This shift in blame invites women to reassure themselves that they are at risk only if they do something "wrong"—that is, fall into one of the scripts of victim responsibility. There is an analogy to the culture of the test pilots in Tom Wolfe's *The Right Stuff,* which persistently attributes death to failure of flying skill, in the face of statistics that indicate that almost all of them are doomed.

The Cost of Precautions Versus the Burden of Excess Enforcement

To my mind, the main problems with the conventional view are that (1) abuse is far too widespread to be understood through the categories of abnormality or pathology, (2) the manoeuver of blaming the victim allows both men and women to deny its reality, (3) this denial keeps men and women from acknowledging the pervasive way abuse structures relations between men and women *in situations that seem not to involve it at all,* and (4) the result is blindness to the real conflict of interests between men and women in this area.

With regard to the last two points, the conventional view greatly understates both the costs to women of present practice and the potential costs to men of changing it. The conventional view is apologetic: it views the status quo through rose-colored glasses and at the same time underplays the structural factors, and particularly the male interests, that support it.

Costs to Women

Suppose that a sensible woman does not go into an unfamiliar bar in a working-class neighborhood at night without a male escort, even to use the ladies' room, because her presence may be interpreted as consent in advance to some kind of sexual contact with some one of the men in the bar, and a refusal of any kind of contact is likely to lead to some kind of abuse. Suppose that a sensible woman who is deeply offended by her boss's patting her behind puts him off by gentle jokes when she would like to read him the riot act. Suppose that a sensible girl of ten with an incestuously abusive father avoids ever sitting in his lap, though she would sometimes like to in spite of the risk.

One issue here is the cost of the abuse that happens when women refuse, because they are mad or gutsy or cocky or have no choice or don't get it, to accept the restrictions and end up paying the price. A second issue is the cost to those who avoid the abuse by foregoing doing things they want to do. It seems plausible that this cost, to black and white, young and old, gay and straight, and so on, of activities foregone because of risk is very high. Significantly reducing the risk might well lead to very different patterns of behavior by large numbers of women who are "at the margin" but are effectively deterred by the tolerated residuum.

It seems clear that women would benefit enormously if they were free of the actual abuse, free to do the things they now can't risk doing, and free of the generalized fear that is a rational response to the pervasiveness of male violence. But the conventional view denies or ignores this whole range of costs. The various activist movements against battery, child abuse, rape, and sexual harassment, with their allies in social work, psychotherapy and the liberal media, have gradually forced them into public awareness,[13] without managing to have a major impact on them in practice. The result is a situation of disequilibrium, a kind of cultural crisis for the conventional view.

The crisis arises because acknowledging the actual prevalence of abuse threatens to undermine the other elements of the gestalt: that abuse is a matter between a small class of abnormal perpetrators and a small class of victims, that apparent instances are often explained by the woman's behavior, and that the whole practice is of only marginal importance to the patterns of social life. Moreover, as the conventional view begins to fray at the edges, it has become clear that it underestimates not just the evils of the current situation but also the obstacles to changing it, and particularly the male interest in the status quo.

Benefits to Men

Speaking as a man, it is easy to see some serious drawbacks to any attempt to change the legal treatment of abuse in a way that would significantly reduce it. But it makes me uneasy to write about them. It may appear that just by listing and describing them I am implicitly equating them with the things that happen all the time to women, or to the things women don't do because men make them dangerous. That's only half of it. The other half is that there is a kind of convention of silence among progressive men about what we might lose through more protection for women. The convention may be based on the idea that to mention these costs will discourage other men from supporting reform.

Most men—I would say practically all men—have the intuition that if you wanted to enforce even the limited existing rules you'd have to increase enormously women's willingness to complain, as well as the resources devoted to investigating complaints at every level. The definitions of abuse would have to be made cruder. And there would be a large increase in the number of accusations, with a proportionate (or more) increase in the number that turn out to involve contestable issues of interpretation or are just plain false. Because this seems obvious, and because most or all men who have thought about it are aware of it (I think), it's better (I think) to acknowledge the issue and discuss it, rather than pretend it's not there.

The underlying idea has a strong paranoid quality, but to name the fear is not to make it go away. The social scripts about harassment include, along with parts for the provocateur and the woman who doesn't know how to handle herself, the roles of the vindictive deceiver, the delusional hysteric, and the "oversensitive" woman who systematically misinterprets innocent behavior.

These are stereotypes, and they are used constantly in ways that distort or falsify the reality of victims' experiences. Men use them to defeat women's enforcement efforts and to deter women from complaining at all. Our whole society uses them in the strategy of denial of the problem. But they are not exclusively "male," except to the significant extent that all social imagery is male (because men dominate the whole culture). I have spent a lot of time listening to "traditional" women mock my leftist unwillingness to admit the existence of deceivers, inventors, and the oversensitive. Many white and black women I know strongly believe (as I do) that there is sometimes reality behind the images, just as there is sometimes reality behind other gender or racial or ethnic stereotypes.

But leaving aside the paranoid images of female malevolence, what about mistaken identity? A white man goes into The Gap to buy a pair of pants. The store sells men's and women's clothes, and on this day it is full of men and women. He has to wait in line for a dressing room. He tries on a pair of pants, doesn't like them, puts his own pants back on, and steps out of the cubicle. A saleswoman is standing directly in front of the door waiting for him. She tells him in an angry voice that a woman customer leaving the store has just told her that he had been peeking at her over the top of the seven-foot-high partition between dressing rooms. The saleswoman says that the store strongly disapproves of this behavior. He denies it, and begins to defend himself: he suggests that the person who was in the dressing room before him had probably indeed peeked over the partition and left quickly when spotted, and he, the next occupant, is taking the rap. But the saleswoman tells him that it is the end of her shift, that she is leaving, and that she doesn't want to discuss it any further.

The man leaves the store hurt, frightened, and enraged, and for some time thereafter buys his trousers only in stores where there is no chance of another false accusation. Eventually he goes back to The Gap, hoping that the saleswoman will have forgotten him or moved on to another job. If the protagonist in this story had been a black man and the complaining woman white, it seems plausible that the events would have been more highly charged, and might have gone "worse," and that the black man might have experienced more hurt, fear, and rage than the white man did.

Social control involves both interpretation of rules and fact-finding. Neither will ever be perfect. Toleration of abuse eliminates any need for interpretation or fact-finding in the whole range of situations in which there is *a case* that a man has done something unquestionably wrong and immoral, but in which it is also obvious that the legal system will not respond.

There is a real conflict of interests here. The conflict exists even for men who detest sexual abuse, for the simple reason that the current regime does more than place the burden of the tolerated residuum squarely on women. By doing this it spares men, abusive and nonabusive, the burden of excess or inaccurate enforcement that any significant increase in social control would almost certainly generate. And it spares them the burden of precautions against the risk of excess enforcement.

There is a peculiar symmetry between the burden of excess enforcement and the burden of tolerated abuse. To get rid of one, you have to have the other. They also have psychological elements in common, including the reactions of shame, self-questioning, avoidance, and depression. The argument that increased enforcement would make men hesitate to take altogether innocent initiatives toward women is usually put forward without considering that the tolerated residuum makes women hesitate to take altogether innocent initiatives toward men. This symmetry does not alter the fact that at present the actual burden on women of tolerated abuse seems far greater than any imaginable burden on men from excess enforcement.

But it does mean that the conflict of interests between men and women is there, even though the costs to women of complaining of abuse are high enough that contestable or false accusations would probably continue to be extremely uncommon in a regime of effective enforcement. Men's fear of being victimized is only indirectly and ambiguously related to whatever the reality might turn out to be. The fear varies from man to man, but there is still an unmistakable group interest in avoiding having to worry about enforcement excesses; it is in direct conflict with women's interest in not having to worry about being abused.

Imagine that increased sanctions against unquestionably wrongful conduct come about in part because women as a group get a larger share of power in the legal system, including the processes of rule interpretation and fact-finding. If men and women tend to interpret cases differently on the margins of the category of "unquestionably wrongful conduct," and if I interpret like other men, I have even more to lose than I would if we men decided unilaterally to stamp out abuse as *we* define it.

It seems to me, without more than anecdotal evidence, that men are as likely as women to believe that the two sexes see these things differently. My own view is that the definition of the unquestionably wrong is more heavily contested between conservatives and liberals than between men and women. Even so, I am safer with the status quo than I would be if women had a lot more power in these matters, simply because the status quo is a known evil. Men who accept the feminist claim of polarized male and female understandings are likely to see the empowerment of women as a very risky business.

This brings me to another cost for men of trying to give women more protection. Such an effort would force us men into conflict with one another. It would force us to define our positions and use our resources and energy in fights about definition and enforcement. We men can avoid these fights so long as the whole level of enforcement is low enough so that most of the time women know from the beginning that they have no effective recourse.

Bargaining in the Shadow of Sexual Abuse Law

Shifting the line between toleration and prevention of male sexual abuse of women should also affect the process of bargaining between men and women.[14] People in friendly or even passionate relationships in workplaces and families often experience disagreement and conflict organized along gender lines. There's no marriage without an understratum of bargaining where the parties see each other as having opposing interests. There's no workplace relationship between a boss and a supervisor, or between two co-workers, that isn't to some degree negotiated.

In those negotiations, some men routinely use or threaten violence in order to increase their "gains from trade." This means that the losses to abusive men from more enforcement go well beyond the loss of the pleasures of hurting women. There would be secondary losses in every area of life where the threat to hurt is an effective way to get what one wants.

In those negotiations, some women regard the notion of a nonabusive man as oxymoronic. For such women, increasing legal deterrence of male violence would reduce the credibility of male threats that they believe are always at least implicitly present in heterosexual relationships. It should thereby increase their bargaining power vis-à-vis all men. Some women, on the other hand, seem to make a sharp distinction or a blurred distinction among men according to how likely they are to be abusive. There may even be men from whom they categorically do not fear violence. It seems likely that such men get a better deal, *because* they are seen as not abusive, than they would get if abuse were eliminated. A better deal can be anything from deference in the workplace to the personal/political benefit of having to do fewer chores at home.

Other things being equal, a party who can leave a relationship at little cost will demand more and receive more than one who can leave only at high cost. Each party's bargaining power depends to some extent on the explicit or implicit threat to leave, in the short or long run, unless a demand is met. Opposing bargainers judge the credibility of such threats in part by reference to what they think the consequences of leaving will be for the other. In other words, if the person threatening to leave would suffer severe harm from doing so, the threat is less credible than that of a person who can leave at little cost.

For a woman in a relationship with a man, one of the costs of leaving is having to run the risk of ending up with a new man who turns out to be abusive. For women in workplaces, one of the costs of leaving is running the risk that a new job environment will turn out to be a hostile one. The seriousness of the risk depends to some extent on the legal system's commitment to prevention and compensation. Reducing the likelihood that a new man or a new workplace will be abusive increases the credibility of women's threats to leave wherever they are.

This analysis leads to the simple law and economics hypothesis that increasing protection from sexual abuse should increase the bargaining power of women vis-à-vis men, *whether or not those men are seen as potentially abusive,* both in domestic situations and in the workplace. Reducing protection, on the other hand, should make women more dependent on men who don't abuse, by making leaving riskier, and so make them more willing to make concessions.

The existence of a real conflict of interests between women and men at the levels I have been describing does not mean that every man who knows which side his bread is buttered on opposes a realistic campaign to seriously reduce sexual abuse—or that every woman favors one. A man might believe that there are "fundamental issues of human rights" involved, or that what happens to women is so bad that the costs to men of stopping it should be regarded as trivial, or that more protection for "his" women is well worth a small extra risk for him. I will argue a little later on that some men have an erotic interest in reducing abuse. But it seems plausible that the line we currently draw between toleration and prevention is in part the result of a tradeoff, made by the men who run our whole system of government, between their group interests and those of women.

Sexual Abuse as Discipline

Up to now, I have been arguing against the idea that because male sexual abusers of women are pathological, the legal response to their conduct is a matter between the abusers, their victims, and the taxpayers. I have been arguing that the interests of men and women in general are also at stake. Now it is time to look more closely at the notion that abuse is merely pathological.

The difficulty with that view is that the tolerated residuum of abuse functions to enforce social norms about appropriate female behavior. In other words, it is disciplinary abuse. In the home and workplace and on the street, the chances of being victimized are dramatically increased if the woman violates a set of customary norms of female behavior.

The Disciplinary Mechanism

It may seem paradoxical to argue that abuse is disciplinary when I have defined it as behavior that most people in our society regard as unquestionably wrong or immoral. The abuse is deviance. But it is often deviance that punishes deviance. The abstract idea of "pathology" doesn't explain by itself how abuse can be sufficiently targeted so that being competent in responding to it mainly means understanding what behaviors are likely to provoke it, and then *regulating your own behavior accordingly.* And it doesn't explain how it can be the case that when women regulate their behavior to avoid sexual abuse, it turns out that the regulations correspond quite closely to a particular patriarchal code.

At least some of the time, in other words, the pathological abuser is a kind of vigilante. The woman victim has violated a customary rule about how women are supposed to behave. Most people would agree that rape or murder triggered by the woman's misconduct is a totally inappropriate response. But we also agree that fear of some kind of abusive reaction has in fact a strong deterrent effect on women contemplating violation of a whole range of patriarchal norms.

This observation seems to be contradicted but is actually confirmed by the fact that many victims report asking themselves repeatedly what they did to bring it on, and finding no answer. The question itself presupposes the asker's understanding that there are norms whose violation creates a risk. The victim asks the question because she has been regulating her behavior, consciously or unconsciously, in a way that should have, but did not, protect her.

Abuse is disciplinary when its perpetrators, whether or not they are "pathological," are sane enough to target some of it at women violating customary rules. It is still disciplinary even if a great deal of it is not targeted in any intelligible way. In other words, it makes sense both to say that "you will be abused no matter what precautions you take; it happens all the time; what you do or don't do has nothing to do with it," and to say that "you would be crazy to do this or that given the risk of abuse." There just has to be enough pattern so that women respond by complying with the norms to a greater degree than they would if they were better protected.

Assume that when abuse is disciplinary, it has the effect of reducing the deviant behavior at which it is aimed. The consequences will be different depending on one's position in relation to that behavior. An increase in compliance with the norm will affect people differently according to how they feel about the norm.

Women who would have violated the customary rule in spite of the risk of abuse are likely to be better off if abuse is eliminated, because they can "get away with it" at less cost than before. Women who would not have violated the norm under the old regime, because of the risk, should also be better off with more protection. Their compliance under the old regime enabled them to avoid harm. But they should be happy to get rid of the risk of disciplinary abuse so they can "do what they want" at less cost than before.

The good consequences of more protection, for women who would like to violate the customary rule, are balanced by the bad consequences for people of both sexes who agree with it and wish it were universally observed. Even supposing that they abhor abuse and would gladly abolish it, they derive an indirect benefit from its disciplinary deployment against female behavior they disapprove of.

There is yet a third group affected, consisting of men and women who benefit, according to their own assessment, from women's deviance. Disciplinary sexual abuse is often targeted to enforce norms about permissible female sexual behavior. The targeted behavior, whether quite concrete or merely symbolic, is something that the woman in question is doing with or to or for other people. Those other people may themselves be participating as deviants or they may be just spectators, but in either case they are affected when disciplinary abuse discourages conduct they get pleasure from.

For example, it seems likely that, in many parts of the United States, gay-bashing reduces the willingness of lesbians to wear very dykey, ultrabutch clothing on the street. Women who are not gay, but who would at least sometimes adopt ultrabutch styles, are also discouraged. But men and women who disapprove of lesbian sexual practices, and also of sexual minorities' expressing themselves through clothing, benefit indirectly from gay-bashing even if they think it is terrible. Men and women who get an erotic kick from other women's butch behavior lose, as do men and women who appreciate butch fashion without being turned on by it.

As this example is supposed to suggest, disciplinary abuse may be particularly important where there is not only deviance but also a challenge to the legitimacy of a norm of female conduct. The abuse is supposed to reinforce the norm that women should not be lesbians or appear to be lesbians, in a situation in which the deviant conduct seems to challenge the rules as well as break them. It is one of the weapons in an ideological struggle about which values should prevail, rather than just a mechanism to enforce a moral consensus against random backsliders.

Characterological Discipline

According to the theory of disciplinary abuse developed by radical feminists, including Robin Morgan, Andrea Dworkin, Catharine MacKinnon, Kathleen Barry, and Diana Russell,[15] the various practices of abuse play a central role in constituting and maintaining the system of male domination. Abuse may be labeled pathological, but it is omnipresent not just to enforce particular patriarchal rules, but also as a means to impose stereotypical or "traditional" female identity on women in the interests of men. However, the abstraction "men's interests," like "the interests of capital," suppresses too many particularities to be useful in understanding the puzzling aspects of eroticized hierarchies, and stereotypical female identity has the same problem.[16]

The theory of abuse as one of the practices that constitute our whole gender regime is in a sense the mirror image of the conventional view of abuse as pathological and exceptional. If forced to choose, I much prefer the radical theory to its conventional opposite. I think it identifies a deep truth about the regime of liberal patriarchy, just as Marx identified a deep truth in *Capital*. The question is how to interpret the insight.

Men's Interest in Traditional Female Identity

This subsection presents a reading—an appropriation and therefore inevitably a reworking and possibly a distortion—of a complex body of radical feminist work. A primary thesis of this work is that it is in the interest of men that women should have traditional identities, and that abuse is the mechanism by which men bring those identities about. But the theory bears a family resemblance to the sophisticated Freudian-Marxist account of capitalism, and particularly of the rise of fascism, because it goes well beyond explanation based on simple coercion.[17]

It goes beyond simple coercion because the particular character that men enforce through abuse is one that embraces rather than merely submitting to male domination. At a first level, men make women weak and passive, even in their virtues, by abusing them. At a second level, women embrace their own domination as part of an unequal bargain. At a third, men and women eroticize the relationship of domination so that it is sustained by (socially constructed) *desire.**

The "genius" of liberal patriarchy, in this view, is that it creates female subjects not just to suit men's interests in particular interactions, but to suit its "system interest" in its own reproduction. Women are coerced to be a particular way, against their will, but they also consent to be that way and find themselves constructed to get off on being that way.† Like a capitalism that constructs for its own purposes workers who are alienated individualists addicted to consumption, liberal patriarchy is far more stable than a system based on force alone.

According to Catharine MacKinnon, the traits of women identified by Carol Gilligan[18] in her studies—empathy, the "relational" as opposed to rights focus, contextuality as opposed to abstraction, and so forth—are the strategies of victims who must minimize

---

*This brilliant passage is one of the first clear statements of the theory: "The line between rape and intercourse commonly centers on some measure of the woman's will. But from what should the law know woman's will? . . . Women are socialized to passive receptivity; may have or perceive no alternative to acquiescence; may prefer it to the escalated risk of injury and the humiliation of a lost fight; submit to survive. Some eroticize dominance and submission; it beats feeling forced. Sexual intercourse may be deeply unwanted—the woman would never have initiated it—yet no force may be present." Catharine MacKinnon, "Feminism, Marxism, Method, and the State: Toward Feminist Jurisprudence," 8 Signs 650 (1983).

†"Sexual desire in women, at least in this culture, is socially constructed as that by which we come to want our own self-annihilation. That is, our subordination is eroticized in and as female; in fact, we get off on it to a degree, if nowhere near as much as men do. This is our stake in this system that is not in our interest, our stake in this system that is killing us. I'm saying femininity as we know it is how we come to want male dominance, which most emphatically is not in our interest." Catharine MacKinnon, *Feminism Unmodified: Discourses on Life and Law* 54 (1987).

"The brilliance of objectification as a strategy of dominance is that it gets the woman to take the initiative in her own degradation (having less freedom is degrading)." Andrea Dworkin, *Intercourse* 142 (1987).

their vulnerability to abuse of various kinds.* If women are empathic, it is because they have to be alert to the moods of the dangerous men in their lives; if they are relational, it is because they need solidarity to deal with the constant reality or threat of violence. If they shun abstraction, it is because men control the textual universe of abstraction in ways that disempower and disadvantage them when they try to enter it.

The theory suggests that the idealization of these feminine traits, by cultural feminists as well as by traditionalists, plays into the interests of men because the traits are empowering only or mainly within the context of liberal patriarchy. If the goal is to challenge and change the regime, such traits are problematic, since they involve renouncing the male-defined techniques of power that anchor the system. For this reason, it is in the larger interest of men that women should embrace an essentialist understanding of themselves as bearers of these passive virtues, even if it renders men less powerful in particular interactions at the microlevel than they might be if women were less empathic and relational.†

It is not surprising, in this view, that women with these traits tend to accept the unconscionable bargain proposed by the culture as a whole and by right-wing women ideologists in particular. The bargain is: A "real" woman is heterosexual, monogamous, maternal, submissive to her man, and sexually pleasing to him. If she manages

---

*"[I]t makes a lot of sense that we should want to negotiate, since we lose conflicts. It makes a lot of sense that we should want to urge values of care, because it is what we have been valued for." Isabel Marcus et al., "Feminist Discourse, Moral Values, and the Law—A Conversation," 34 *Buff. L. Rev.* 11, 27 (statement of Catharine MacKinnon). "Why do women become these people, more than men, who represent these values? . . . For me, the answer is clear: the answer is the subordination of women . . ." Id. at 74. See also MacKinnon, *Feminism Unmodified* at 39: "Women think in relational terms because our existence is defined in relation to men. Further, when you are powerless, you don't just speak differently. A lot, you don't speak."

†"Given existing male dominance, those values amount to a set-up to be shafted." Marcus et al., "Feminist Discourse" at 74. "Difference is the velvet glove on the iron fist of domination. This is as true when differences are affirmed as when they are denied, when their substance is applauded or when it is disparaged, when women are punished or [when] they are protected in their name." MacKinnon, *Feminism Unmodified* at 8. "One genius of the system we live under is that the strategies it requires to survive it from day to day are exactly the opposite of what is required to change it." Id. at 16. "When difference means dominance as it does with gender, for women to affirm differences is to affirm the qualities and characteristics of powerlessness." Catharine A. MacKinnon, *Towards a Feminist Theory of the State* 51 (1989).

to be or to appear to be these things, she can claim in return her man's protection, backed by the legal system if necessary, from other men.*

Street hassling sometimes seems to say: "Have a man with you as your protector, in which case we'll leave you alone because that's the appropriate way for women to be on the street. If you choose to present yourself as a single woman, then you have to deal with our conception of what single women are, which is up for grabs. You choose yourself to be hassled. But the minute you have a man with you, we wouldn't dream of bothering you. You won't have to worry. So get yourself a man."†

Incest, rape, the sexual enslavement of prostitutes, domestic battery, and sexual harassment in the workplace are all targeted, according to this theory; they put "teeth" into the message of street hassling. They do this because playing the submissive role in a conventional marriage seems like an obvious and sometimes effective way to prevent them. "Sometimes effective" is enough; the culture teaches that the risk is reduced even if these things can happen to any woman anywhere.‡

In this light, the female roles in the scripts of sexual abuse take on a new importance. They are not "just" stereotypes. The provocateur, the vindictive liar, the hysterical inventor, and the oversensitive woman all fail to keep their part of the bargain and therefore forfeit patriarchal protection. Watching women victims victimized

---

*"Right-wing women see that within the system in which they live they cannot make their bodies their own, but they can agree to privatized male ownership: keep it one-on-one, as it were." Andrea Dworkin, *Right-Wing Women* 21–23, 69 (1982). See also MacKinnon, *Feminism Unmodified,* 225–226.

†"Finally, for exceptionally privileged and protected young women and girls who do not learn elsewhere the threat under which they live, street hassling gets the message across. It is a potent daily reminder of the quality of the state-of-nature outside the protective institutions in which they will be expected to encase their lives." Robin West, "The Difference in Women's Hedonic Lives: A Phenomenological Critique of Feminist Legal Theory," 3 *Wis. Women's L. J.* 106 (1987).

‡Dworkin, *Right-Wing Women,* 212–213: "So each woman has to make a deal with at least one of the strong ones for protection; and the deal she makes, being based on her inferiority, originating in it, acknowledges the truth and inevitability of that inferiority." See also West, "The Difference" at 104: "One way that (some) women respond to the pervasive, silent, unspoken and invisible fear of rape in their lives is by giving their (sexual) selves to a consensual, protective, and monogamous relationship. This is widely denied—but it may be widely denied because it is so widely presumed. It is, after all, precisely what we are supposed to do."

again in the legal process or just in the media teaches men and women that redress for sexual abuse is conditional on being or appearing to be a "perfect" victim, and that means conforming to patriarchal norms.

In her wild, brilliant, subtle book *Intercourse,* Andrea Dworkin proposes (among many other things) that when a woman gets the message and enters a monogamous relationship with a man, the act of sexual intercourse is the microcosmic enactment of his conquest and possession of her. Her socially constructed experience of pleasure in being conquered and possessed, when that is her experience, is the culture's erotic reward for accepting the bargain. If she "fails" to experience that pleasure, it is her own fault, and her problem. The bargain works only for "real" women, so if it doesn't work for you, you must not be a real woman.[19]

In this view, liberal patriarchy can tolerate very extensive female participation in the workplace and presence in public space. Because they are "real" women, women workers and public figures will reproduce in those settings the attitudes of deference and acceptance of inferior status that are modeled in marriage. Men and women will eroticize the hierarchical element in the boss/secretary, doctor/nurse, pilot/stewardess, actor/actress and bartender/waitress relationships.[20] Attacks on gender segregation in the workplace will seem to "go against nature."[21]

Thus men use abuse directly to tilt the balance in their favor when they bargain with women, and also indirectly, to tilt women's characters so that they can't get or no longer even want what men don't want them to have. The keystone of the theory is the eroticization of abuse itself, through pornography.[22] Pornography is the "truest" form of patriarchal ideology, analogous to apologetic political economy in classical Marxism. It systematically constructs male heterosexuality so that it "is" to be sexually excited not just by male dominance and female submission, but also by the possibility or reality of male violence and female vulnerability to that violence.

An Endorsement and a Critique

I agree with a lot of this analysis. But it seems flawed in its insights by many of the vices that, beginning in the 1920s and 1930s, radical leftists came to see as requiring a reinterpretation of the central insights of Marxism.[23] As a result of this parallel my critique of (my own version of) MacKinnon and Dworkin tracks, in many ways, the debate within and about Marxism, and may be skewed by that prior experience.

Radical feminist theory explains how eroticized domination operates to maintain hierarchy by rendering it invisible or apparently consensual, in families and workplaces and public arenas. It explains why women often don't ask for or even seem to want what it seems to me, as a man, they *ought* to ask for and want if they were "our equals." Sometimes this seems plausibly attributed to different values that one should respect in the name of pluralism. But sometimes, especially when there is a basis of comparison because other women are making these demands and do seem to have these wants, it looks like oppression, albeit at a characterological level.

It seems there are stereotypically feminine traits that are propagated in some women I know partly by the need to anticipate, manage, and avoid abuse. Some of these seem admirable. Some of them seem to me to be negative aspects of femininity. Further, I value the occasions when women surprise, disconcert, and sometimes terrify men by suggesting possibilities of identity that have nothing to do with what men think women "ought to" be like, but come at us (men) out of their irreducible differentness. The system of abuse makes these occasions less likely than they might be in its absence, and indeed seems targeted to prevent them from happening at all.

I'm not saying that all women are affected in one particular way by the multiplicity of abusive male practices. Nor am I promoting the idea that there is a way that women are. It's a question of margins, of the way the tolerated residuum of abuse pushes traits one way or the other, increasing or reducing their statistical probability, not remaking people as single, unified beings as men or women.*

---

*I agree with Butler's formulation: "The presumption here is that the 'being' of gender is *an effect,* an object of a genealogical investigation that maps out the political parameters of its construction in the mode of ontology. To claim that gender is constructed is not to assert its illusoriness or artificiality, where those terms are understood to reside within a binary that counterposes the 'real' and the 'authentic' as oppositional." Judith Butler, *Gender Trouble: Feminism and the Subversion of Identity* 32 (1990).

The claim that gender is an effect does not suggest downplaying the role of force in its construction: "as a strategy of survival within compulsory systems, gender is a

Particular women sometimes seem to be less self-confident, less competent, less clear about what they think, less aggressive in the service of their ideals or just their interests (as I construe them), less willing to take risks where explosive male tempers are involved than they might be if they didn't live in an abusive universe. I think men profit in all their dealings with women from this impact of the tolerated residuum on character. I think women achieve less, both in terms of my own values and in their own terms, than they would in a regime less permeated by terrorism against them.

For some straight men—for many, including myself—the vulnerability of women, and phallic power in relation to it, have, sometimes, deep erotic appeal. Many straight women seem to be excited, some of the time, by that same vulnerability and phallic power. In all the situations in which straight men and women live and work together, there are possibilities of eroticized domination and submission constructed into male and female character.

For this reason, the discussion above drastically understated the interest of nonabusing men in the toleration of abuse. Indeed, the male interest in avoiding excess enforcement, crude definitions, the subtle constriction of their freedom of action vis-à-vis women, is not the half of it. Because abuse is important to the whole regime of liberal patriarchy, the male interest in the whole regime is implicated in efforts to abolish it.

Moreover, women who have accepted the bargain of liberal patriarchy, who have tried their best to "be" "real" women and succeeded at it, have their own stake in the regime. In the MacKinnon/Dworkin analysis, they are "collaborators," accomplices in their own oppression and opportunists who profit from the suffering of other women.*

This is a harsh way to say that the successful "traditional"

---

performance with clearly punitive consequences. Discrete genders are part of what 'humanizes' individuals within contemporary culture; indeed, we regularly punish those who fail to do their gender right . . . . The historical possibilities materialized through various corporeal styles are nothing other than those punitively regulated cultural fictions alternately embodied and deflected under duress" (id. at 139–140).

*Dworkin, *Right-Wing Women,* 227–231; idem, *Intercourse,* 143: "Instead occupied women will be collaborators, more base in their collaboration than other collaborators have ever been: experiencing pleasure in their own inferiority; calling intercourse freedom"; MacKinnon, "On Collaboration," in *Feminism Unmodified* at 205: "It keeps the value of the most exceptional women high to keep other women out and down and on their backs with their legs spread."

woman benefits, indirectly to be sure, and regardless of how much she disapproves of it, from the abuse that constitutes her social world, even though she is herself at risk. This half-conscious interest seems sometimes to translate into a sharp antifeminist skepticism about claims of abuse, aimed to preserve the conventional understanding that it is pathological and rare.

It is at this point, with the insight that some women benefit from the regime, and thus, like men, benefit indirectly from abuse even if they loathe it, that my endorsement runs out. There is an eerie resemblance between the radical feminist response to the problem of internal division and the response of Marx and Lenin.[24] In both, no-holds-barred polemics and a fierce willingness to split defend the seamless quality of the theory against the fissures of gendered existence within liberal patriarchy.

But that very seamlessness in interpreting "men's interests" and "female identity" are obstacles to understanding the puzzling aspects of eroticized hierarchy. One puzzle is the precise role of abuse in generating and stabilizing structures that are clearly "overdetermined"—the product of many overlapping causes. Another is that both men and women find heterosexual pleasures within them that they claim to experience as egalitarian and even redemptive, despite their endorsement of the critique of male supremacy.[25] Another is the persistence of resistance, compromise, and opportunism as strategies for negotiating the regime, rather than buying into it without reserve, so that the image of a fully rationalized, totalitarian gender system seems paranoid.

Perhaps the deepest puzzle is that it seems that pleasure within patriarchy, for both straights and gays, can sometimes be resistance, even when the pleasure is based on the very erotic charging of domination and submission that look like main pillars of the regime. This is the challenge of both lesbian sadomasochism and Nancy Friday,[26] not just to MacKinnon and Dworkin but also to the vanilla quality of much liberal and cultural feminist writing about sex. This challenge strikes a chord in the subcategory of straight men who want to be politically correct but don't want to renounce *all* the possibilities of excitement, *all* the dangerous sexiness that women and men produce using unquestionably patriarchal forms. They would like to use the master's tools to dismantle the master's house.

An account of liberal patriarchy that responds to these puzzles has to be more modest than the strong theory described above because it has to keep a sharp distinction between the regime, with its oppressive structure, and the men and women it constitutes and whose day-to-day actions *are* it. There is a regime, in this modest version, but it is not a coherent totality that manages to subsume each of its individual human parts to its system logic.

Men and women do not have the kind of freedom to be whoever they want to be that is sometimes presupposed in liberal theory. Everyone operates within the constraints of the regime. But we can't understand male and female behavior in terms of male imposition of a system within which women have no choice but to be what men want them to be.

No man wants "women" to be any particular thing, except in the context of the repertoire of roles, practices, and even wants, that condition him as soon as he begins to operate in the social world. The practices of abuse and the general structure of the regime are there before he is, always already a given. Abuse is prior to his interests, a condition of the development of his understanding of his interests, as well as something he can develop an interest in. We can embrace the notion of a regime and still recognize that different categories of men develop *different* interests, positive and negative, in it.

Women operate in the world through sign systems (language, dress, the scripts of abusive interaction) and social structures, and act strategically within them. They are always active, from within their intractable identities, in spite of the omnipresent constraints of patriarchy. They too develop different identities and interests in the regime, and the interests, like those of men, are both positive and negative.

Problematizing Men's Interest in Abuse

There is a version of the radical feminist argument in which disciplinary abuse disserves men, by promoting "feminine" traits they might prefer to see disappear, as well as serving men's interests. Robin West describes habitual lying, particularly about one's feelings, as a trait produced by abuse. The woman who defines her desires in terms of the desires of others, of men, lies about how she feels when she doesn't and can't feel what men want her to feel.[27] This idea, that a particular set of practices induced by abuse could be simultaneously beneficial and injurious to men, and differently so to different men, seems very important.

Most people in our culture believe that sexual abuse can have a negative constitutive effect on a woman's sexual identity. Incest victims are likely to have a particular range of "problems of sexual adjustment." *Time* magazine can report, without the need for an expert to quote, that: "Survivors of incest fall victim to extremes. They grow up unable to trust others or, alternatively, tending to trust too easily. They shut down sexually or become wildly promiscuous."[28]

Similar things are said about rape victims, victims of domestic battery, and women who have been sexually exploited by doctors, lawyers, psychiatrists, clergymen, and teachers. It seems to be the case that a large percentage of prostitutes and other sex workers have had childhood abuse experiences.[29] It is common to argue that their choice of sex work as a way to earn a living is at least sometimes and partly a result of vulnerability derived from early experience, and at least sometimes and partly a way to respond actively to early experience (by controlling men in the act of sex rather than being controlled by them, for example).

These female identities constituted through abuse, both "shut down sexually" and "wildly promiscuous," are "negative" in the sense that they diverge from strong social norms about what women are supposed to feel and like in sex with men. Men have had preponderance in developing these norms and in changing them through time as liberal patriarchy has become steadily more "sex positive." The very notion of a "problem of sexual adjustment" presupposes the normative project of making women who will enjoy and seek out "normal" heterosexual monogamous intercourse with men. "Low sexual desire" is a diagnostic category in part because women complain of it, but they complain of it in part because lack of sexual desire is socially constructed as something negative.

On this basis it would seem that men have both positive and negative interests in the female characters constituted by abuse. If the prevailing social norms of female identity, and particularly female sexual identity, serve men's interests, correspond to what they want from women, then abuse gets them what they want but also denies them what they want. It gets them (some) women who are relational, empathic, contextual, submissive, heterosexual, and monogamous. But it also gets them (some) women who don't want sex with them or want sex only because men want them to want it, and who lie about their feelings about it. It may be that the combination of the norms with the tolerated residuum of abuse gets them both of these in some measure from all women (or just from all white women, or all straight women).

We are talking about norms rather than about the wants of particular people. We have to look at different male attitudes toward the result of enforcing the norms. The norms exist independently of the will of any particular man, and there is nothing that compels any particular man to agree with them. Some men may prefer this universe, in which abuse has turned many women off sex with them, to the universe that would follow a large reduction in abuse. Other men may not care one way or the other, so long as they can find women who are submissive and who will fake orgasms to make them feel good. Many men have little erotic investment in women to begin with, and may care mainly about the complex indirect impact of male sexual abuse of women on male sexual identities.

It is certain that in the current sexual situation many men want there to be women who will work at prostitution as well as women who will be "traditional" wives. If abuse is a condition of the social production of prostitutes as a significant part of the labor force, then these men profit from abuse, just as early capitalists profited from the social and economic conditions that produced a large pool of child labor.

In this model, these men have an interest in father/daughter incest analogous to some men's interest in reproductive "free" choice for women, derived from the desire for easier sexual access than they had under a regime of forced pregnancy to term.[30] But some of these same men may feel trapped in a situation in which it seems the only alternative to "traditional" women who are rendered submissive but turned off by abuse is "outlaw" women who are made available for prostitution by abuse.

It is possible that the whole system consisting of norms, the tolerated residuum, and the variety of female sexual identities constituted by the combination is exactly what all men "really" consciously or unconsciously desire, and that women have played no part but that of object. But it seems to me that, for all the strength of this approach, it takes in the end too many epicycles, too many devious twists in the argument, to make it plausible.

It twists and turns because nothing must threaten its reliance on stereotyped, though resolutely antiessentialist, ideas of what men are like and of what their interests therefore have to be. It is in the structural Marxist tradition in which the capitalist class confronts the proletariat, knowing without having to be conscious of its interests, and imposes unilaterally everything from material conditions to consciousness itself.[31]

It is possible to recognize the excessive power of men as a group over women as a group, and the way in which abuse serves a whole range of male interests, including interests in the constitution of particular female identities and sexualities, without agreeing that liberal patriarchy has or could have that degree of totalitarian power. "[T]he paternal law ought to be understood not as a deterministic divine will, but as a perpetual bumbler, preparing the ground for the insurrections against him."[32]

In writing this essay I have come to recognize another, less abstract motive behind my critique. So long as I am a straight man, a part of my being is hostage to women: I want them to exist as women, not men, as bearers of the possibility of my own sexual excitement. This same part of me is, seemingly inescapably, the plaything of the culture that "constructs" women one way or another, and then "packages" them, both as actual people and as media images, by limiting the repertoire of signs through which they can communicate and I can interpret their particular sexualities. And I am no less constrained in what I can produce as intelligible sexuality. So far, so good.

The radical feminist analysis of the eroticization of domination has the enormous value of theorizing the abject in this situation. On the one hand is the longing that my own beings for women and their beings for me should multiply, turn toward transparency, and grow more powerful and surprising in generating and erasing differences. On the other are the conditions of domination that in every routine daily interaction drive both sides, that allow both sides, to lapse, in different measures, into passivity, exploitation, deception, and resigned blindness.

Is it just self-interested self-deception that makes the situation seem less hopeless than that? If it's not hopeless, it seems to me that the hope lies in those same routine daily interactions—for example, in the dailiness of dress.

Sexual Abuse and Female Dress

It is common to make a connection between the practice of sexual abuse and the production and reproduction of sexuality through female dress and men's responses to it. In particular, the relationship between abuse and "sexy" or "provocative" dressing plays a quite important role in the ideology of the patriarchal regime.

It is a part of the conventional view that women sometimes provoke abuse by their dress. This view is currently undergoing a serious challenge sometimes directly and sometimes indirectly inspired by feminist thinking. Within the challenge, there are ideological distinctions that correspond to the numerous possible responses to the norms and images of the regime. The case of sexy dress is an occasion to look at the multiplicity of male and female identities within the regime, at the conflicts of interests between and among men and women that occur when we think about changing the regime, and at the practices of opposition that occur in its interstices.

The Production and Regulation of Sexy Dress

What I mean by sexy dressing is female dress-in-a-setting that large numbers of people label as "sexy" or "provocative." A person who disapproves of a particular sexy-dress performance may call it "cheap," "slutty," "exhibitionist," or even "self-objectifying." In mainstream American culture today, costumes conventionally regarded as sexy in the sense of provocative generally choose exposure over covering, tightness over looseness, brightness (or black) over soft color, transparency over opaqueness, and symbolic shaping of breasts, waist, buttocks, and feet over "natural" lines. (As a practitioner put it, "If you can't see up it, down it, or through it, I don't want to wear it.") There are similar complex dimensions for accessories, hair, makeup, and so forth.[33]

The sexiness of a costume is a matter of degree. Women combine the elements to produce a spectrum with infinitely fine gradations from less to more. But which fashion performances people regard as sexy is also very much a matter of arbitrary convention. A revealing, tight, bright, transparent, shaped costume that doesn't follow the specific fashions of the moment is likely to be seen as weird or "gross" rather than sexy.

Finally, whether a given costume counts as sexy dressing in the sense in which I will be using the term depends on the setting in which it is worn. Sexy dress is sexy *only* in terms of the dress codes that regulate virtually all social space. These codes pervasively regulate the degree of sexiness permitted in each setting, but they do *not* operate to suppress female sexuality or impose a puritan morality. Rather, we are talking about the spatial and temporal distribution of behavior that is itself socially produced. In American society today there are norms, requirements of more or less sexy dressing (and sexy behavior generally) in some places at some times, as well as a variety of prohibitions of it in other times and places. A very tentative map might look something like this:

Women's Dress

	More Sexy	*Less Sexy*
Family life	In bedroom before sex	In kitchen with kids
	Dinner party	Family picnic
Public space	Nighttime	Daytime
	Night club	Airport
	Beach	Church
	Health club	Folk concert
The workplace	Sales work	Professional work
	Street prostitutes	High-priced call girls
	Actresses and models	Women scriptwriters
	enacting sexuality	

Sexy Dressing as Deviation from the Norm of the Setting

Dress codes try to match the spectrum of costumes, from less to more sexy, to the spectrum of settings, from less to more sexually charged. In a given setting, the code specifies some part of the costume spectrum as permissible. Dress is sexy for the setting when it is close to, at, or over the line that separates dress for this setting from dress for a more sexually charged one. Office wear that suggests a nightclub is sexy because it deviates in a particular direction from the office norm. Dress is conservative for the setting when it is at the line in the other direction.

In a given setting, to put on a costume composed of the conventional elements of dress is to produce a sign, in the same way that to speak a word is to produce a sign. The particular costume, say a halter top, like a word, will have a different meaning and convey different things about the speaker according to the context. Sexy dressing is production of a sign that has the two meanings of "sex" and "deviance," because it is a sign that "belongs in" (is prescribed for) a more sexually charged setting than the one in which it is being worn. The halter top is likely to be sexy dressing when worn in the office, but it may be "modest" when worn at the beach.

Once we recognize the sign-in-context as "sexy dressing," with the meaning of deviance in a particular direction, the costume will have many other layers of meaning as well. The reading of the dresser's more complex message will vary according to all her socially significant characteristics, including, for example, race, age, and body type. Given the mainstream white stereotype of black women, a provocative costume is more likely to be interpreted as a uniform indicating actual employment as a prostitute, or at least as "slutty" rather than "sexy," if worn by a black woman than it is if worn by a white woman.[34]

Old women and very large and very thin women are expected to accept the conventional social assessment that they are sexually unattractive and to dress so as to minimize their sexuality. If they dress sexily—that is, if they produce a costume-sign that is deviant in the direction of a more sexually charged setting—they are doubly provocative and are likely to be interpreted as rebels, eccentrics, or "desperate," and sanctioned accordingly. Since sexy dress calls attention to the body of the wearer, it is likely to prompt both the wearer and the audience to apply the conventional beauty standards of the moment. Sexy dressers who don't understand themselves as physically perfect will find themselves, as one practitioner put it, "trying to hide it and show it at the same time."

It is possible to engage in sexy dressing "by accident," that is, through ignorance or misapprehension of the dress code for a particular setting. But the dress code may also be contested or in transition, as when older people persist in interpreting a given costume as sexy dressing long after it has been "normalized" for a younger generation. Furthermore, there is no necessary connection between the judgment that a particular woman has produced the sign of sexy dress and the judgment that she herself is "sexy," in the sense of sexually desirable. A woman dressed "conservatively" may be seen as "very sexy," and a woman dressed "provocatively" may be seen as "sexless."

There is, nonetheless, a conventional discourse about the sign system, things that many people repeat about sexy dressing. In other words there is a discourse about why women dress sexily (deviate), about what it is to experience dress as sexy (rather than just recognizing the sign), and about the consequences of acts of sexy dressing (production of the sign). This is the discourse that justifies the dress codes that establish and enforce norms for each setting.

In this discourse, a first basic idea is that sexy dressing is intended to and probably does arouse sexual feelings in some men. This is what keeps the sign system from "floating" completely free of reality. Indeed, speaking as a straight man I can testify that deviation from the norm in the direction of the next sexier setting does often produce an experience of sexual interest, arousal, excitement in me and in some fraction of the men who see it. And also that I often experience it as intended to do this by the woman who is doing it.*

This straight male reaction of excitement to sexy dressing (as conventionally defined sign) seems to have something to do with both fetishism and voyeurism. The sexy dresser has modified her costume in a way that suggests looking at her in a setting that has a greater sexual charge than the one she is actually in. The associations of the more sexually charged setting are brought into the pre-

---

*Anyone, man or woman, can recognize the sign as the sign of sexy dressing without experiencing sexual feelings in response, and without thinking it is "really" sexy, and regardless of whether they approve or disapprove of sexy dressing. At this level, all we are talking about is the existence of a conventional sign system. There is no necessary link, but only an indirect and complex one, between what is conventionally understood to be "it" and what men and women experience in response. Dress can be regarded as sexy for a long time without producing the experience, or it can produce the experience in one or many men without acquiring the social meaning.

It is not necessary for the moment to establish the exact process that connects (some) men's experience of dress as arousing and its categorization as sexy. I will proceed on the assumption that there are mechanisms, like the market and direct negotiations among men and women, that give specific forms this designation.

sent one by the details of dress, which "represent" the costume of the other setting, and that costume in turn "represents" (as in fetishism) a part of or the whole sexualized female body.

Because sexy dressing violates the norm for the setting, the straight male reaction is complicated, indeed given a different "nature," by the addition of the particular man's reaction to the association of sexiness and deviance. Her dress is more than display. The woman who produces the sign seems to invite the watching straight man (cast as voyeur) to look at what, in that particular setting, she is supposed to hide.*

Only some men have this kind of reaction to the sign. Many who recognize it do not respond to it at all, or react to it with panic or distaste. Many "don't get it," in the sense of being oblivious. Others have voyeur-fetishist reactions that they are aware of but feel guilty about or think are politically incorrect, and fight hard against them.

Furthermore, men can have voyeur-fetishist reactions to *any* female self-presentation, without regard to the sign system, or in per-

---

*The analysis in the preceding two paragraphs, which is crucial to the rest of this section and the next, is heavily influenced by the work of Tracy Davis on the sexual meanings of Victorian actresses' clothing and by the general semiology of fashion of Roland Barthes:

"While clothing functioned [in the Victorian theater] as the sign of gender and sexuality was the referent of revealing clothing, certain articles of costume were more heavily weighted by the erotic lexicography of male culture. The clothing inextricably associated with a 'guilty' body part became the indexical sign of the sexual part; in other words, it was fetishized. In the opinion of Anthony Storr, a sexologist, women use fetishized objects to attract men, so 'a fetish may, as it were, be a flag hung out by the woman to proclaim her sexual availability.'" Tracy Davis, *Actresses as Working Women: Their Social Identity in Victorian Culture* 114–115 (1991), quoting Anthony Storr, *Sexual Deviation* 56 (1964).

Whether or not any particular item signifies a body part and also signifies "availability" depends on the vestimentary code of the particular culture. It might signify the "guilty" part, but not availability, or vice versa. Whether the wearer of a fetishized item of dress is using it as a "flag" to proclaim sexual availability is a matter of the intentions of the wearer, which cannot be conclusively inferred from either the production of the sign or the reaction to it. See generally Roland Barthes, *The Fashion System* (M. Ward & R. Howard trans. 1983).

But Davis seems right that articles of clothing operate in our culture as signifiers of sexualized body parts. For instance, brassieres and underpants get an erotic charge (for some people) from what they signify. A costume that exposes neither bra nor breasts may therefore get a strong sexual charge by visually *alluding to* or *evoking* a bra and the breasts it signifies (supposing that some people in the culture in question eroticize female breasts). This will be true regardless of the intentions of the woman who produces the sign.

verse reversal of its conventional meanings. Straight male sexuality, as we have constructed it, locks women into the role of performer no matter what they do to avoid it. Following the rules of sign production does no more than increase the probability that a woman will produce the reaction or nonreaction she is looking for. But straight male voyeur-fetishist reaction to female dress (he notes defensively) is at worst a perversion, at best of a piece with all culture appreciation, and not in itself abusive.

The Sexy Dress Subculture and Female Agency

Within the feminist theory that emphasizes the total power of men to shape gendered reality in their interests, it may seem obvious that what I have been describing is men's ideas about sexy dressing, which they impose on women, who then enact them. In this model, men have socially constructed reactions of excitement, and they coerce women to produce them, period. The coercion may be direct (men penalize women for not being sexy for them) or may work through the destruction of self-esteem so that women have no other means of feeling good, or through material deprivation that leaves them nothing else with which to bargain. In this view, there is little room for either female pleasure in sexual self-objectification or female agency in developing the repertoire of sexy dress ("Why would any woman *want* to totter around on high heels?").

Both the conventional and the feminist view have a more sophisticated variant that emphasizes the production of sexuality through a subculture—a semiorganized group—of sexy dressers. The subculture has an ideology, its own media, and relationships with other groups, including particularly women who enforce the norms from which sexy dressers deviate and the men who are aroused by their practices. This view seems to me preferable to the more individualist one.

The subculture exists within a situation of conflict about the eroticization of everyday life. Like others within the larger liberal capitalist system, its members only sometimes defend their practice with the argument that their way is best. More often, they play the liberal trump against majorities bent on enforcing compliance with their standards. "Women have come a long way, from burning bras to flaunting them. If a woman now chooses to look sexy, that is her right," says a *Vogue* editorial.[35]

As with other subcultures (beatniks, hippies, gangs, out gays), deviant practices get their meanings through their relationships both to mainstream practice and to mainstream ideology. In this case, sexy dress has an element of defiance, both of the conventional morality about dress* and of the feminist critique.† But at the same time that it defies it, the subculture influences the mainstream by providing an evolving vocabulary that can be incorporated piecemeal by sympathizers who don't want to "drop out" altogether.

It is possible to recognize the subculture but to deny its autonomy. The fashion industry and its media—mail-order catalogues, women's magazines, soap operas, magazine and television advertising aimed at women, women's pulp fiction—are heavily influenced by men. Men are dominant in their structures of ownership, and the male-oriented media that purvey arousal through sexy dressing (men's magazines, Video Hits 1, Black Entertainment Television and Telemundo, movies, advertising aimed at men) obviously influence the women's media.[36] The female subculture of sexy dress may be best understood as an instance of women collaborating in their own oppression.

But given that sexiness is a matter not just of the setting but of the choice to move closer or further from the boundary of deviance within it, women *as a group* are not compelled to dress sexily for men. If all the women in a setting deviated toward the next sexier setting, what they did would not be deviance at all, but a redefinition of the norm. Some women deviate, but most don't. Vast numbers, traditionalist and feminist and in between, do no more than "follow" whatever the fashion may be, either not caring about sexual self-presentation or not daring it or feeling incapable of it or very consciously rejecting it.‡

*"Don't be shy—it's fashion, not lingerie! And you want to show some cleavage!" Sandra de Nicolais, "The Bra . . . Meant to be Seen!" *Cosmopolitan*, Feb. 1992, at 174–175.

†"At the Women in the Law Conference, I found myself in the ladies' room with a feminist friend, smoothing my bright red lipstick on more slowly than usual so I could enjoy her horror, as though I were shooting drugs right before her eyes" (name of practitioner withheld).

‡One might note in response that the very uniforms that define the norm in any given setting are powerfully shaped by men's eroticization of femininity. High heels are often given as an example. I agree with this point and discuss it at length later. But high heels are sexy dress only when they are at least close to out of place, or adopted for the specific purpose of signifying sexuality.

Why dismiss the vast amount of energy, imagination, and work that women put into the constant evolution of the repertoire of dress? This happens at the micro level, where there are an indefinite number of possible combinations of clothes and body, with distinguishable finely graded meanings in the language of sex. Women produce themselves as gendered artifacts using this vast repertoire—indeed they produce gender itself.[37] And it happens at the level of the media, where the repertoire itself develops.

This work seems to me driven by numerous forces, all of which involve both men and women, without its being possible to sort out the issue of control in any simple way. For example, because sexy dressing is a subculture that influences the mainstream, it has to keep evolving or risk being normalized. Normalization threatens its existence as a subculture, which is dependent on deviance or defiance. It also deprives any particular sexy dress practice of its sexiness. This is partly because sexually arousing objects have a tendency to lose their charge over time. Familiarity breeds indifference. It is also partly because moving a particular costume (or costume element) away from the margin back toward the norm for the setting undermines its suggestive power for the voyeur-fetishist. When all the women on the beach have been wearing bikinis for years, the two pieces connote "all the other women on the beach" rather than "bra and panties." There is a contradiction between the words *risqué* and *respectable* in the view of the *Ladies' Home Journal:*

DRESSED TO THRILL
Victoria won't tell all her Secrets, but we can guess: Sales are skyrocketing. Her catalogues have made risqué undies respectable for all.[38]

Men influence this constant evolution rather than controlling it. Women negotiate with them, trying out new ideas and responding to the response. This is not a random Mendelian evolutionary process, but one in which women conceptualize men's desires and react to them with choices of their own among possible variations, according to their own authorial impulses. Women as authors compete among themselves for male approval, but they also influence one another, stealing and modifying one another's ideas.

Some men negotiate back, influencing women with praise but also with all kinds of other rewards, ranging from marriage proposals to "unearned" job promotions. Other men negotiate in the opposite direction, discouraging or penalizing the very same innovations. Women negotiate with other women as well, encouraging or severely punishing any hint of deviance. They are the primary enforcers as well as the violators of the codes.

All of this occurs in settings that are loaded with their own sign systems unrelated to heterosex. Every move along the spectrum of sexiness-for-straight-men is heavily constrained by the need to produce messages in all these other codes about all these other subjects. For example, dress encodes status in the workplace.

Perhaps the most important constraining context is that women dress for one another, participating in a discourse that is much more complex than that of sexy dressing for straight men and, for many or most women, involves a greater investment of interest and energy. It is impossible to separate out the contributions of producers and consumers in this intersubjective complex, as it is with pop culture in general. (Straight male) consumer sovereignty is a myth, as is the idea of simple imposition of mass culture by (male) tastemakers.

This is not to say that everything is all right because women have a free choice about how to dress, so whatever they actually decide to do represents what they "want" to do. Without denying that the regime gives men vastly more power than women, or that (as I will argue later) sexual abuse has an important constitutive role both in the definition of sexy dress and in its regulation, it seems wrong to dismiss female agency in the social construction of male excitement, and the possibility of female pleasures in the construction.

The Conventional View: Sexy Dress Provokes Sexual Abuse

> She is a constant distraction to the male employees, with her spiked heels, fishnet stockings and plunging neckline. Her makeup is more appropriate for a nightclub, and her skirt is so short and tight that her colleagues wonder how she ever sits down . . .
>
> Bauer and others say that employees have a responsibility to ensure that their personal appearance—especially in the workplace—does not indirectly encourage sexual harassment.
>
> Not everyone agrees with that position, but a recent survey of

1,769 psychiatrists suggests that many of them do believe in a link between "provocative" clothing and sexual harassment and sex crimes . . .

The survey included these statements and responses:

Female attire that appears to the male to invite direct sex[ual] attention tends to increase the risk of sex crimes. Yes: 63 percent; no: 21 percent; the rest undecided . . .

When a female minor is involved in intercourse or molestation in the home, one factor may be informality as to nudity or revealing attire. Yes: 81 percent; no: 17 percent.[39]

This story by Julie Hatfield, the fashion reporter of the *Boston Globe,* won a journalism award, perhaps because it so well reflects the ambivalence of our cultural moment. Hatfield's description of the sexy dresser's costume might conceivably be interpreted as part of the feminist critique of the regime's coercion of women into self-objectification for men. The article refers to "a debate over sexual harassment" and purports to reflect the views of "consultants who counsel management on how to curb sexual harassment in the workplace."[40] But her endorsement of female responsibility for controlling dangerous male sexual desires is firmly in the conventional camp, and disregards twenty years of feminist critique of that allocation of images and roles.

Hatfield has updated the conventional view by substituting "empirical data" for a simple appeal to "human [that is, male] nature" to establish the link between dress and abuse. The study to which she refers is truly postmodern social science: instead of attempting to gather data about the effect of dress on abuse, its authors polled "psychiatrists" about their views, with no indication that any of them had ever done or seen any empirical work on the subject. Their responses have the same kind of authority as those of the man who when asked for medical advice happily gives it on the ground that although he is not a doctor he has played one on television.

The Conventional View as Narrative

Hatfield's article restates, with a slight feminist and a slight social science patina, a narrative that is both reflective of and a constitutive element in the regime's ideology of sexual relations. In this narrative, a woman wears provocative clothing and suffers sexual abuse. She demands redress of some kind from the abuser. He is put on trial on the basis of her accusations, but he is exonerated or excused on the basis of what *she* did. From within the ideology of the regime, this narrative is highly intelligible—it makes sense, in spite of the enraged and seemingly uncomprehending reactions of critics—and it is also highly functional.

The affect involved goes beyond "blaming the victim," as she might be blamed for not "taking care of herself"; in this case, she actually "got what she deserved." She is a bad person. In the conventional view, what she has done wrong is to produce a particular sign, the sign of sexy dress, knowing that the sign both has a meaning and will produce an effect. She is responsible because in the narrative of sexy dress she understands the meaning and anticipates the effect.

The meaning of the sign, in this view, is that the woman desires to have sex with men outside the context of domestic intimacy. This is understood both by the woman and by the men who apprehend the sign. A secondary meaning of the sign is performative: it is, in itself, consent to having sex with some man outside domesticity, and she does or should understand that if she denies all the men in the setting, she will be forced or otherwise abused.

In this view, a woman who behaves in a sexually provocative way has agreed in advance to be raped or harassed if she decides she doesn't want sex with any of the men to whom she has communicated her availability. She has to go through with it. If she didn't want to go through with it, all she had to do was not produce the sign in the first place.

Well, why would a woman produce the sign? To traditionalists, this seems like a very naive question. The woman is a sexual mercenary or a slut or a tease. A mercenary is a woman who intends to get something out of a man by offering him sex in return. A slut is a woman who wants sex indiscriminately, like a man. A tease is a woman who pursues her mercenary or sluttish proclivity by exciting men, but does not intend to "deliver" on the promise that is the meaning of the sign of sexy dress. She may be uninterested in actual sex, or she may get sadistic pleasure from arousing and then frustrating male desire.

In each of these cases, in the conventional view, the type of female sexuality deployed is evil. It invites sex without either social legitimacy or love; it is manipulative or indiscriminate or sadistic. But it may work. When it does, the woman uses her sexual power over men, the power she exercises when she produces the sign of sexy dress, to achieve an immoral success. Abuse occurs when the woman who has set out to tease is "caught" and forced to perform her part in the bargain, or when the woman changes her mind and decides that she wants to withdraw the offer/promise she made when she produced the sign.

The man's corresponding desire for illicit sex is also immoral, though "natural," and just as wrong in the abstract as the woman's; and the abuse is wrong in itself. But there is an asymmetry in the situation that explains why she is the one more at fault. The woman in this narrative has taken the initiative by producing the exciting sign, and the man's reaction is involuntary. His violence is the expression of desire aroused and then frustrated. Women produce these antisocial reactions through their conscious acts, so both the lust and the violence are their responsibility.

But there is more to it than this. The male abuse of the sexy dresser is not just contract enforcement or an unfortunate consequence of involuntary male excitement; it fulfills a sadistic angry impulse on the part of the blaming public. She "got what she deserved," "it served her right," "she was asking for it." This punitive reaction of traditionalist men and women seems to be related to her apparently intentional violation of the patriarchal bargain of gender in which women will be madonnas (mothers, wives, or virgins) or whores.

The sexy dresser threatens the interest of traditional men and women in the stable reproduction of the regime. She is toying with the explosive, "natural" forces of sexuality outside the framework. It's not only that she is giving in to temptation or getting caught when she changes her mind; her whole course of conduct, what got her there in the first place, was a form of cheating, free-riding, selfish subversion of the tenuous arrangements that provide women in general with security against abuse and men with protection against the destructive force of their own competitive desire for women.[41]

The expanded narrative—in which the woman accuses the man of rape or sexual harassment, society affirms that if he has done what she says he is an offender, the facts are investigated, it turns out that she acted provocatively, he is let off, and she is disgraced—raises and resolves the questions of whether there are women like this and how they should be treated. It also raises and responds to other questions that come to mind every time a woman accuses an apparently sane man of abuse.

Is it really true that women benefit from a bargain—autonomy surrendered in exchange for protection from abuse? If men can freely abuse women who are blameless, then perhaps there is no bargain and women give up their autonomy for nothing. On the other hand, if women who refuse the bargain and insist on sexual autonomy can get protection in their free-agent negotiations with men, then women also give up their autonomy for nothing.

What are men really like? If men will deal with women as equal bargainers in sexual transactions, then there is not that much danger in renouncing the bargain. On the other hand, if men who are not insane rape and abuse just for the pleasure of it, then even the bargain won't keep women safe.

The narrative answers these questions as follows:

The norm of patriarchal protection of women is clear: men shouldn't rape or sexually harass women who perform their part of the bargain.

The norm that women should find sexual fulfillment with a single male protector is clear: women shouldn't present themselves as sexually available outside domesticity.

Bad women who refuse the bargain—mercenaries, sluts, and teases—are punished, by abuse and then by disgrace, so there are real benefits to the bargain even for women who feel ambivalent or angry about giving up their autonomy.

Men are indeed dangerous and violent, especially in relation to women who are asserting themselves as sexual free agents, so the bargain has a lot to offer.

But sane men are not randomly abusive; women are safe so long as they comply with the terms.

The narrative has appeal because these answers restore the equilibrium, the status quo ante, that was threatened by the woman's initial accusation. It seems plausible that people who hold the conventional view are likely to want, consciously or unconsciously, particular accusations of abuse in the real world to fit the narrative. They are likely to work hard at interpreting the event to promote this fit. They are likely to make assumptions, place burdens of proof, and imagine context in ways that will do all this. In short, the narrative is a tool for the ideological task of legitimating the regime.

Responses to the Narrative

The enemies of the regime can't "disprove" the regime narrative any more than a poll of psychiatrists can prove that "revealing attire" causes incest. The narrative is not a formal theory, but a way to understand a specific course of events in the world. In any given case, everyone might agree that it "didn't apply" or wasn't what actually happened. But it is still there to facilitate the traditionalist ideological project in the next case. The responses are no less ideological than the narrative itself, in the sense that they, too, attempt to construct templates, exemplary stories, "models," that will ease but also subtly influence future interpretations.

One response is a counternarrative of abuse in which dress is irrelevant, a story in which it made no difference what she was wearing. In this version, male conduct is reinterpreted so that it is no longer an uncontrollable reaction to the production of a sign well understood by all participants, but rather a combination of the arbitrary sexualization of female bodies and the will to power over the victim. When men later produce the regime narrative to explain what happened, they are lying or rationalizing. According to a letter to the editor in response to the Julie Hatfield story quoted above:

> Hatfield claims that female employees should leave their transparent clothing at home. But what if the harasser happens to be excited by sweatshirts and jeans, or by men's suits? . . . Sexual harassment is not caused by women's clothing. On the contrary, it is caused by a perpetrator's hunger for power. Rather than tell women how to assuage aggressors, Hatfield and her cohorts should educate those aggressors in respecting women's rights.[42]

The difficulty with this response is that it ignores the existence of the sign system. It is certainly true that some men will eroticize any form of female dress, and that there is no uniform that categorically repels unwanted sexual attention.[43] It may even be true that producing the sign of sexy dress actually provides protection against some harassers in some settings, because it intimidates them. And a woman who wears extremely modest clothes in a setting where the norm says she should dress quite sexily is likely to find herself approached coercively by men who see her as signaling sexual vulnerability. Male entrepreneurs abuse women sex workers who aren't sexy enough to sell.

So it is right to describe as a myth the regime's theory that "provocative female dress is a significant cause of sexual abuse."[44] It is a myth in the sense that a narrative singling out dress from the complex context of abuse is patently ideological, and in the sense that making everyone dress "conservatively" wouldn't end and probably wouldn't even reduce the amount of abuse.

But it is not just mythological thinking that explains the responses to an interview questionnaire about rape that lists possible measures the respondent might have taken "to increase [her] safety." One question asked, "When you are out alone, how often do you try not to dress in a provocative or sexy manner?" Fifty-eight percent of women answered "always," 18 percent "never," the rest in between.[45] Short of rape, many women perceive violating the dress code in the direction of being "too sexy" as creating a particular risk of persistent propositions, unwanted touching, suggestive remarks, exhibitionism, obscene phone calls, and the like, from both "creeps" and macho harassers, both on the street and in the office.

It is not that the dress "causes" the reaction, in the way a germ causes a cold.[46] But in a particular case it may be obvious that the abuser interpreted the costume as a sign, as an expression with a meaning about the woman, about women in general, or both. He then reacted to—abused—the woman as he interpreted her through the sign. If she hadn't produced the sign, she wouldn't have gotten the reaction, though maybe the man would have found someone else who did produce it and abused her instead or, failing that, taken to abusing on a different basis. Although I don't know what portion of all abuse happens this way, I have seen it happen this way.

This is not to say that the woman who produces the sign intends to invite sexual attention, let alone abuse. The meanings of dress signs are currently contested, and consequently highly uncertain. According to another letter to the editor in response to the Hatfield story, "Enjoying what one wears is one thing, but many misguided women dress provocatively to seek attention and approval from men, not necessarily their advances. Men are told that such outfits are a signal that advances are welcome. Why, after all, would any sane person dress that way for her own comfort or pleasure?"[47]

If abuse sometimes occurs in this kind of interactive context, then the antiabuse position is in part a demand for a revision of the conventional meanings of dress language, or a resolution, in favor of women's freedom of action, of the current contest about those meanings. Even though they are "misguided," men should allow women to produce this sign without its having the meaning that some men attribute to it—they should not interpret it as an invitation or as consent in advance to violence.

This position accepts that there is a sign—sexy dressing—that is mutually understood on one level (we know what it is) but whose meaning is contested at another (is it or is it not invitation and consent?). Men should agree that women can produce the sign without thereby offering an excuse for any modification in "proper" male behavior. A man who responded to the sign with unwanted advances or abuse would be breaking the rules and inviting punishment, just as he would be if he claimed that a bank's advertised "friendliness" justified his robbing it at gunpoint.[48] Sexy dressing would no longer be (or at least everyone would agree that it shouldn't be) dangerous in the way it is now. Or, if you believe that there really is no connection between production of the sign and abusive reactions, imagine that this view was general, so that the imagined threat of abuse was no longer a factor in women's dress decisions.

Different Reactions to the Relaxation of Sanctions against Sexy Dressing

If we imagine that such a change in our social system actually occurred, so that there was no longer a developed script for the disciplinary abuse of sexy dressers, it seems likely that there would be changes in women's behavior as well as in men's. It is not that women would now be "free to dress any way they want," because even in the absence of abuse there would be the whole complex of internal and external pressures for compliance with the various dress codes. But production of the sign of sexy dressing would be less dangerous than it now is. There might be a consequent increase in violations of the dress code in the direction of sexiness. If there were, the change would be controversial, indeed would bring out deep ideological conflict within the camp of critics of the regime.

The cost/benefit analysis of disciplinary abuse suggests that doing away with abuse of sexy dressers would have positive consequences for women who already violate the norm, and for those who would begin to violate it once the penalties were reduced. There would be losses for those who approve of the norm and don't want to see more sexy dressing, even though they disapprove of vigilante enforcement. The whole subculture of practitioners and advocates would gain, including those who are turned on, and like being turned on, and those who appreciate it without a turn-on, and would like to see more of it in spite of the norm.

The trouble with this approach is that it simplemindedly assumes that women now violate the norm because they "want" to, and would violate it more, for the same "reason," if there were fewer sanctions. If we are to get at the real conflict of interests between and among men and women, we have to explore these "wants" rather than taking them at face value. To begin with, there is the problem that the behavior regulated is the production of a sign for other people, and not an activity like eating ice cream in private.

A similarity to eating ice cream in private might be that the sexy dresser is engaged in "consumption," and values her freedom from sanctions because she wants to be able to enjoy this activity at the least possible cost. But because we are dealing with the production of symbols, this hypothesis is less plausible than it is with more conventional kinds of consumption. Female dress is also expression, and it may in any particular case be a misrepresentation of the speaker's inner state and a strategic one at that. Reducing disciplinary abuse of sexy dressers will affect women differently according to how they characteristically relate to this constrained set of opportunities.

Conventional liberal thinking about this kind of issue tends to assume a sharp and unproblematic contrast between choice and duress.[49] Thus we can say that if some women respond to a reduction in disciplinary abuse of sexy dressers in the workplace by dressing more sexily, they benefit because they have chosen to change their behavior. If they are within their "rights" in doing so, the private benefit is also a social good. But in this case it seems much more plausible to suppose a continuum (perhaps a loopified continuum) between choice and duress.

When we put together the variation in women's experiences of freedom or duress with the possibilities of strategic rather than simply expressive use of the dress code, it is clear that a change in incentives might be experienced in many different ways.

1. A woman might experience a reduction in sanctions as coercing her into sexier dressing. The coercion might come from a particular man who wants her to dress deviantly for him, or from an employer, or from a clique of women friends. Sanctions against sexy dressers might be welcomed by such a woman because they counteract the pressure by giving her a "good reason" for her preferences. When she responds to the relaxation of dress discipline by dressing more sexily, she is moving not to a higher but to a lower indifference curve.

2. The change might be experienced as allowing her to make men happy, by reducing the dangers to her of doing what they want, or of appearing to express the feelings they want her to be having. In other words, it might be the occasion for the pleasure of consent to the desires of another. In economic language, the woman's utility function might not be discrete from that of her audience. As in the previous case, no sexual feelings of the type conventionally understood to be expressed by sexy dressing are involved. It is not a question of what the woman herself, autonomously, feels and then expresses, but a question of what she thinks men want her to feel. Compliance (submission) might be eroticized or might not be.[50]

3. A woman might derive sexual pleasure from the combination of her agency in creating a representation of sexuality and the sexual reaction of her audience. In other words, she might be an exhibitionist. She might experience this as a compulsion that she would rather be rid of, or as a part of her sexual nature that she is happy with. She might regret a reduction in sanctions as putting her more at the mercy of her compulsion, or welcome the reduced riskiness of pursuing her kink.

4. Some women might experience reduced abuse as increasing their power by allowing them to exploit an asset, the ability to dress sexily successfully, at the expense of other women (not as good at it) and of men (putty in their hands). Again, the gain has nothing to do with the ability to express "true" sexual selves, but rather with greater freedom to exploit the asset of *perceived* sexiness. For other women, the choice to dress more sexily in the postabuse workplace might be no more than a way to minimize the losses caused by the increase in bargaining power of the advantaged group.

5. The conventional understanding of dress as expression might apply, so that some women experienced a gain in welfare because they could now "say what they mean" in a way that would previously have been dangerous.

6. A woman might experience an increase not in the ability to express herself, but in the ability to produce a complex sexual persona, reflecting in part her "true" feelings about her sexual being, but also in part her ideas about women, sex, fashion, and everything else, and in part her desire for sexual and aesthetic reaction from others.[51] Here the pleasure is in self-objectification as performance, the pleasure of cultural creation and relationship, rather than of being able to translate the inner sexual self into the world by representing it.[52]

In assessing each of these six hypothetical reactions, we have to take into account that the pleasures of sex are connected with the pleasures of ideological contest and of transgression. Changing the norm might de-eroticize behavior that had the pleasures of defiance or deviance. This might be true for both the sexy dresser and her audience. When the "punk" teenage subculture adapted the working-class butch lesbian look, it changed its erotic significance by switching its meaning from one form of defiance to another. When punk fashion crossed over into the mainstream, leather jackets with chains lost and gained erotic and other kinds of meaning once again.

An increase in sexy dressing in the workplace, brought about by reducing disciplinary sanctions, might end up "normalized." The sexy-dress subculture and its opponents would adjust to it, as would everyone else, and the "action" would shift to the outer boundary of a new rule. Exhibitionists, whether or not compulsive, would have to test the new as they tested the old, or lose their voyeurs; self-expressers would have to defy it in order to convey their true feelings; gender artists would have to play its edges to convey their particular cultural messages.

This "semiotic" property of the norm means that there is less at stake than at first appears. Women and men will communicate and produce themselves as culturally laden objects and perform, using the opposition the norm establishes between the required and the forbidden, no matter where we choose to draw the line. But it does not mean that nothing is at stake.

First, the relaxation of sanctions might have no effect at all on the quantum of sexy dress in the sense of deviation from the norm, but have a major effect in the long-run conflict over the eroticization of media, workplaces and public space. The particular types of eroticism characteristic of the regime might flourish, through the actions of the different types described above and their male collaborators, at the expense of the current variety of de-eroticized modes of female self-presentation.[53]

Second, the bodies and the psyches of the abused are at stake. The stage for the play of signifiers is sometimes a killing field. A reduction in the total amount of violence against women, or even its delegitimation by repudiation of the regime narrative in which "she asked for it," would have consequences, direct and indirect, for millions of women. These two sets of effects—those on the erotic quality of life under the regime, and those on the women who are the object of different kinds of disciplinary violence—evoke passionate responses. They involve the general ideological contest over sexuality.

Ideological Conflict over the Discipline of Sexy Dressers

The conflicts of interests over sexy dressing arise in large part from ideological differences about its meaning for the actors and watchers who are involved. There are deep conflicts among men and among women about how to interpret "women's hedonic lives,"[54] about how we should respond to coercion, or engulfment in male utility functions, or exhibitionism, and so on; likewise about how to interpret and respond to the reaction of the audience of male and female dominators, voyeurs, prudes, aesthetes, and so on.

A very tentative map of ideologies might look like this:

Reaction	*Liberal Patriarchy*	*Radicalism*
Neopuritan traditionalism (sex = danger of sin)	Clean and dirty sex naturally separate (home and house)	Neopuritan feminism (sex = danger of abuse)
Pro-sex traditionalism *(The Total Woman)*[55]	"Consensual" sex healthy not dirty (sex manuals and the "sexual revolution")	Pro-sex postmodern *(Pleasure and Danger)*[56]

We might lay the grid of positions across the grid of times and places for the production and expression of sexuality. In the straight workplace, for example, each ideological position has a valance, pushing for more or less permissive norms. People in different ideological positions are likely to have very different assessments of the costs and benefits of an increase in sexy dressing brought about by a reduction in disciplinary sexual abuse.

Pro-sex traditionalism endorses traditional women's roles in the home, on the job, and in public space but rejects the neopuritan connection of sex and sin. It is an accommodation of the reactionary position to the evolution of liberal patriarchy toward greater permissiveness. Marabelle Morgan's "total woman" is all in favor not just of physical pleasure but of the sexual gestures and paraphernalia that are current in the culture. Sexiness *within marriage,* in her view, is a component of the wife's power over her husband; it is fair play in the battle of the sexes and a basis of stability (along with religion) for family life.[57] The *Ladies' Home Journal* represents a milder, more sophisticated version of this position, with a strong liberal feminist element.

Men and women with this view tend to accept the conventional script according to which workplace sexy dressers invite, even if they don't deserve, disciplinary abuse—they are disregarding the God-given distinction of realms according to which a woman should be a whore only in the marital bedroom. A marginal increase in office sexy dressing in response to a relaxation of sanctions is likely to look like exhibitionism, commodification, or postmodern blasphemy. Moreover, it is a threat to marriage, to the wife's legitimate monopoly on her husband's sex life.

The neopuritan strand in radical feminism takes a much more uncompromising attitude toward the "sexual revolution" and the liberal feminist emphasis on consent as the criterion of healthy sexuality. In this view, the relaxation of sexual prohibitions along with the general eroticization of the culture have disserved women because their "consent" takes place in a context of radical power inequality. There is inequality in the way society constructs sexuality to conform to the male model (the eroticization of domination). Men and women socialized in this way then confront each other in one-on-one encounters in which men pervasively are violent or threaten violence, deploy their superior economic status, and manipulate the discourse of consent to get what they want.[58]

In this perspective, the central reality of sexual relations is danger to women from men. Moreover, "under male supremacy, heterosexuality ensures that each woman is intimately colonized by the dominant class."[59] For neopuritan feminists, a reduction in sexual abuse is likely to be an important good, while any concomitant increase in sexy dressing is likely to look like the evil of objectification. From this ideological perspective, the change in the marginal woman's behavior is likely to look coerced or compulsive or commodified.

The *nonabusive* regulation of sexy dress, through negotiation among women and the application of merely social sanctions to deviants, looks to me, as a male observer, to be a common feminist practice. Many feminists enforce dress codes among themselves and work for their more general acceptance because they think they express a healthier, better attitude toward sexuality than that of the sexy-dress subculture. They see the particular conventions of sexy dress, the actual content of the sign system, as expressing patriarchal views about female attractiveness, and particularly the view that what makes women attractive is vulnerability to domination and accessibility to male sexual appropriation.

I would put myself in the pro-sex postmodern (po-mo) category. This position affirms not just the possibility but the actual occurrence sometimes of great pleasure in heterosex, and the (sometimes) liberatory, oppositionist character of that pleasure. But it affirms the same possibilities in the practices of sexual minorities, as well as in the day-to-day practices that are coded to permit erotic life to flourish in everything from cooking to teaching to dressing.

An important difference from the neopuritan strand in feminism (and from much of the rest of left thought) is a postmodern take on the meaning of the term *social construction*. The clichéd version (from an article in *Ms.*) is: "Until we elect to take over the job, the dominant culture constructs our reality and forms our values."[60] But the "dominant culture" never has either the coherence or the power to construct us in the way suggested, and we never achieve the "outside" position vis-à-vis ourselves-in-the-culture that would allow us to "take over the job." We are positioned at any given moment by everything that has gone before so that we can only do and be some things, and not others. When we most fully experience ourselves as choosing, as improvising, we are ringing the changes on the limited scripts the culture makes available. But we nonetheless sometimes change those scripts.[61]

The pro-sex po-mo manifesto has already been written, by Marny Hall, under the rather mysterious name of "anti-sex":

> Anti-sex, despite its oppositional designation, is apposite, rather than opposite, patriarchal sex. Consequently, at the same time that anti-sex challenges old constructions, it contains elements of the old which may be teased and twisted into new pleasure scripts that are tailored to the histories, fantasies and neurophysiologies of intimates. In this scrambling process, old phallocentric practices, instead of serving as the invisible template of lovemaking, can be impelled into consciousness, rearranged, refurbished, and combined with elements from other dimensions of experience.[62]

People in the pro-sex po-mo position are no less attached than anyone else to making moral and political judgments about social structures and individual conduct. Their idea is not that "anything goes," but rather that "anything *might* go." Coercion, engulfment, compulsion, and sexual abuse are real, there to hate. Pleasure and resistance relate to them, it seems, symbiotically, even parasitically, rather than through a permanent obliteration and replacement of the regime.

The next section develops this idea in the context of sexy dress, with the focus on the ways in which the language of dress simultaneously promotes eroticized male domination of women and permits its subversion.

Abuse and Resistance in the Language of Sexy Dress

In our culture, particular items of dress are used to signify the abstract ideas "man" and "woman." This is not a complex or mystical idea. How do you know, when you want to pee, which is the ladies' and which the gents'?

```
            X                              X
          XXX                            XXX
          XXX                            XXX
            X                              X
   XXXXXXXXXXXX                   XXXXXXXXXXXXXXX
       XXXXX                          XXXXX
       XXXXX                          XXXXX
       XXXXX                          XXXXXXX
       XXXXX                          XXXXXXXX
       XX XX                          XXXXXXXXXXX
       XX XX                            X  X
       XX XX                            X  X
```

Not all women wear dresses, but a dress or a picture of a dress is a sign, which, when used along with the opposite sign of pants or a picture of pants, has the conventional meaning "woman." Particular items of dress—a skirt with a particular cut, a hat with a particular shape—have similar functions as signifiers in the system of oppositions within the lexicon consisting of all items of female dress.[63] Items of dress (or pictures thereof) signify that the woman who wears them is a particular type of woman. This is obvious in the case of uniforms, in the literal sense, specified for particular occupations (policewoman, flight attendant). But dress also signifies "character types," as in this description by Molly Haskell:

As a type, the man's woman may or may not be a vamp; but she is defined by her relations with men, and it is in their presence that her fire blazes. Essential to her aura is a hyperfemininity; by implication she sets herself apart from women who are "mannish" or homely or too smart, or who have malelike ambitions, or who might otherwise threaten the hegemony of men.

This siren has suffered something of a setback with the rise of feminism, which places a premium on more direct and non-sexual routes to power . . . Think of the stars of the '80s: Meryl

Streep, Sally Field, Sissy Spacek, Goldie Hawn, Mia Farrow—
good girls all. None of them would wear a torpedo bra or a
waist cincher, or call when you're out of town on a business trip
and, finding your husband/lover alone and lonely, suggest a ren-
dezvous.[64]

Yet a third signifying mode is that in which a woman says something about her state of mind by what she chooses to wear on a
particular occasion. The *Ladies' Home Journal* recently asked its readers their "advice for keeping a marriage really passionate," and
published ten responses. In one of them the wife-respondent
"smuggles" a suitcase with her "sexiest lingerie" on a romantic get-
away, and in another the couple "do special things for each other."
The wife would "wear a pretty nightgown or fix a romantic din-
ner."[65] This is the pro-sex traditionalist version of the sign system,
and people of other ideological persuasions or from different subcultures might choose radically different signs to express different
things. The point is that dress signifies day-to-day attitudes (for
both men and women) as well as gender and character type.

Items of clothing do more than signify, however, even in the
simplest case of the signs on the men's and women's room doors.
Dressing is one of the most important ways in which people
reflect, reproduce, and change through time our particular social
constructions of the differences between men and women, of the
appropriate relations between men and women, and of hetero- and
homosexuality.[66]

There is no need here for an elaborate gloss on reflection, reproduction, and change. The notion is that if you want to figure out
the regime of gender, you will find it set forth, or reflected, coded,
in dress. But to dress is more than to reflect an order located elsewhere: it is to produce a sign, willy-nilly, to act, to express something.

As an expression, it is double. On the one hand, it says something about or represents the dresser, fits the dresser into one of the
available, intelligible categories of people. But this is only half of it.
Dress is performative in the sense that it does something in the
world, rather than just representing an "interior." When a man or a
woman puts on a costume, he or she implicitly affirms the ideas
coded into it, not just as ideas about the self, but as ideas about

gender. Dress is both an operation carried out using the conventions, and a comment on them.*

It may express adherence to the regime, or it may express some form of disengagement or opposition. It is like voting. It puts the wearer on one side or the other. When a dress performance reflects the ideas of the regime, it also reproduces the regime, in the sense of extending it in time as "the same thing." Where the ideas are divergent, they may change the regime, though usually they don't. I'm not sure whether this has to be so, but it seems clear that it is an aspect of our particular cultural situation.

For example, sexy dress (deviation from the norm in the direction of a sexier setting) may be read as a critique of the boring, utilitarian asexuality of the setting and the people in it. Conservative dress may seem to be a critique of the gender stereotypes coded into the female fashion conventions of the setting. It may also be read as a critique of the conventionally feminine behavior of the other women in the setting.

A dress or a picture of a dress functions quite unambiguously, when opposed to pants, as a signifier of the idea "woman," and a person who fails to interpret the sign correctly is likely to be thought stupid or weird. But the theory that there are ideas beyond "woman" that are reflected, reproduced, or resisted by this particular sign is obviously contestable. The women in the examples above might well deny that they meant any such thing by their dress ("it's personal, not political"). Most people engage in the contested practice of interpreting dress "ideologically" at least some of the time, but there is no consensus about what particular ideas particular items of dress affirm.

Thus any given act of dressing can have different meanings for different observers, and different effects on them. It can look like opposition to one person but like conformity to another. A particular act of dress interpreted as conformity can incite one person to disgusted resistance and persuade another that resistance is hope-

---

*Dressing is analogous, in its impact on its "audience," to moviemaking: "Thus, one's gendered subjectivity is not only implicated, such as it is, in the spectator's encounter with each film, but also constructed, reaffirmed or challenged, displaced or shifted, in each film-viewing process." Teresa de Lauretis, *Technologies of Gender: Essays on Theory, Film, and Fiction* 96 (1987).

less. What acts will change the culture rather than reproduce it can never be predicted with certainty, and the very definition of change is likely to be contested in its turn.[67]

The following example of unintended ideological effect is from an article in *Time* about whether sex differences are innate:

> Even professional skeptics have been converted. "When I was younger, I believed that 100% of sex differences were due to the environment," says Jerre Levy, professor of psychology at the University of Chicago. Her own toddler toppled that utopian notion. "My daughter was 15 months old, and I had just dressed her in her teeny little nightie. Some guests arrived, and she came into the room, knowing full well that she looked adorable. She came in with this saucy little walk, cocking her head, blinking her eyes, especially at the men. You never saw such flirtation in your life." After 20 years spent studying the brain, Levy is convinced: "I'm sure there are biologically based differences in our behavior."[68]

Feminist reactions to dress issues often assume that women are to men as this toddler is to her mother. Women's dress acts, like speech acts, produce the world, reinforcing or undermining gender stereotypes just as the toddler converts her mother from a nurture to a nature position, and a traditionalist one at that. I often feel this kind of feminist critique of female dress hovering in the air, but rarely hear it directly stated. It goes something like this: All women's dress that is clearly women's dress simultaneously demarcates the sexes and *defines* them. Women's dress reflects and reproduces the regime's stereotypes about women: they are supposedly softer, warmer, more emotional, expressive, mercurial, nurturing, exhibitionist, and so on, than men.

Women's dress (in this interpretation) also reflects and reproduces a theory about how men should and do relate to women. Skirts and dresses differ from pants at a primary symbolic level: skirts mean vulnerability, and pants mean protection. Skirts mean: my sex is hidden from you, but it is not protected by clothing that, like pants, can be removed only by a complex series of unzipping, pulling down, and pulling off. My sex in a dress is symbolically accessible to another in a way it is not in pants.

So skirts and dresses symbolically reflect and reproduce (in this interpretation) a straight male idea, or value: that women should be sexually accessible to men. Yet they also reflect a more complicated idea. Why should dress that means "protection" (pants) be worn by the sex that is the less vulnerable of the two? Answer: men are responsible for protecting their own genitals from aggression by other men, and pants provide protection. Women can't defend themselves against men even if they are wearing pants. Their protection is not self-defense, but social relations.

Protection is based (in this interpretation) on men's possession of and consequent willingness to defend "their" women. Women don't have to wear pants because the men who own them, toward whom their skirts and dresses express vulnerability, protect them from other men. A woman is a person who can't defend herself but can get defense by accepting a male protector or by relying on the protective role of men in general.*

An interpretation of this kind can't really be "true" or "false" in a straightforward way, unlike the interpretation of which is the men's and which the ladies' room. Who's to say whether it's more or less valid than Woody Hochswender's voyeur-fetishist version of the skirt? "Long skirts are like a secret waiting to be unraveled. Among the things that men love: the sensual rustle of fabric against leg, the romance and sophistication of a lengthened silhouette, the mystery of what's beneath. The more modern versions are all about danger. Most of the new designs are slit, up the sides, back or front, and there is always the shifting drama of these openings."[69]

Before taking these interpretations in counterpoint, so to speak, with women's readings, and with other male ones, I want to try an interpretation of sexy dress (deviation within the setting) as reflecting and reproducing the eroticization of domination in general and of sexual abuse in particular. This interpretation is based on the idea that a costume or a particular item of dress produces its effect by making an allusion, or reference, that evokes a character in a narrative that is known to the audience. As Holly Brubach puts it, "A dress by Valentino or a jumpsuit by Jean-Paul Gaultier has implicit in its design a description of the sort of woman who would wear it and of the life she leads."[70] I'm claiming that the straight male audience "reasons" subconsciously that "this woman chose this cos-

---

*This theory helps explain the erotic significance—for men—of garter belts: the garter belt is to panty hose as a skirt is to pants.

tume, which makes reference to the costume worn by a character in a narrative, so she must be saying that she is like that character. Why wear it if you aren't the person that it says you are?"

One of the things that make a female costume sexy for the straight male audience is the idea that the wearer has chosen, through the production of the sign of her dress, to signify herself as "the woman to whose costume this costume alludes" and, by implication, as "a woman who would like to have the sexual experience that woman had in the narrative in which she wore it." The sign does not mean that she is *available* for this experience. Indeed, the context may indicate the contrary.[71]

A skirt or dress that suggests a soft animal skin, a zebra or leopard pattern (or a mere allusion to those patterns), an irregular or biased hem or bustline, wrapping, or ostentatiously crude stitching, may have the connotation "me Jane, you Tarzan." This reference is complicated because it evokes not only the relationship between Tarzan and Jane in books and movies, but also the image of a caveman with a club throwing his woman over his shoulder and carrying her off for sex. The effect may or may not be cut by allusion to *The Flintstones* (in which this scenario was suburbanized).[72]

In a notorious series of Jordache/Guess advertisements, a young woman (Claudia Schiffer) is hooked up with an older man. Susan Faludi, asked why Guess ads were "popular among women," answered: "They tap into this ancient vision that if you're a coltlike, knock-kneed, wide-eyed little girl, men will flock around you and you'll be protected and safe and taken care of by all these cowboys. Everyone wants to be loved, everyone wants to be admired and pursued, and, boy, there's a really easy way to do it—all you have to do is buy these jeans."[73]

Guess still advertises. The powerful ads to which the question refers, however, have been replaced—not because of the portrayal of the young woman, but because the older "cowboy" had a sinister, sensual, lower-class but criminally rich, brutal aura. She did seem like a "wide-eyed little girl," but she also looked like Brigitte Bardot, and her clothes had older "sex-kitten" allusions. The whole strongly suggested sexual exploitation of the model by the older man, with an undertone of incest, as several letters to the editor of *Elle* pointed out at the time.[74]

The current Jordache/Guess ads, often using the model from the earlier series, construct a different, less sexually disturbing universe. Yet they contain persistent allusions to the earlier one. A woman who dresses and makes up to look like the model in these ads seems to be inviting the "taken care of" relationship that is pictured in them, but also the more exploitative relationship suggested in the original series.

It is possible to catalogue in a rough-and-ready way some of the main sexual narratives to which female costumes and particular items of dress refer in order to achieve their exciting effects. The process of allusion operates in two dimensions, the synchronic (in relation to current narratives) and the diachronic (in relation to past narratives).

"Sexy dress" as I have been defining it means dress that diverges from the norm for the setting in which it is worn "in the direction" of the next sexier setting. This means that the dress alludes to that sexier setting, and then to the next after that, all in the direction of settings in which men and women actually engage in sex. The sexy dresser invites the straight male audience to imagine being with her in the setting her dress alludes to. This is the synchronic dimension.

The diachronic dimension is more complicated. One can arrange narratives in "genealogies," sequences in which clothing and text in the present refer to an earlier combination, which in turn refers to another still further back in time. Starting points are not "origins," but merely where we get to when we reconstruct backward as far as we can.[75]

One costume genealogy "begins" with Frederick's of Hollywood, moves on to the *Cosmopolitan* girl, and culminates in Victoria's Secret. Frederick's was the mail-order catalogue associated with middle-class stereotypes of "animal" working-class sexuality, with "girlie magazines," strip joints, and street prostitution.[76] *Cosmopolitan* was originally a complex attempt to formulate a sexual style for lower-middle-class pink-collar employees that would combine elements from the world of Frederick's with the sex-positive ideology of the liberal intelligentsia and the "youth culture" of the 1960s.

The mass success of the lingerie section of the Victoria's Secret catalogue represents the gentrification of this cultural terrain—its simultaneous appropriation and transformation by the middle class. However, its name suggests the catalogue's aspiration to a position in a second genealogy. This one begins, perhaps, with *Casanova's Memoirs*.[77] The allusion is to aristocratic decadence and kinky sexuality rather than to the animality of the working class. Queen Victoria's secret was that beneath the repressed exterior of nineteenth-century life there was "rampant" illicit sex. The late twentieth-century Victoria's secret is that she is a middle-class professional woman dressed in a conservative business suit with "naughty" underwear underneath.

Some intermediate terms in this genteel progression include the upper-class institution of expensive "French lingerie" and the 1960s reception of *My Secret Life, Fanny Hill,* and *Story of O*[78] as "erotic classics" rather than "hard core." The mass success of Victoria's Secret lingerie is a comedown in this sequence, an appropriation of upper-class sexual culture from below.

A third "outlaw" genealogy, androgynous and sadomasochistic, begins with Elvis Presley, Marlon Brando, James Dean, *Scorpio Rising, Last Exit to Brooklyn* (the 1960s book, not the 1980s movie),[79] and the iconic Hell's Angel "biker girl." It passes through groupies and plaster-casters[80] into lesbian sadomasochism,[81] punk, Mapplethorpe, and the "metallica" subculture. The women in the *Rolling Stone* photos of the "heavy metal societies of New York and L.A.," by Mark Seliger,[82] look strikingly like the *Vogue* photos accompanying the Declaration of the Right to Sexy Dressing. According to *Elle:*

> Hell's Angels and Hollywood starlets have one thing in common this year—Harley hunger. Brando started it, of course, when he straddled his gleaming road hog in *The Wild One.* But what used to be a symbol of in-your-face rebellion is fast becoming the ultimate fashion accessory. Whether it's the '92 Sportster 1200 or the latest model Softail Custom, a Harley-Davidson looks both classic and sexy, even standing still. That's not to say it isn't a serious machine.[83]

This genealogy reaches the present, momentarily enters high fashion, and momentarily fuses with the other genealogies in Madonna's Blond Ambition tour costumes designed by Gaultier and in the current work of Karl Lagerfeld. As Maureen Orth described it in *Vanity Fair:*

> That's how Lagerfeld answers the critics who say his recent work for Chanel—which borrows liberally from downtown hookers and hustlers as well as from uptown debs on drugs, in tank tops and tulle ballerina skirts—is vulgar . . . Maybe you are longing for those chic-of-the-week $1,000 Chanel motorcycle boots?— exact replicas, except for the trademark *C*'s, of the $70 variety he appropriated from the look of S&M boys in leather bars fifteen years ago. But in Lagerfeld's head they are already gone, out.[84]

It should be clear from these examples that the genealogies of sexy dress involve a double movement—backward through time and outward toward the social margins as defined by the straight white middle class. In addition to the upper margin of Victorian aristocracy, the lower margin of proletarian sexuality, and the horizontal margin of outlaw culture, there are geographic margins—the France of "Oo-la-la" (can-can costume), the South Seas (sarong), the Middle East (belly dance costume), and South of the Border (Flamenco skirt, fan, headdress). In the United States there is a racial margin—the locus of white fantasy representations of black male sexual athleticism (for example, the movie *Mandingo*) and black female promiscuity.[85]

Genealogies connect sexy dressing to abuse through a four-step process. The first step is an item of dress. The *Ladies' Home Journal* article that credits Victoria's Secret with making "risqué undies respectable" lists the "biggest undercover best-sellers":

1. Lacy pushup bras
2. Teddies/camisoles
3. Slinky slip gowns
4. Bikini panties in hot colors
5. Bustiers[86]

The costume item in the setting evokes, perhaps only by a minor detail, the costume worn by women in another setting in a different period. A hint in the shape of the bodice of an otherwise "conservative" dress might evoke a Victorian bustier. Second, the bustier might evoke an image of a woman wearing a bustier in an upper-class boudoir in a Victorian "naughty" postcard. Third, the image of the Victorian woman in the postcard wearing a bustier in an upper-class boudoir might evoke a female character in a narrative, specifically a narrative from Victorian pornography. The woman in the bustier is a maid or a young woman of good family. Fourth, the image of that character might evoke what happened to her in the narrative: she was seduced, devirginized, looked at, bound, whipped, shared, enslaved—against her will until she lost control and loved it.

The Frederick's-*Cosmopolitan* genealogy has the same movement backward in time and toward the social margins (still viewed from the perspective of the straight white middle class). Two narratives evoked by the push-up bra and the too-red slit skirt are those of the small-town "tramp" from the other side of the tracks and of the sailor and the bar girl. The tramp chews gum, and any boy can have her in the back of the family car. She is "hot" but powerless—no one has to marry her, and if she gets pregnant, his father, the mill owner, will take care of it *(Peyton Place)*.[87] The sailor and the bar girl meet in a raunchy dive where she has been sexualized by abuse (forced by a pimp who beats her, and holds her baby hostage, to dress like a whore who "wants it"). He gets her true, liberated desire in exchange for rescuing her, only to leave her for the desexualized women of home *(The World of Suzie Wong)*.[88]

The biker men in the outlaw genealogy of sexy dress beat their "old ladies" and pass them around among themselves in a gang rape ritual loaded with homoeroticism (their bond among themselves is stronger than any biker's bond with a woman). The women are group slaves and love it, defying the straight world by advertising their submission. Their black leather or vinyl lingerie signifies masochistic partnership with sadistic biker jacket men, and they enact it by displaying themselves on command so that nonbiker men can "eat their hearts out."

Given these fashion references, it is not hard to construct the feminist rationale for the nonabusive social regulation of sexy dress. There is a lot more at stake than a generalized critique of self-objectification or "appealing to men." The particular forms we collectively designate as sexy dressing are particularly connected—to abuse. When a woman dresses sexily, she reflects and reproduces an idea: that men and also women are sexually excited by abuse, that women want to produce that excitement in men, and that the complex of female communication and male response is a legitimate and perhaps even a "natural" aspect of male and female sexuality.

In Susan Bordo's article "Material Girl," this position is put forward in self-conscious opposition to pro-sex po-mo:

All the elements of what I have here called "postmodern conversation"—intoxication with individual choice and creative *jouissance*, delight with the piquancy of particularity and mistrust of pattern and seeming coherence, celebration of "difference" along with an absence of critical perspective differentiating and weighting "differences," suspicion of the totalitarian nature of generalization along with a rush to protect difference from its homogenizing abuses—all have become recognizable and familiar elements of much of contemporary intellectual discourse. Within this theoretically self-conscious universe, moreover, these elements are not merely embodied . . . but are explicitly thematized and *celebrated*—as inaugurating new constructions of the self, no longer caught in the mythology of the unified subject, embracing of multiplicity, challenging the dreary and moralizing generalizations about gender, race, and so forth that have so preoccupied liberal and left humanism.[89]

She has me dead to rights, I thought. Bordo goes on to analyze the video *Open Your Heart,* in which Madonna plays a dancer in a peep show:

I would argue, however, that despite the video's "hedging along the lines of not communicating a clear signified," there *is* a dominant position in this video and it is that of the objectifying gaze . . . Indeed, I would say that ultimately this video is entirely about Madonna's body, the narrative context virtually irrelevant, an excuse to showcase the physical achievements of the star, a video centerfold. On this level, any parodic or destabilizing element appears as utterly, cynically, mechanically tacked on, in bad faith, a way of claiming trendy status for what is really just cheesecake—or, perhaps, pornography.

Indeed, it may be worse than that. If the playful "tag" ending of "Open Your Heart" is successful in deconstructing the notion that the objectification and sexualization of women's bodies is a serious business, then Madonna's *jouissance* may be "fucking with" her youthful viewer's perceptions in a dangerous way. Judging from the proliferation of rock lyrics celebrating the rape, abuse and humiliation of women, the message—not Madonna's responsibility alone, of course, but hers among others, surely—is getting through.[90]

These last two paragraphs are a good example of the kind of thing pro-sex po-mo types see as "totalitarian" and "homogenizing." In an ideological conflict, each side tends to think the other's position is based on mistakes, and it is tempting here to go after the role played in Bordo's argument by words like "ultimately," "entirely," "virtually," "utterly," and "just" (cheesecake). But I don't think her reading of the video is "just" wrong—I can see what she's getting at, though my own reading is utterly different. The problem with her attribution of causal responsibility is that it is speculative and paranoid, not that it *couldn't* be true.

In other words, I don't think it is wrong to read sexy dressing in general, and this supreme example in particular, as reflecting and reproducing (some) men's, and the regime's, "celebrat[ion of] the rape, abuse and humiliation of women." Many men, including me, have rage at women and at least a streak of violence somewhere in their character, and sexy dress, like a million other things, may, in a particular real life context, provoke either. But the video has other meanings as well, constructed by its male viewers at the intersection between its images and their associations. These meanings involve other aspects of sexuality than male abuse of women, and I think they are at least as important, probably more important components of the "objectifying gaze" to which Bordo refers. Madonna's sexy dressing facilitates these meanings by references to past and present narratives familiar to the audience, in other words through the same mechanism that links her costume to abuse. Four such references are: to masturbation, to social margins, to women's sexual power over men, and to female defiance of patriarchy.

I am going to describe how these references operate for (some) straight white middle-class men. They may operate in similar ways for people in other identity positions, but not in the same way, because the references (such as to social margins) presuppose the *self-imagined differences* between straight white middle-class men and various "others." I haven't tried to describe how the systems of reference might work for people in these "other" positions, because I don't think I can do it convincingly. For example, it seems obvious that the racist stereotyping that goes into the white middle-class construction of the margin between races as a locus of sexual excitement, as well as of hate and violence, must affect the ways people of color "read" and also the way they "do" sexy dress. But I don't trust my fragmentary impressions enough to put them forward even in the armchair vein of this piece.

The Reference to Masturbation

Though she is dancing in a peep show, Madonna never comes close to exposing her breasts or sex in "Open Your Heart." She wears a heavily constructed, high-cut, black silk bodysuit, fishnet stockings, and high heels—a costume that, in the setting, brings together all three genealogies of sexy dressing. It suggests simultaneously a Frederick's red-light district, designer lingerie, and a biker girl.

Many straight white male middle-class men react to this triple play with embarrassment, shame, and distaste. They don't want to watch the video and wish it didn't exist. Maybe they oppose the "objectification and sexualization of women's bodies." If so, they know this video achieves both. It objectifies and sexualizes because Madonna's costume strongly evokes pictures in girlie magazines (centerfolds, cheesecake) and movies *(Paris, Texas),*[91] just as Susan Bordo suggests. But the narrative associated with the pictures involves not sexual intercourse, abusive or otherwise, but masturbation.

Many men associate masturbation with sexual deprivation, rejection by women, dirtiness, shame, secrecy, the danger of discovery and punishment by Mother or Father, and the danger of addiction *(Portnoy's Complaint).*[92] It "ought to be" (though the "data" show it isn't) transcended in "normal" heterosexual relationships ("If you really loved me, you wouldn't need to masturbate"). Moreover, the good things about masturbation, physical, narcissistic, and fantastical, are deeply connected to its transgressive, solitary, antisocial character as practiced in our society.[93]

Many, many straight white middle-class men don't want any of this to enter mainstream culture. They honestly disapprove of masturbation, though they do it, and they are just as much repelled as fascinated by the "dirty" images associated with it. The sexualization of the media disturbs them, in the sense of provoking unwanted excitement, shame, and confusion. They feel guilty as charged with respect to sexualization and objectification of the female body, but they don't feel guilty of wanting to abuse women.

Further, if going to porn films or arcades were emblematic of male power, one might expect that the experience would be characterized by an easy confidence reflective of macho security.

For me, however—and, I'm guessing, for many men who have visited porn arcades or film houses—these periodic visits are always minor traumas. While there is erotic excitement involved in the decision to attend and in the experience itself, this is mixed with considerable amounts of fear and embarrassment. From the instant my car is carrying me toward pornography, I feel painfully visible, as if everyone who sees me knows from my expression, my body language, whatever, precisely where I'm going.[94]

The Reference to Social Margins

Sexy dress, for straight white middle-class men, evokes danger, as well as or instead of male power. The danger is coded in its allusion to social margins. The Frederick's allusion to the red-light district evokes robbery or assault by a prostitute or pimp, and the possibility of venereal disease. It evokes the imagined physical milieu of rundown small hotels, organized crime, blackmail, drugs; and the possibility of being caught doing something vile, and exposed. It evokes racial fears as well, of the black underclass culture of street hustlers and pimps.[95] The same straight white middle-class man for whom the reference to the lower class suggests a sexuality more animal than his own or that of "his" women may associate everything lower-class with fear for his safety, for his social standing, for his sense of racial superiority, for his self-respect.

The same is true of the biker genealogy, but this time with the added thrill/danger of abusive gay sex. The stronger bikers, in the straight white middle-class fantasy, bugger the weaker ones. The upper-class decadent genealogy of sexy dressing evokes more subtle fears, of embarrassment and exclusion. Only the peacetime geographic margins (the South Seas or France) are truly benign, but maybe also less powerful as references today than they used to be.

The Reference to Women's Sexual Power over Men

In simplest terms, the interpretation of fashion as eroticizing male domination of women ignores the fact that fashion signs that are understood to refer the "reader" to images of men dominating women are combined with fashion signs that invite the opposite. The reference is sometimes direct: "Metallica is in fashion this season, whether your taste runs to the precious or the proletarian . . . Silver accessories range from the classic to the subversive: . . . a sterling bondage bracelet (chain attached) is by Gregg Wolf. There's a touch of the dominatrix—albeit a rich one—in Cartier's platinum and diamond choker, too."[96]

The more complex references to proletarian sexuality, to the kinky decadence of upper-class Victorian pornography, and to the bondage-and-domination sadomasochistic biker genealogy all evoke narratives of female domination of men, as well as the reverse. The most basic are those of Adam and Eve and the Sirens, in which women exercise sexual power to make men do the wrong thing "against their will." Female nudity, alluded to in all the complex modes of stereotypically sexy dress, evokes the paintings that illustrate these narratives, and thereby the narratives themselves. Women use their nudity to make men do things.

Sexy dress that alludes to prostitution conjures images of unlimited male access to women's bodies on male terms, along with the world in which pimps control women through abuse. But the allusion is also to the extreme version of Adam and Eve in which a "respectable" man becomes obsessed with a "fallen woman" and sacrifices not just his money but also his job and his social standing in a vain attempt to win her heart. Marlene Dietrich in *The Blue Angel* and *The Professor and the Prostitute*[97] are examples. Every biker girl is a potential dominatrix, ready to turn the tables on the fantasy biker, who is a wimp in real life. The appeal of her imagined entry into the life of the sex slave of the group includes her adoption of leather jacket "attitude" (Melanie Griffith in *Something Wild*).[98]

In these stories, men eroticize female domination and exploitation. In the images associated with them, we get an interpretation of why the men in question submit: it is because women present themselves, their costumed and uncostumed bodies, in a way that makes men want them so badly that they lose their reason. It is clear that the body and the costume are *media* through which the women as *subjects* deploy a power that is intersubjectively based— they know how to drive men crazy. The point is that women are

capable of offering men something that other men cannot offer—
they have a base of power in dealing with men that men can't
neutralize or escape.

One of the writers Susan Bordo criticizes for being soft on Madonna is Catherine Texier, a novelist who writes a lot about sexual
danger and pleasure:

> It's a tease, the slit that opens and falls with each step coming
> down with the high heel hitting the pavement. Eva has it down
> to an art. The tilt of the hip, the tightening of the calves, the line
> of the seam up from the heel, an arrow pointing up to her ass.
> While the cinched jacket points down to the waist, then curves
> round to the crotch.
>
> There is something in her walk. A bounce, if you know what I
> mean, that attracts men. Not like an exaggerated hip swing that
> some women develop starting at age three and perfect later with
> the use of five-inch high heels.
>
> Why do you women dress like that?
>
> How can you ask such a dumb question?[99]

The male response to sexy dress is a response to the possibility
of being overpowered as well as to the possibility of power.[100] I
think it's totally great that feminism has, in Molly Haskell's phrase,
put "a premium on more direct and nonsexual routes to power."[101]
Women might conceivably altogether *renounce* the sexual route.
Anything is possible.[102] As long as they haven't, and perhaps even if
they do, fashion will sometimes convey to some men exactly the
opposite message from that ascribed to it in the radical feminist
analysis.

The Reference to Female Defiance of Patriarchy

"And if a man chooses to misinterpret the signals, that is his problem. Corsetry on the runway is not about fashion titillation but
about a world in which sexual harassment is a burning issue."[103]
When I read this in *Vogue*, I thought it was a joke. It seems obvious
that corsetry on the runway is in part about fashion titillation (it titil-
lates me). Then I got it: *Vogue* is asserting that sexy dressing makes a
statement against sexual harassment because it defies the threat of

abuse. It says that the woman in question refuses to allow her dress to be dictated by the conventional view or to accept its sanctions.

Sexy dress (deviation within the setting) sometimes seems to me to have just this meaning. The woman seems to be saying that a norm of patriarchy deeply grounded in men's interests doesn't apply to her. This is the norm that a woman should not excite men except in contexts in which they have at least a chance of real or imaginary sexual access to her. Corsetry on the runway defies this norm, and sometimes looks to me like a feminist statement, *because* it is titillating.

According to the regime, women are allowed (or required) to call attention to their sexuality only in some contexts—for example, within marital privacy, when they are single women looking for men in bars or clubs or at parties, when they are prostitutes, and when they are producing images of sexuality in movies or advertisements or the like. In other settings—the street, the workplace, the classroom, the supermarket—they are to desexualize themselves.

Dress that deviates toward sexiness in a desexualized setting carries with it the message of the setting: that the woman is *not* sexually available. She is wearing a costume. It may say a lot about her, and about what her attitude might be in a different setting, but it most definitely does not have the meaning in this one that it would have there. Indeed, the meaning of sexy dress out of place sometimes seems to be that the woman claims the right to present herself as sexual without the permission, which she can have only at the cost of being available, that goes with being a wife alone with her husband, a single person on the make, a prostitute, or an actress acting. And then she claims the further right to deny sex to the men she has aroused.

Of course, this is not *the* meaning of sexy dress. It might mean something entirely different. Moreover, women are not equally free to signify in this way. Bell Hooks claims that since black women "are coded always as 'fallen' women in the racist cultural iconography we can never, as can Madonna, publicly 'work' the image of ourselves as innocent female daring to be bad."[104] But sexy dressers do sometimes put men in the position of picking up an allusion to settings in which women are available, while having to obey the norms of the actual setting, which make them unavailable. There are many possible male reactions to this kind of female defiance. Here is an example from *Lear's*:

> [D]uring a sojourn in San Diego as a visiting professor, I was astonished by the rather relaxed outfits of some of my students. Seated in the front row, they sported here a miniskirt, there extremely short shorts, which pushed against the limits of decency (by European standards) and made it very difficult for me to concentrate. Yet what I thought I heard was this, spoken with great temerity (or with terrific unconcern): "I am beautiful, young, practically nude, and this is of no importance."
>
> Their casualness, which in Europe would have been heavy with insinuation, did not seem to provoke any excitement among the men in the class . . . Could it be that in the United States women exhibit their bodies in order to make their sexuality banal? In matters of the flesh, after all, to display what's usually hidden can be the best way to detoxify desire in the act of arousing it.[105]

This Frenchman's reaction is oblivious to the current women's discourse of sexy dress—not to the familiar argument that "no matter how" a woman dresses, she has a right not to be abused, but to the sexual interpretation of what's involved. According to Heather Bradshaw, twenty, of Tallahassee, Florida, interviewed in *Parade:* "I, and any other woman, can dress as skimpy as I want, flirt my head off and let a man buy me expensive dinners, and I don't owe him a thing. Women have the right to control their bodies no matter how hot they've gotten a man. There are plenty of men who are full of desire for women, and they don't rape."[106]

Ms. Bradshaw's defiance is not aimed at making "sexuality banal," or for that matter at moving toward an ideal feminist vanilla sexuality, but at changing a social structure. One American male reaction is described in a survey question to the "1,769 psychiatrists" in the *Boston Globe* story quoted above: "A male may interpret sexually teasing attire as uncaring and unfair. This may result in thoughts of revenge against the female who brought on the distress, sometimes expanded to hostility against females in general. Yes: 85 percent; no: 11 percent."[107]

The charge that the sexy dresser is "uncaring and unfair" is a reaction to the apparent intent to convey neither availability nor unavailability. She is not available in the sense of inviting or needing or being vulnerable to sexual advances. She is not unavailable in the sense of "taken by someone else" who has proprietary rights over her sexuality, or in the sense of being asexual. She conveys sexuality and, at the same time, defiantly, autonomy.

It seems to me that many men react to this apparent message not with fantasies of dominating or abusing women, or even with hostility, but with disquiet or fear. It is not fear of the particular sexy dresser, but fear for their investment in women particularly conceived—as beings whose sexuality is open to their appropriation, as beings whose love for particular men abolishes their autonomy, or who are the common property of all men. The sexually autonomous woman disrupts the madonna/whore dyad by advertising her refusal to be either one.

It is easy to dismiss the negative male reaction as the consequence of patriarchal indoctrination. The regime does indeed demand that men be "proprietors," in Dalma Heyn's phrase, for whom their women's "morals are always in question and decency always invoked: 'Why did you look at that guy like that?' 'You're really going *out* in that short skirt?'"[108] But anyone, man or woman, who has experienced intense sexual jealousy knows better than to be patronizing about it. The sexually autonomous woman is potentially threatening to all men because her defiant existence suggests that no woman is "true" in the way patriarchy promises that the madonna type will be true.

In some men, the reference to defiance of patriarchy evokes not only fear and anger but also a set of positive reactions, rooted in a paradoxical combination of connection and disconnection. The woman whose dress defies patriarchy conveys the comforting message that women are more like men in their sexuality than either patriarchy or feminism has much acknowledged. No woman will be true in the way the culture promises that the madonna type will be true. But neither are women the aliens they would be if they *could* be like that.

Second, there is the allusion to sex without either the whole range of domesticating, regularizing, defining roles and rules of the regime, or the context of prostitution. By this I don't mean sex without responsibility or intimacy; sex without either is widely available within the regime, both in and outside marriage. The straight white middle-class male fantasy of the female free agent is

of a woman who doesn't owe you sex under the terms of the patriarchal bargain (not "a wife") and isn't looking to get something
out of you (not "a whore"). The reference is to sex in which the
man doesn't have to worry whether the woman "really" "wants it."

Third, the sexy dresser is doing something the man would do if
he could. His stereotypical feminine traits—forbidden by the regime—get projected onto the woman who enacts femininity
against the norm of the setting. Whatever she may actually be feeling, the sign of sexy dress is the sign of narcissism, exhibitionism
and desire, body power. We men can have it through identification
with women, if only women will "take it on." Most straight white
middle-class women don't seem to want to. And why should they?

But wanting women to enact body power, and enjoying—being
sexually excited by—their performances when they do, is not the
same thing as wanting to dominate or abuse them. Indeed, sexy
dressing *sometimes* affirms the possibility of this kind of female
power brought home from the temporal, spatial, and racial margins—in other words, as a possibility in straight white middle-class
life in the present, rather than located necessarily, only, and forever
in the abusive narratives of the red-light district, the Victorian boudoir, and the motorcycle gang.

What about abuse? It is all very well, I hear my feminist critic
insist, to celebrate the collaboration of the defiant antipatriarchal
sexy dressing woman with the man in the audience whose fantasy
is that her free agency will free him, too. But in the eyes and minds
of *most* men and women in the audience, "the dominant meaning"
is that women are exciting, dangerous, irresponsible creatures who
want and need sexualized abuse and protection in about equal
measure. Some men will respond to the sign by raping or harassing;
many more men will respond to it as confirming (reflecting, reproducing) the regime's version of the sexes.

Anne Wagner, in a brilliant essay on Rodin, points out that his
art and the popular understanding of his life fit a particular contemporary stereotyped version of the natures of men and women
and their natural relationship.[109] Rodin was a sculptor whose work
and life could be and often were interpreted "to endorse both male
mastery of woman and the fiction of male sexuality that takes mastery as its premise."[110] But Rodin also elicited another interpretation. "What, then," Wagner asks, "for the female convert, of the

charges of brutality, the metaphors of penetration and violation?"[111]
I like her answer a lot:

> [T]hese selfsame drawn and modeled bodies were also seen by
> certain [women] viewers, at least, to give heterosexual relations a
> new inflection . . . [T]he sculpture offered . . . an imagery
> confirming and celebrating the very existence of an unbridled
> female sexuality as the complement, rather than the object of
> male desires . . . [T]he bourgeois woman could embrace her car-
> nality without its being equated with the pathetic and dismissible
> pleasures of a Nini or a Popo . . . [F]emale sexuality is reclaimed
> as bourgeois, and the centurywide gap between woman's identi-
> ties as Madonna or Magdalen begins, ever so slowly, to close . . .
> That the same representations could give rise to two such vary-
> ing accounts—the patriarchal and the bourgeois feminist—should
> not strike us as odd or unexpected . . . It is when alternative
> accounts can no longer feed themselves on the imagery proposed
> by the dominant culture that there is cause for concern.[112]

As with all pleasure and all interstitial resistance, there is a dark
side to this collaboration. There is the problem that the male fantasy of the female free agent is only apparently disentangled from
the madonna/whore duality. She is defined only negatively. The
minute the woman is a real person, we are caught again, inevitably,
in the web of roles. People do owe each other and want things
from each other as soon as they know each other even a little. This
stuff has to be negotiated, and the fantasy of free agency on either
side can make the process harder rather than easier.

The web of roles is given (at least for the time); the reality of
inequality between men and women within the regime is given (at
least for the time); inequality between specific men and women
(with women sometimes advantaged) is given; and that a sign is not
a signified is given. Given all this, even the most purely pleasurable,
purely oppositional reference of sexy dress is shadowed, for the
male audience, by the possibility that the signifier (dress) is a lie
about the signified (the woman). She is "really" coerced or a com-
modifier or engulfed or compulsive, rather than the self-expresser
or gender artist we let ourselves hope she was. It turns out she was
only masquerading as a masquerader.[113]

I think this is often the case for the woman herself: she does not
know whether or not she's lying, or whether it is possible either to

lie or to tell the truth.[114] I also think that any particular woman's pleasure in her defiant sexy dress is often shadowed by the possibility that no one, not one single person, experiences it as she would want—that the whole audience consists of "dirty old men," abusers lying in wait, and critics who think she is a slut or politically incorrect or too old or not pretty enough or doesn't really know how to do it right.

I think nonetheless that some of the time, some sexy dressers and some of their audience are engaged in pleasure/resistance in the interstices of the regime. They are eroticizing female autonomy. In so doing they undermine not only the structure that opposes madonna and whore but also that which opposes straight white bourgeois vanilla sexuality to the (imagined) kinky, animal, androgynous sexuality of the margins.[115]

This must be always an uncertain form of politics because the signifying woman may be doing more harm than good, feeding the conventional view in which the tease deserves what she gets and men get off on woman-wanting mixed with woman-hating. For both men and women, the experience is compromised because it occurs within, is indeed dependent for its meaning on, the larger web of references to male sexual abuse of women and to male degradation in relation to them. It is never just "the truth" (something to be relied on) that the experience is indeed pleasure/resistance rather than something else, something bad, instead.

Doing and appreciating sexy dress is flawed as pleasure/resistance in another way. It is asymmetrical. The straight white middle-class men (or man) watch, and the woman performs. It seems plausible that this pattern reinforces, helps reproduce, one of the bad aspects of patriarchy: its construction of woman as the object of the attentive, adoring, excited male gaze, the actress active by being-for-the-men, while the men dispose of her fate, and the fate of the world, on the side.[116]

What is wrong with this is not that men and women should be-for-themselves, whatever that would mean. What is wrong with it politically is that it contributes to disempowering women as actors within the "male sphere." What seems to me wrong with it *erotically*, as a straight white middle-class man, is that it requires each party to give up a possible pleasure—that which might be found in the activity the regime allocates to the opposite sex. To say this is to make a choice between two plausible routes beyond asymmetry.

One is to try to get rid of sexual objectification and to de-eroti-cize power in sex. Getting rid of objectification on the male side means avoiding experiencing the woman as the involuntary bearer of multiple sexual significations hooked up to multiple sexual nar-ratives, and trying to experience her as a "real person." From the woman's side, it means sacrificing the possible pleasure, avoiding the possible degradation, and renouncing the possible power that are to be had by playing the sexual fantasy object.

De-eroticizing power in sex means looking for the sexual charge, the excitement, that is sometimes present when the other is "just the same" while at the same time "different," without difference implying hierarchy. It also means trying to "deprogram" one's own excitement at images of domination and submission. Though this is unmistakably the liberal humanist sexual program, it seems to me what is often behind cultural and socialist feminist theorizing about sex as well.[117]

But there is another way to imagine getting beyond asymmetry, beginning with Judith Butler's point that:

[t]he pro-sexuality movement within feminist theory and practice has effectively argued that sexuality is always constructed within the terms of discourse and power, where power is partially un-derstood in terms of heterosexual and phallic cultural conven-tions. The emergence of a sexuality constructed (not determined) in these terms within lesbian, bisexual, and heterosexual contexts is, therefore, *not* a sign of a masculine identification in some re-ductive sense . . . If sexuality is culturally constructed within ex-isting power relations, then the postulation of a normative sexual-ity that is "before," "outside," or "beyond" power is a cultural impossibility and a politically impracticable dream, one that post-pones the concrete and contemporary task of rethinking the sub-versive possibilities for sexuality and identity within the terms of power itself.[118]

Robin Morgan wants us to accept as aesthetic-social ideal "*'[t]he most heterogeneous ideas . . . yoked by violence together'*—such as strug-gle with the person one loves."[119] In her discussion of the politics of women's masochistic fantasies, she starts from the position that "[i]f the fantasy-theme seemed enjoyable to me, I was not about to punish myself with guilt for that pleasure."[120] She proposes a mythi-cal female program that seems better (meaning I agree with it) than getting rid of sexual objectification and de-eroticizing power: "[t]he possibility of their naked minds and bodies engaging one another—a joyous competition which must include an assumption of defeat as (1) temporary and (2) utterly lacking in humiliation; of any triumph as, obversely, impermanent and meaningless. *The taking and giving of turns.*"[121]

It seems to me that what this means, put simply, is restoring symmetry by men dressing sexily for women, and women watching, and vice versa, rather than restoring symmetry by rooting out male voyeurism and female exhibitionism (so that no one is performing and no one watching). Within the regime this is, of course, an utterly utopian idea. And though utterly utopian it doesn't even promise getting beyond—it merely assumes away—the real possibility that accepting competition, defeat, and triumph in the "battle between the sexes"[122] as erotic will slip over the boundary into the plain and simple eroticization of male domination of women.[123] (For the straight man, it doesn't promise release from *Blue Angel* fear.)

Yet taking turns is no more utopian than trying for unalienated relatedness within the regime—and, still within the regime, it is no more dangerous, either. In the very restricted domain of sexual signification through dress, taking turns is even a real tendency in contemporary American life, because there are overlapping gay and black male subcultures that have made it part of their program to appropriate the female prerogatives of self-objectification and fashion exhibitionism.

An Erotic Interest in Ending Abuse

As consumers, men and women operate on the cultural map by picking and choosing among the kinds of arousal the culture offers them. In this mode they do more than simply register their personal relationship to the social field they are born into. They participate willy-nilly. But they are more passive than in the modes of self-creation, such as fantasy, play, experiment, and invention. In our active being on the map, whether in public or in private, we seek sexual excitement and also moral value, and produce them, in all these four ways, or flee them, rather than merely registering them in ourselves or choosing among pre-set alternatives. Like it or not, we find ourselves changed by the experiences that ensue, and sometimes we change our surroundings.

We fantasize, play, experiment, and invent using the repertoire our culture makes available. Fantasy and play involve the reversal of expectations and of social valuations, and entering imaginatively into situations that one might flee in real life. Experiment and invention are not either unless they contravene a norm of some kind. It is part of the dark side that the connected repertoires of stereotypical gender identities, archetypal narratives, and costumes associated with the identities and the narratives all allude to the real-life practice of abuse. Because there is no way to operate without these tainted repertoires, there is always the risk that what we think is escape or daring resistance in the interstices is turning us into victims or victimizers.

For many people, myself included, the relationship between what it is exciting to produce or consume and what is "good" is profoundly complex, and problematic. The relationship is not as simple as a perennial conflict between an internal moral code and a set of internal propensities to excitement. It is always hard to tell whether the code that says "no" or "yes" is "really" inside us or an imposition from outside, from an authority that is open to question. The same is true for the charges we find associated with things we want or equally passionately don't want to do. Our turn-ons are conditioned, always open to the critique of external imposition, just as codes are sometimes mere indoctrination.

Moreover, even what we "really" believe is open to our own interpretation and reinterpretation. This can be, as in the writing of legal opinions, ex post rationalization, or casuistry, or "evolution of timeless principles to meet new circumstances," or what we ourselves regard as our own moral growth. The same is true of erotic charges. We learn them, and unlearn them. Abuse, tangled into the cultural images through which we produce and interpret our own and other people's sexuality, seems to me to weigh heavily on this tricky, risky enterprise.

Men and women might fantasize, play, experiment and innovate more, and *perhaps* more happily, if there were less of this danger. By this I mean specifically if there were less incest and rape and sexual harassment. I don't mean that there would be fewer fantasies involving these things; rather, the positive uses of such fantasies, for both men and women, would be less impeded by guilt and fear.

As the radical feminists have rightly insisted, sexual abuse is an instrument of male disciplinary terror against women, and our culture inculcates erotic pleasure in male domination of women in every aspect of life. Fantasies, play, experiment, and innovation that use abuse as an element, including the practice of sexy dress, sometimes reflect and reproduce the most hateful aspects of the way men treat women under the regime. But they are not just, or essentially, or always, politically incorrect. According to Ann Ferguson, there are two ways to interpret the recent increase in the male pornography industry:

> Either one can see it as a relatively benign male fantasy "backlash" to the increased sexual autonomy of women or else as a determined attempt by male chauvinists to sexually objectify women so as to legitimize sado-masochistic gender roles in heterosexual sex.
>
> Though it cannot presently be proved which of these two analyses is correct, the sexual symbolic code as presented in the public media is clearly a site of contestation . . .[124]

On the other side, the choice is just as stark:

> Is it true that persons who get off on masochism in bed are by that practice perpetuating a vulnerable ego in other areas of their social life? Or is that person merely venting an unconscious (and possibly unchangeable) aspect of her emotional life thus expurgating its influence from the rest of her life? . . .
>
> Despite the heated claims by both proponents and opponents of S/M that it is empowering *vs.* disempowering to the women who engage in it, there is no clear proof either way . . .[125]

There is more wrong with Ferguson's position than the insistence that fantasy *must be* one thing or the other, and that someone might prove which one it is. It might be one *or* the other for a particular person in a particular context. It might be other things as well. Here are three others, from the straight white male side, the first from Scott MacDonald. He starts from the idea that "the same cultural history which has defined women as Beautiful has had . . . as its inevitable corollary, the Ugliness of men; women have been defined as beautiful precisely in contrast to men."[126]

> To me, the nature and function of pornography have always seemed understandable as a way for men to periodically deal with the cultural context which mitigates against their full accep-

tance of themselves as sexual beings. The fantasies men pay to experience in porn arcade booths and movie houses may ostensibly appear to be predicated on the brutalization of women. But from a male point of view, the desire is not to see women harmed, but to momentarily identify with men who—despite their personal unattractiveness by conventional cultural definitions, despite the unwieldy size of their erections, and despite their aggressiveness with their semen—are adored by the women they encounter sexually.[127]

Second, what of the theory that upper-middle-class white male masochism boomed in the 1980s, along with the New York dominatrix business, in response to the social insistence that these men behave in a supermacho way while working as Michael Douglas in *Wall Street?*[128] The inverse of this theory is that *sometimes* male fantasies of dominating women represent not backlash, but symbolic compensation for male efforts to comply with the feminist ethical demand that they renounce their supermacho stance in relation to women. Signe Hammer suggested, fifteen years ago, a parallel theory about women: "Our basic rape fantasy reflects our anxiety about asserting ourselves in all areas—in work, sex, and relationships." [129]

Third, many written pornographic narratives of male humiliation, domination, and abuse of women are told relentlessly from the female point of view *(Story of O).*[130] They invite the male reader to participate in the consciousness of the victim, and particularly in her experience of overwhelming, ego-obliterating pleasure when she surrenders to the will of the male abuser.

It seems obvious that *sometimes* the goal is to permit the male reader vicarious access—access safely distanced by the combination of the gender and the helplessness of the victim—to the pleasure he might derive from giving up the fight to dominate other men. This might be pleasure/resistance, however distorted, in a regime that tells him that competition with men is his reason for being and his greatest role-appropriate pleasure. In this interpretation, it is men, rather than women, who can fantasize their own pleasure in self-surrender only when they fantasize it as forced, and only when they can pretend that it is they themselves who are doing the forcing.[131]

I don't mean to suggest that a given fantasy (or a given costume) has one or another of these meanings for its audience because that is the meaning that is "in" it. Quite the contrary, my point is that men and women *use* fantasies (and costumes), constrained by the elusive requirement of some minimal "fit," on the way toward these diverse imaginary pleasures. In the extreme case, abolishing real-life male sexual abuse of women would reduce the dangerousness of this enterprise, for both men and women, by cutting the connection between rape fantasies and real-life rape, between incest fantasies and incest.

In such a world, some people would stick fast to what turns them on, and others would "stretch the envelope." I would feel freer to fantasize the boy hooker in myself if I weren't so scared of pimps—but also freer to fantasize the john in me. Whichever way one chose to go, Susan Keller's image of the process of gender change would be easier to accept:

> I suggest that there is no pure gender culture. Instead, I think of all cultural artifacts as being like the Watts Towers in Los Angeles, a structure/sculpture in the middle of Watts that was decorated over many years with various throwaways—pieces of plastic medicine bottles, pottery shards, used tile, Seven-Up bottles. Everything, like the Watts Towers, is a re-creation from stuff that was already created, which itself was recreated from stuff that was already created. Every possibility that exists, and that we will be transformed into, will be, like the Watts Towers, composed of the leftovers, scavenged treasures of the dominant culture.[132]

The argument for a male erotic interest in reducing the sexual abuse of women is thus quite complex. Abuse screws women up sexually, and that's bad for men. It discourages women from risking, disciplines them not to risk the forms of pleasure/resistance through which we might eroticize autonomy and soften the contrast between the straight white middle-class cultural center and the imagery of exciting but dangerous margins that are often real-life sites of oppression. And it burdens both men's and women's fantasy, play, experiment, and innovation with questions, risks, fears, and guilt that trap us in the reproduction of patriarchal sex. Being against abuse is not, for men, just a matter of human rights, empathy, protecting "our" women, romantic paternalism, or political correctness, however valid and important each of those may be.

Both the idea of reducing the violence so we can get on with playing within while evolving the repertoire, and the idea of over-throwing the repertoire altogether, are open to the critique that people would in fact end up worse off with more freedom and less repression. We would still have our inner demons, and lots of outer ones as well. There is no *hors-repertoire*. Power to the imagination all the same. When Madonna hurries down the hall at the end of the "Justify My Love" video, smiling to herself, it would be better on balance that she not end up . . . dead.

Notes

2. A Cultural Pluralist Case for Affirmative Action in Legal Academia

1. Gary Peller, "Race Consciousness," 1990 *Duke L.J.* 758. Two articles by Alan Freeman strongly influenced this essay: "Legitimizing Racial Discrimination through Anti-Discrimination Law," 62 *Minn. L. Rev.* 1049 (1978), and "Racism, Rights, and the Quest for Equality of Opportunity: A Critical Legal Essay," 23 *Harv. C.R.–C.L. L. Rev.* 295 (1988). The writer who has most influenced my thinking about race is Harold Cruse; see his *The Crisis of the Negro Intellectual* (1967) and *Rebellion or Revolution?* (1968).

2. See generally Jean-François Lyotard, *The Postmodern Condition: A Report on Knowledge* (G. Bennington & B. Massumi trans. 1984); Jane Gallop, *Thinking Through the Body* (1988).

3. Randall Kennedy, "Racial Critiques of Legal Academia," 102 *Harv. L. Rev.* 1745 (1989) (hereafter cited as R. Kennedy). For other responses to Kennedy's article see "Colloquy: Responses to Randall Kennedy's Racial Critiques of Legal Academia," 103 *Harv. L. Rev.* 844 (1990) (responses by Scott Brewer, Milner Ball, Robin Barnes, Richard Delgado, and Leslie Espinoza); and Richard Delgado, "When a Story Is Just a Story: Does Voice Really Matter?" 76 *Va. L. Rev.* 95 (1990).

4. Derrick Bell, "*Bakke,* Minority Admissions, and the Usual Price of Racial Remedies," 67 *Calif. L. Rev.* 1 (1979); idem, "The Unspoken Limit of Affirmative Action: The Chronicle of the DeVine Gift," in *And We Are Not Saved: The Elusive Quest for Racial Justice* 140 (1987); Richard Delgado, "The Imperial Scholar: Reflections on a Review of Civil Rights Literature," 132 *U. Pa. L. Rev.* 561 (1984); Mari Matsuda, "Affirmative Action and Legal Knowledge: Planting Seeds in Plowed-Up Ground," 11 *Harv. Women's L.J.* 1 (1988); idem, "Look-

215

ing to the Bottom: Critical Legal Studies and Reparations," 22 *Harv.*
C.R.–C.L. L. Rev. 323 (1987).

5. Critical Race Theory is an "emergent" phenomenon, and it may
turn out that these articles do not have as much in common as they
appear to me to do. This list is illustrative only; it is not an attempt
to establish a canon. Regina Austin, "Sapphire Bound!" 1989 *Wis. L.*
Rev. 539; John Calmore, "Exploring the Significance of Race and
Class in Representing the Black Poor," 61 *Ore. L. Rev.* 201 (1982);
Anthony Cook, "Beyond Critical Legal Studies: The Reconstructive
Theology of Dr. Martin Luther King, Jr.," 103 *Harv. L. Rev.* 985
(1990); Kimberle Crenshaw, "Race, Reform, and Retrenchment:
Transformation and Legitimation in Antidiscrimination Law," 101
Harv. L. Rev. 1331 (1988); Mohammed Kenyatta, "Critical Footnotes
to Parker's 'Constitutional Theory,'" *Harv. Blackletter J.,* 49 (Spring
1985); Maivan Clech Lam, "The Kuleana Act Revisited: The Sur-
vival of Traditional Hawaiian Commoner Rights in Land," 64 *Wash.*
L. Rev. 233 (1989); Charles Lawrence, "The Id, the Ego, and Equal
Protection: Reckoning with Unconscious Racism," 39 *Stan. L. Rev.*
317, 324 (1987); Gerald Lopez, "Training Future Lawyers to Work
with the Politically and Socially Subordinated: Anti-Generic Legal
Education," 91 *W. Va. L. Rev.* 305 (1989); Harold McDougall, "The
New Property vs. the New Community," 24 *U.S.F. L. Rev.* 399
(1990); Gerald Torres, "Local Knowledge, Local Color: Critical Legal
Studies and the Law of Race Relations," 25 *San Diego L. Rev.* 1043
(1988); Patricia Williams, "Alchemical Notes: Reconstructing Ideals
from Deconstructed Rights," 22 *Harv. C.R.–C.L. L. Rev.* 401 (1987).
See generally Frances Ansley, "Stirring the Ashes: Race, Class, and
the Future of Civil Rights Scholarship," 74 *Cornell L. Rev.* 993
(1989).

6. Like Randall Kennedy, I see it as a weakness of current attempts at
radical politics in the United States that we tend to sentimentalize
all "victims of oppression." Another weakness is a tendency to exag-
gerate the relative importance of current racism in explaining racially unjust outcomes and, by contrast, to underestimate the relative
importance of past racism and of nonracial economic and institutional factors.

7. With Derrick Bell, I regard race, a proxy for connection to a subordinated cultural community, as an intellectual credential in hiring
and promotion decisions. (See "The Political and Cultural Arguments for Affirmative Action" later in the chapter.) I agree with
Mari Matsuda, as paraphrased by Kennedy, that "by the exclusions
imposed by existing practices, legal academia loses the sensibilities,

insights, and ideas that are the products of racial oppression" (R. Kennedy, 1778). (See "What Might Be Gained through Large-Scale Affirmative Action" later in the chapter.) And I agree with Richard Delgado that we are entitled to judge with suspicion the work produced in a field like constitutional law on the basis of the "status," i.e., the cultural community, of the authors. (See "Rational Meritocratic Judgment Cannot Be Culturally and Ideologically Neutral" later in the chapter.)

8. This section is indebted to Peller, "Race Consciousness," and to Freeman, "Racism, Rights, and the Quest."

9. R. Kennedy, 1772–73.

10. Peller, "Race Consciousness," 767–771.

11. See Neil Gotanda, "A Critique of 'Our Constitution is Colorblind': Racial Categories and White Supremacy," 44 *Stan. L. Rev.* 1 (1991).

12. Of course there are meritocrats who favor what Peller would call nationalism. Likewise, one might favor color-blindness and still believe wholeheartedly in the critique of meritocracy.

13. None of the authors Kennedy criticizes takes this position either.

14. R. Kennedy, 1806.

15. Id. at 1807.

16. Id.

17. Id.

18. Id. at 1768, 1770, 1814 n.296.

19. Id. at 1807.

20. See *The Politics of Law: A Progressive Critique* (David Kairys 2d ed. 1990); Duncan Kennedy, "Form and Substance in Private Law Adjudication," 89 *Harv. L. Rev.* 1685 (1976); idem, "The Structure of Blackstone's *Commentaries,*" 28 *Buffalo L. Rev.* 209 (1979); idem, *Legal Education and the Reproduction of Hierarchy: A Polemic against the System* 14–32 (1983).

21. See Freeman, "Legitimizing Racial Discrimination"; Ruth Colker, "Anti-Subordination above All: Sex, Race, and Equal Protection," 61 *N.Y.U. L. Rev.* 1003 (1986); Randall Kennedy, "Persuasion and Distrust: A Comment on the Affirmative Action Debate," 99 *Harv. L. Rev.* 1327, 1335–36 (1986); idem, "*McCleskey v. Kemp:* Race, Capital Punishment, and the Supreme Court," 101 *Harv. L. Rev.* 1388, 1424 (1988); Catharine A. MacKinnon, *Feminism Unmodified: Discourses on Life and Law* 32–45 (1987); Frances Olsen, "Statutory Rape: A Feminist Critique of Rights Analysis," 63 *Tex. L. Rev.* 387, 390–401, 429–430 (1984); Ansley, "Stirring the Ashes," 1063–64.

22. "Independently of 'merit'" means regardless of whether the candidates in question would be hired or promoted if the law schools

applied their current standards without taking affirmative action goals into account. I put the word "merit" in quotation marks because, in my twenty years as a law school faculty member, I have quite consistently found myself voting "on the merits," without regard to affirmative action, for minority teaching candidates who did not get the job and against white candidates who did. This means that I disagree with my own school's institutional application of the merit standard before we even get to questions of affirmative action. Extensive indirect exposure to hiring and promotion decisions at a range of other schools suggests to me that they are not different. Most law school faculties give too much weight to paper credentials, overvalue old-boy connections, make bad intuitive judgments based on interviews, and tend to misevaluate the substantive quality of presentations and written work when applying formally color-blind standards. For these reasons, the current institutional interpretation of standards yields no more than a very loose approximation of what I myself regard as merit. For a somewhat different but accurate critique of elite law school hiring, see Steven Carter, "The Best Black and Other Tales," 1 *Reconstruction* 6 (1990). For a critique of Carter, see "Taking Color-blindness Seriously" later in the chapter. See also Elizabeth Bartholet, "Application of Title VII to Jobs in High Places," 95 *Harv. L. Rev.* 945 (1982).

23. Cf. Anthony Appiah, "The Uncompleted Argument: Du Bois and the Illusion of Race," in *"Race," Writing and Difference* 21 (H. Gates ed. 1986). I see the groupings that Americans identify as "racial," such as the black, Hispanic, Asian-American, or Native American communities, as different from communities characterized as "ethnic," such as the Irish-American or Italian-American. The difference I am asserting derives not from the biology of group members, but from their different places in the American ideology of racial and group identity and from the historic practice of differential treatment in the context of subordination. See Neil Gotanda, "A Critique of 'Our Constitution Is Colorblind,'" 1.

24. This is not a "reparations" argument for affirmative action, since it is not dependent on establishing for any particular cultural community that a history of racial oppression justifies special measures in the present. The idea is that if the politically dominant groups decide to annex, transport, or admit into the United States large numbers of people who form a subordinated cultural community, then they should make sure those people have the resources to function in the national political arena. But the argument is not averse to reparations, and I favor them where there has been a history of oppression. For a reparations argument, see Matsuda, "Looking to the Bottom."

25. See R. Kennedy, 1765–70.

26. Incorporating a floor into the proposal will require faculties that adopt it to negotiate over what should be considered minimum qualifications. If a faculty set the floor very high, the result would be little change in existing practices, since all but the candidates who would have been considered anyway would be excluded. For the proposal to have an impact, the faculty adopting it would have to intend to change its practices by identifying a significant pool of candidates of color considered minimally qualified, and then choosing "the best" from among them until the faculty had achieved a reasonable representation of minorities.

The vagueness of the terms *reasonable representation* and *minimum qualifications* does not seem to me a drawback to the proposal. We are talking about changes at the level of particular law faculties rather than about legislation or administrative or even Association of American Law Schools guidelines. No faculty would adopt the proposal unless there was a majority committed to a quite radical change in existing practices. That majority could choose to define the new policy much more specifically, say in terms of quotas and lists of credentials, rather than leave it vague. But another faculty might see the vagueness of the standard as valuable for "equitable flexibility," rather than viewing it as a drawback.

The floor, as I define it in the text, refers only to instructional functions of the law professor. I would leave writing out altogether, for at least three reasons. First, existing criteria of merit do not seem to me either to predict or to reward ex post the particular qualities that make for what I regard as scholarly excellence. Second, arbitrariness and ideological disagreement about what scholarship is good scholarship chill the academic freedom and undermine the quality of life of candidates and assistant professors. Third, since the rationale of the proposal is partly political empowerment of cultural communities that are subordinated by the dominant white community, it is undesirable to invite the white male majorities of our law faculties to engage in exclusion from the pool of "minimally qualified" scholars of color according to criteria of "quality" that have a heavy ideological load.

27. See notes 4 and 5.

28. Yet a third important reason for affirmative action is that it will improve the quality of legal pedagogy. The political case anticipates that increasing the number of law teachers of color will influence the experience of law students of color in directions that will empower subordinated communities. This is a part of the general strategy of building minority intelligentsias so that subordinated communities

can participate effectively in the political process. The cultural case anticipates that scholars of color will have an impact on the substantive content of what is taught about particular legal issues and on the composition of the curriculum and on the syllabi of particular courses. In all these areas, "white moderate" bias is rampant—that is, white moderate ideological blinders render minority issues invisible. But affirmative action is also important to improve the educational experience and the practical value of legal education for people of color. The availability of "role models" is only a part of what is at issue here. Improvements should derive in part directly from what minority teachers do in and out of the classroom, and in part from their influence on what white teachers do. And the benefits should run to white students as well as to students of color. See Kimberle Crenshaw, "Foreword: Toward a Race-Conscious Pedagogy in Legal Education," 11 *Nat'l. Black L.J.* 1 (1989).

29. The mainly white male candidates who win jobs and tenure under the existing system do so through a difficult, effortful, often draining process of academic competition before and during law school. The criteria of success—mainly getting good grades on exams, writing good student papers, and making professors think you are intelligent and "sound" (not too far out of the political mainstream)—have real bite. I do not see them as arbitrary in the sense that there is enormous variance in how different professors evaluate a given student, or that just anyone can do equally well, or that grades are random. But the fact that there is a difficult process of selection does not mean we should regard those who get through the screening as having "merit" that "entitles" them to the jobs we offer.

The undergraduate and law school work that qualifies students for jobs usually has no academic "merit" in the sense of making permanent contributions to knowledge. Its function is to develop skills that will pay off, if they do pay off, later on. Possession of the skills is no guarantee of success, and people who have less skill at the competition often produce better work in the end than those with more. The academic performances that get one into law school and then into the legal academic job market are at best a weak proxy for the merit of actually producing valuable legal scholarship or teaching.

Even the criteria we apply in granting tenure are no more than proxies for merit in the lifetime careers we are distributing. We grant future job security on the basis of past performance, without subsequent readjustment if the candidate turns out to lack merit over the coming decades. We do reward actual academic merit, but we do it through the process of lateral appointment up the prestige ladder, through the distribution of high reputation, and by academic honors and prizes.

In short, the white male applicant is in a very different situation from the white male author of a law review article rejected because the editors accepted an article by a black that has no claim to cultural distinctiveness and is "not as good" by color-blind standards. Even in this case, the decision may be justified as an investment by the white community in developing minority scholars who may eventually use the resources generated by publication to produce distinctive work, and as the distribution of a share of the social power represented by publication to people who have traditionally been excluded. But the case is harder because we are dealing with a direct judgment of scholarly merit rather than with a proxy.

30. That these vices are widespread does not invalidate meritocracy. They may be present in valuable meritocratic systems and in corrupt ones, or largely absent in either type. I am asserting that they are distressingly prevalent in our system and constitute a significant cost of doing business the way we do.

31. R. Kennedy, 1807.

32. It is an interesting question (though one I will not deal with here) whether the proposed program violates the equal protection clause of the U. S. Constitution or Title VII of the Civil Rights Act of 1968, as they are currently interpreted by the U. S. Supreme Court. See Derrick Bell, "The Racial Barrier to Reparations," in *And We Are Not Saved* 123–139. See generally Kathleen Sullivan, "Sins of Discrimination: Last Term's Affirmative Action Cases," 100 *Harv. L. Rev.* 78 (1986) (arguing that affirmative action can be justified on the basis of "forward-looking" goals of an integrated future rather than solely on the basis of past sins); Paul Brest, "Affirmative Action and the Constitution: Three Theories," 72 *Iowa L. Rev.* 281 (1987) (analyzing "original intent," "discrete and insular minorities," and "color-blind equality" approaches to affirmative action).

33. The tone of Kennedy's article is unrelentingly hostile to the "racial distinctiveness" thesis, but surprisingly unhelpful in assessing it. He writes as if it must mean either that there is a single minority or black or Hispanic "voice," or that anything any minority person says is said in a minority voice. He suggests (note irony) that we should develop a definition of what a meritorious black voice is, and then apply color-blind criteria in judging whether candidates have it, or that we should just abandon the idea altogether. See R. Kennedy, 1802–03. As the text following this note indicates, the issue seems to me a good deal more complicated than his position makes it seem.

34. Kennedy, and probably most others of his camp, are not willing to
go that far. At a number of points his article recognizes, tentatively,
one might even say grudgingly, that the groups that make up our
society have differing characteristics and that under some circumstances it might make sense to take them into account: "[E]ven taking into account class, gender, and other divisions, there might remain an irreducible link of commonality in the experience of
people of color: rich or poor, male or female, learned or ignorant, *all*
people of color are to some degree 'outsiders' in a society that is
intensely color-conscious and in which the hegemony of whites is
overwhelming" (id. at 1784).

And again: "I do not maintain that no appreciable differences exist
in the prevailing opinions and sensibilities of various racial groups.
Nor do I maintain that it is improper ever to make decisions based
on racial generalizations" (id. at 1816).

See also id. at 1805 n.271 (noting that in some cases the "fact of
being black—like that of being tall, being able to see, or simply being alive—may help one to accomplish something admirable").
There is black literature, music, film, in the sense of contributions
of individuals who happen to be black (id. at 1758–59), but no
"black art" in a stronger sense (id. at 1803 and n.262). There are
patterns of behavior and particular opinions (e.g., opposition to the
death penalty, id. at 1816) that characterize one ethnic subculture
more than another. It is even true that "racial and other ascriptive
loyalties continue to organize a great deal of social, political and intellectual life throughout the world; in many areas such loyalties have
intensified" (id. at 1782). When talking about the production of academic knowledge, the article places the burden of proof on the person who would assert that membership in a defined community is
associated with a particular way of knowing or with particular intellectual strengths or weaknesses. The crucial question in the debate
about standards is: "But what, as a function of race, is 'special' or
'distinct' about the scholarship of minority legal academics? Does it
differ discernibly in ways attributable to race from work produced
by white scholars? If so, in what ways and to what degree is the
work of colored intellectuals different from or better than the work
of whites? . . . [A]t least with respect to legal scholarship, [Matsuda]
fails to show the newness of the 'new knowledge' and the difference
that distinguishes the 'different voices'" (id. at 1778–79). It seems unlikely that we will get far by trying to resolve the substantive dispute
by the placement of the burden of proof. If we take the idea of
proof seriously, then whoever bears the burden will lose. The deci-

sion to allocate the burden to one side or the other is no less ideological than a decision on the merits.

35. Peller, "Race Consciousness."

36. Jean-Paul Sartre, *Critique of Dialectical Reason I: Theory of Practical Ensembles* (A. Sheridan-Smith trans. 1976).

37. See generally James Clifford, *The Predicament of Culture: Twentieth-Century Ethnography, Literature, and Art* (1988).

38. See Chapter 1, pp. 21–25; Andrew Ross, *No Respect: Intellectuals and Popular Culture* (1989).

39. See Daniel Fusfeld and Timorthy Bates, *The Political Economy of the Urban Ghetto* (1984).

40. See generally Regina Austin, "Employer Abuse, Worker Resistance, and the Tort of Intentional Infliction of Emotional Distress," 41 *Stan. L. Rev.* 1 (1988); Michel Foucault, "Two Lectures," in *Power/Knowledge: Selected Interviews and Other Writings* 78 (R. Gordon trans. 1980). On the homologies in the legal treatment of class and race, see Karl Klare, "The Quest for Industrial Democracy and the Struggle against Racism: Perspectives from Labor Law and Civil Rights Law," 61 *Ore. L. Rev.* 157 (1982).

41. See Duncan Kennedy, "The Politics of Hierarchy," in *Legal Education and the Reproduction of Hierarchy* 78–97.

42. See generally Antonio Gramsci, *Selections from the Prison Notebooks* (Q. Hoare & G. Smith eds. 1971).

43. See generally Karl Mannheim, *Ideology and Utopia: An Introduction to the Sociology of Knowledge* (1954).

44. See generally Louis Althusser, "Ideology and Ideological State Apparatuses (Notes towards an Investigation)," in *Lenin and Philosophy and Other Essays* 127 (B. Brewster trans. 1971).

45. Some important discussions of the role of intellectuals in situations of domination are Paolo Freire, *Pedagogy of the Oppressed* (M. Ramos trans. 1970); Frantz Fanon, *The Wretched of the Earth* (C. Farrington trans. 1968); E. Franklin Frazier, *Black Bourgeoisie* (1957); Cruse, *Crisis of the Negro Intellectual.*

46. Angela Harris, "Race and Essentialism in Feminist Legal Theory," 42 *Stan. L. Rev.* 581 (1990).

47. For an example of the kind of work I am talking about see Harold McDougall's articles about the *Mt. Laurel* decision: "The Judicial Struggle against Exclusionary Zoning: The New Jersey Paradigm," 14 *Harv. C.R.–C.L. L. Rev.* 625 (1979); "*Mt. Laurel II* and the Revitalizing City," 15 *Rutgers L.J.* 667 (1984); and "From Litigation to Legislation in Exclusionary Zoning Law," 22 *Harv. C.R.–C.L. L. Rev.* 623 (1987).

48. See Mark Tushnet, *The NAACP's Legal Strategy against Segregated Education, 1925–1950* (1987).

49. An example of the kind of work I am talking about is Mario Baeza, "Telecommunications Reregulation and Deregulation: The Impact on Opportunities for Minorities," *Harv. Blackletter J.* 7 (Spring 1985).

50. I am referring here to the century-and-a-half-long discussion about the character of African-American identity and its implications for strategy. The debate involves famous pairs, among them Martin Delany (see *The Condition, Elevation, Emigration, and Destiny of the Colored People of the United States* [1852]) and Frederick Douglass (see *My Bondage and My Freedom* [1855]); Booker T. Washington (see *The Future of the American Negro* [1899]) and W. E. B. Du Bois (see *The Souls of Black Folk* [1903]); Marcus Garvey (see E. Cronon, *Black Moses: The Story of Marcus Garvey and the Universal Negro Improvement Association* [1957]) and the later W.E.B. Du Bois (see *Dusk of Dawn: An Essay toward an Autobiography of a Race Concept* [1940]); E. Franklin Frazier (see *Black Bourgeoisie* [1957]) and Harold Cruse (see *Crisis of the Negro Intellectual*); Malcolm X (see *The Autobiography of Malcolm X* [1965]) and Martin Luther King, Jr. (see *A Testament of Hope: The Essential Writings of Martin Luther King. Jr.* [J. Washington ed. 1986]). This list is just an appetizer. The primary and secondary literatures are enormous. A valuable summary and reinterpretation is Cornell West, "The Four Traditions of Response," in *Prophesy Deliverance! An Afro-American Revolutionary Christianity* 69 (1982). See also Robert Allen, *Black Awakening in Capitalist America: An Analytic History* (1969). For an extensive collection of sources, see Peller, "Race Consciousness."

51. See Thomas Sowell, *Markets and Minorities* (1981) and *Race and Economics* (1975). For a progressive critique of Sowell, see Crenshaw, "Race, Reform, and Retrenchment," 1339–46.

52. See William J. Wilson, *The Truly Disadvantaged: The Inner City, the Underclass, and Public Policy* (1987); William J. Wilson, *The Declining Significance of Race? A Dialogue among Black and White Social Scientists* (1978); See R. Kennedy, 1814 n.296.

53. For a classic statement of the conflict, see Zorah Neale Hurston, *Their Eyes Were Watching God* (1937). See generally Paula Giddings, *When and Where I Enter: The Impact of Black Women on Race and Sex in America* (1984); bell hooks, *Ain't I A Woman: Black Women and Feminism* (1981); see also Lee Rainwater and William Yancey, *The Moynihan Report and the Politics of Controversy* (1967); Harold Cheatham and James Stewart, *Black Families: Interdisciplinary Perspectives* (1990).

54. Derrick Bell's point of view has always contained elements of na-

tionalism—particularly his writing on school desegregation. See, e.g., Derrick Bell, "Serving Two Masters: Integration Ideals and Client Interests in School Desegregation Litigation," 85 *Yale L.J.* 470 (1976) (educational improvement for blacks must take precedence over failed integration policies); idem, "The Burden of *Brown* on Blacks: History-Based Observations on a Landmark Decision," 7 *N.C. Cent. L.J.* 25, 26 (1975) (recognizing *Brown's* limitations and arguing that it should be used as "critical leverage for a wide range of [continuing] efforts" by black communities to improve education for blacks). The debate is internal to Bell's book *And We Are Not Saved*. With the publication of the articles cited in notes 4 and 5, and the response in R. Kennedy, the issue seems finally to have its own momentum in legal scholarship. On black feminism in law, see Kimberle Crenshaw, "Demarginalizing the Intersection of Race and Sex: A Black Feminist Critique of Antidiscrimination Doctrine, Feminist Theory and Antiracist Politics," 1989 *U. Chi. Legal Forum* 139; Angela Harris, "Race and Essentialism in Feminist Legal Theory," 42 *Stan. L. Rev.* 581 (1990).

55. For example, compare Richard Rodriguez, *Hunger of Memory: The Education of Richard Rodriguez* (1982), with Alfredo Mirande, *Gringo Justice* (1987).

56. R. Kennedy, 1784. Kennedy's article says only that there "might" be a link of commonality among people of color. Id.

57. The dividing line between questions that seem "objective" and those that seem "political" or "subjective" or "cultural" or "ideological" cannot be fixed "objectively." Although we experience merely cognitive questions (Did the article cite and discuss the leading treatise on its subject?) as very different from "value" questions (Did the article discuss the leading treatise fairly?), we also argue about which domain we are operating in. I might claim that the article did discuss the treatise even though it disposed of its (silly) argument in a single sentence. You might respond that a single, dismissive sentence just does not count as discussion. I might counter that your view that there was no discussion is a disguised judgment on the merits of the discussion. And so forth. For an analogous argument about adjudication, see Duncan Kennedy, "Freedom and Constraint in Adjudication: A Critical Phenomenology," 36 *J. Legal Educ.* 518 (1986).

58. See generally Thomas Kuhn, *The Structure of Scientific Revolutions* (2d ed. 1970).

59. See generally Michel Foucault, 1 *The History of Sexuality* (R. Hurley trans. 1978).

60. For example a person from a group that has successfully used the

idea of merit to wrest from a dominant group advantages previously denied on the basis of race might well have a different view of how much is lost in the use of cultural criteria from a person who was born into the dominant group. But the differences could cut many ways in generating positions. The person from the previously excluded group might conclude that merit is the only way to overcome prejudice, and that adherence will lead eventually to a society in which skin color is irrelevant. But a person from the same group might believe that as long as merit is the only basis on which to claim advances, advances will be made at the expense of cultural identity and will lead to assimilation, which is cultural suicide. A person born into the dominant group might believe that the only basis on which advances are justified is merit, and that the dominant group is itself organized according to merit. Departures from race neutrality that favor the previously excluded may be necessary, but they have a heavy cost of unfairness to meritorious members of the dominant group. By contrast, some ruling-class people believe that the internal meritocratic culture of the dominant group has large elements of sham and serious antisocial consequences, and that departures from its forms are likely to be beneficial even if it turns out, unhappily, that they do not lead to serious cultural pluralism.

61. One defense of the system would be that there is basic social consensus on the way faculties do their job, so that self-consciously culturally pluralist procedures are unnecessary. This would deny that color-blind fundamentalism is significantly contested, either by alternative visions or with respect to the resolution of its internal gaps, conflicts, and ambiguities when we have to decide what it means in particular cases. For the opposite view see Peller, "Race Consciousness" and articles cited in notes 4 and 5. Another (somewhat inconsistent) defense would be that the process of color-blind meritocratic selection, along with ideological divisions among white males, has already produced a representation of minorities and enough dissidents so that debate occurs or soon will occur within faculties. The formal adoption of power sharing is therefore not needed. For the opposite view see Richard Chused, "The Hiring and Retention of Minorities and Women on American Law School Faculties," 137 *U. Pa. L. Rev.* 537 (1988).

62. See "Color-Blind Meritocracy and Affirmative Action," above. See also R. Kennedy, "Persuasion and Distrust," 1328–29 (affirmative action "on balance . . . is useful in overcoming entrenched racial hierarchy").

63. For example, Kennedy argues that "the use of *race* as a proxy is spe-

cially disfavored because, even when relatively accurate as a signifier of the trait sought to be identified, racial proxies are especially prone to misuse. By the practice of subjecting governmentally-imposed racial distinctions to strict scrutiny, federal constitutional law recognizes that racial distinctions are particularly liable to be used in a socially destructive fashion" (R. Kennedy, 1794).

64. Id.
65. These include his remarks on the use of the racial distinctiveness thesis by the Nazis, among others. See id. at 1789 n. 197. He also discusses the possibility that using race as an "intellectual credential" will backfire and harm minorities. See id. at 1796.
66. Id at 1816. To derogate means "to cause to seem inferior" or "disparage" or "detract" from. *Webster's Ninth New Collegiate Dictionary* 342 (1984).
67. R. Kennedy, 1804 (citing Ralph Ellison, *Shadow and Act* 146 [1972]).
68. Id. at 1807.
69. Id. at 1772 n.114.
70. Id. at 1772 (emphasis added).
71. Id. at 1773.
72. Id. at 1806.
73. Id. at 1807 (emphasis added).
74. Kennedy defines "merit" as "achieved honor by some standard that is indifferent to the social identity of a given author" (id. at 1772 n.114). He seems to think that from this it follows that race should not (cannot?) be an "intellectual credential": "The strategy of elevating racial status to an intellectual credential undermines the conception of intellectual merit as a mark of *achieved* distinction by confusing the relationship between racial background and scholarly expertise; the former is a social condition into which one is born, while the latter is something that an individual attains. Confusing accidental attributes and achieved distinctions in turn derogates the process by which all individuals, simultaneously limited and aided by the conditions they inherit, personally contribute to human culture" (id. at 1805-06).

But the confusion here is Kennedy's. The word *credential* was introduced into the discussion of affirmative action as part of the argument that as a matter of probabilities we can expect to get more of some desirable capacities from minority rather than from majority scholars: "Arguing that race should be a consideration in matching instructors to course offerings, Harvard Law School Professor Christopher Edley, Jr., maintained that '[r]ace remains a useful proxy for a whole collection of experiences, aspirations and sensitivities . . . we teach what we have lived . . .' Similarly, Professor Derrick Bell argued that '[r]ace can create as legitimate a presumption as a judicial clerkship in filling a teaching position intended to interpret . . . the impact of racial discrimination on the law and lawyering.' Racial background can properly be considered a credential, he observed, because of '[t]he special and quite valuable perspective on law and life in this country that a black person can provide'" (id. at 1758).

Richard Delgado's "The Imperial Scholar" likewise speaks in terms of probabilities in arguing that the minority community should not rely on white scholars to develop fields of law that deeply affect their interests. See R. Kennedy, 1788–89. Delgado then argues that the actual outcome of white scholarship is less favorable to minority interests than minority scholarship would be, but here he is doing just what Kennedy approves: he is making sustantive judgments of actual works (although he may be wrong or may not have proved his points). There is no confusion between "accidental attributes and achieved distinctions."

In a footnote Kennedy concedes that for some jobs under some circumstances, race would be a valid basis for favoring one candidate over another. But instead of asking whether legal academic jobs fall into this category, he argues that we should not use the word *merit* to describe what makes the candidate better for the job. No one is arguing about how to define the word *merit*. The issue is what should count as a "credential" in a hiring situation, and Kennedy's own text here recognizes, without refuting, the type of argument his opponents are making. See id. at 1805 n.271.

75. This does not mean that only cultures produce culture. We can still identify authors of artifacts within a culture and compare them. If the culture has only group authors, then we can distinguish between the groups. The mere existence of culture poses no a priori problems for making judgments of value between artifacts or between their creators.

It is equally wrong to think that the fact of culture (if it is a fact) makes it impossible to judge the merit of work or capacities of a person from another culture. We can assess the ability of *anyone* to produce a given type of artifact of our own culture. We look at the work, not who produced it, and we just treat it as an attempted performance within our own culture and ask if it succeeded. Then we make inferences about the likely capacity of the individual or group author to do more work of the same quality. We can even rank cultures according to their production of particular kinds of valued artifacts and capacities.

Yet another mistake is to believe that one can't assess the value of people or work in another culture according to its own, alien standards. A person from one culture often has the experience of knowing what is going on in another. It is possible to pick up on the way the other culture assesses work and people, and to predict accurately what the consensus view of quality in a foreign culture will be. But it is also true that what we think we know about actions or performances in another culture is suspect in a way not true of what we think we know in our own, because we may "misread" behavior in the other culture. Given the "inherited" quality of cultural capacity, we never "read" in the unselfconscious way we do in our own context.

Finally, it's wrong to think there cannot be shared values between cultures. Each culture may understand the other as using the same standards for assessing particular kinds of artifacts. On the other hand, a conviction that we are applying the same standards across cultures must be held more tentatively than the same view within a culture. Because of "our" difference from "them," the appearance of sharing a standard may be illusory. When we discuss an evaluative or even a descriptive issue with a person from another culture on the mutual assumption that we share standards, there is always the possibility that we will find ourselves in a stalemate that seems best explained by admitting that the standards were not shared in the first place.

The point in all these cases is that we can *problematize* the operation of making judgments of value, of applying standards, without abandoning it altogether. See note 57. See also Richard Rorty, *Consequences of Pragmatism* 166–67 (1982): "'Relativism' is the view that every belief on a certain topic, or perhaps about any topic, is as good as every other. No one holds this view. Except for the occasional cooperative freshman, one cannot find anybody who says that two incompatible opinions on an important topic are equally good. The philosophers who get *called* 'relativists' are those who say that the grounds for choosing between such opinions are less algorithmic than had been thought . . . So the real issue is not between people who think one view [is] as good as another and people who do not. It is between those who think that our culture, or purpose, or intuitions cannot be supported except conversationally, and people who still hope for other sorts of support."

76. R. Kennedy, 1805.
77. See "Premises of Cultural Pluralism," above.
78. See R. Kennedy, 1772–73, 1806–07.

79. The first interpretation is influenced by Claude Lévi-Strauss, *The Savage Mind* 1–33 (1966), the second by Jean-Paul Sartre, *Being and Nothingness* 3–30 (H. Barnes trans. 1956), and both by Jacques Derrida, "The Law of Genre," in *On Narrative* (W. Mitchell ed. 1981).

80. *Nation,* Sept. 4, 1982, at 169.

81. A striking example of the genre is Martin Kilson, "The Black Experience at Harvard," *New York Times Magazine,* Sept. 2, 1973, at 13. It is interesting to contrast the genre in which a more or less conservative white author attacks the same black radical and white liberal characters, but in a quite different tone. See Tom Wolfe, *Radical Chic and Mau-Mauing the Flak Catchers* (1970).

82. R. Kennedy, "Persuasion and Distrust," 1335–36.

83. Cf. Gerald Frug, "Argument as Character," 40 *Stan. L. Rev.* 869 (1988).

84. Delgado, "The Imperial Scholar."

85. R. Kennedy, 1796; see also id. at 1796–97.

86. Id. at 1796.

87. Along the same lines, I see nothing wrong with trying to figure out the social psychology of the preference for efficiency and "unequal bargaining power" arguments over distributional arguments in "moderate" legal scholarship (see Duncan Kennedy, "Distributive and Paternalist Motives in Contract and Tort Law, with Special Reference to Compulsory Terms and Unequal Bargaining Power," 41 *Md. L. Rev.* 563 [1982]), or with attributing the white Critical Legal Studies hostility to rights rhetoric to some combination of neomarxist ideology and middle-class white cultural context (see Williams, "Alchemical Notes," 401, 414). As in the case referred to in the text, the question for me is not whether the type of analysis is legitimate but whether the particular instance is convincing.

88. R. Kennedy, 1793 (commenting on Delgado, "The Imperial Scholar," 568–69). Since what is involved is a cultural/ideological analysis, there is no inconsistency, indeed there is "merit," in noting that the traits are not shared by all whites and that the same traits appear in the work of some scholars of color. For a rejection of this position, see id.

89. Id. at 1795.

90. Id. at 1747.

91. Id. at 1754. In his text and footnotes Kennedy repeatedly calls attention to the racial composition of the groups trying to control this public image, referring to the "Black Power Movement" (id. at 1755), "black scholars" (id. at 1756 nn.46 & 48), "black writers" (id.).

92. Id. at 1807 (emphasis added).

93. See id. at 1808.
94. Kennedy writes, "Professor Delgado rejects both 'conscious malevolence or crass indifference.' Rather, he posits that the imperial scholars' exclusionary conduct is mainly unconscious and prompted by their desire to maintain control, to prevent scholarly criticism from becoming too threatening to the academic and political status quo" (id. at 1771).
95. Id. at 1773 n.114.
96. Id. at 1816.
97. See id. at 1755 and n.44, 1790.
98. Id. at 1818–19.
99. Id. at 1819 n.308.
100. Id. at 1807.
101. Kennedy claims that he does not seek to evade politics. He quotes Lionel Trilling with approval: "[O]ur fate, for better or worse, is political. It is therefore not a happy fate, even if it has an heroic sound, but there is no escape from it, and the only possibility of enduring it is to force into our definition of politics every human activity and every subtlety of human activity. There are manifest dangers in doing this, but greater dangers in not doing it" (id. at 1787 n.191, quoting Trilling, *The Liberal Imagination* 96 [1950]).
102. This discussion is a response to Carter, "The Best Black and Other Tales," 6.
103. This view is dependent on the existence of real disagreement among minorities about affirmative action. If there were an indisputable consensus among blacks, say, that culturally conscious decision making is "derogation" and "insult," and an equally indisputable willingness to abide by the consequences, it would be a tough call whether affirmative action should continue. My problem would be my (ideological) conviction that the type of judgment required is not only politically incorrect, but also impossible to do and bad for legal scholarship. I might nonetheless feel that the value of cultural pluralism paradoxically required agreeing to the self-exclusion that would result from color-blind judgment.
104. R. Kennedy, 1802.
105. On the vexed question of the boundary between situations in which judgment seems somehow "compelled" and those in which we experience it as closer to "choice," see notes 57 and 75.

3. The Stakes of Law, or Hale and Foucault!

1. The works of Robert Hale on which this article is based are *Freedom through Law: Public Control of Private Governing Power* (1952);

"Prima Facie Torts, Combination, and Non-Feasance," 1946 *Colum. L. Rev.* 196; "Bargaining, Duress, and Economic Liberty," 1943 *Colum. L. Rev.* 603; "Force and the State," 1935 *Colum. L. Rev.* 286; and "Coercion and Distribution in a Supposedly Non-Coercive State," 38 *Pol. Sci. Q.* 470 (1923).

See also John R. Commons, *Legal Foundations of Capitalism* (1924); Richard T. Ely, *Contract and Property in Their Relations to the Distribution of Wealth* (1914). For more on Hale's life and times as well as his thought, see Neil Duxbury, "Robert Hale and the Economy of Legal Force," 53 *Modern L. Rev.* 421 (1990) (hereafter cited as Duxbury). Warren Samuels' article "The Economy as a System of Power and Its Legal Bases: The Legal Economics of Robert Lee Hale," 27 *U. Miami L. Rev.* 261 (1973) (hereafter cited as Samuels), contains an invaluable collection of unpublished Hale material and a thorough summary of nondoctrinal aspects of his work.

Two earlier attempts at appropriation are Duncan Kennedy and Frank Michelman, "Are Property and Contract Efficient?" 8 *Hofstra L. Rev.* 711 (1980); and Duncan Kennedy, "The Role of Law in Economic Thought: Three Essays on the Fetishism of Commodities," 34 *Am. U. L. Rev.* 939 (1985).

The best extant discussion of legal realism is Joseph Singer, "Legal Realism Now," 76 *Cal. L. Rev.* 465 (1988).

2. This essay is based on the following works by Michel Foucault: *Discipline and Punish: The Birth of the Prison* (A. Sheridan trans. 1979); 1 *The History of Sexuality,* (R. Hurley trans. 1978) (hereafter cited as *History*); "The Subject and Power," in *Art after Modernism: Rethinking Representation* (B. Wallis ed. 1989); "Two Lectures," in *Power/Knowledge: Selected Interviews and Other Writings, 1972–77* (R. Gordon ed. 1980); "Nietzsche, Genealogy, History" and "Intellectuals and Power: A Conversation between Michel Foucault and Gilles Deleuze," both in *Language, Counter-Memory, Practice: Selected Essays and Interviews* (D. Bouchard ed. 1977).

3. Hale, "Bargaining," 625.

4. Samuels, 302–323, 354–368.

5. Id. at 323–344.

6. Although Hale was intensely aware of the distributive importance of the rules governing bargaining conduct (see "Prima Facie Torts"), I think it is fair to say that the main emphasis of his work is on the way the general legal regime permitting unlimited acquisition and relatively free disposition of property produces inequality by structuring alternatives. See, e.g. Samuels, 332, 343.

7. Samuels, 342–344.

8. Wesley Hohfeld, "Fundamental Legal Conceptions as Applied in Judicial Reasoning," 26 *Yale L.J.* 710 (1917). See Singer, "Legal Realism Now," 482. See generally Joseph Singer, "The Legal Rights Debate in Analytical Jurisprudence from Bentham to Hohfeld," 1982 *Wis. L. Rev.* 975. I think both Samuels and Duxbury miss the importance of Hohfeld to Hale's position. Duxbury, 425; Samuels, 274–275.

9. See Hale, "Prima Facie Torts."

10. Hale did not use unstable equilibrium analysis, at least so far as I am aware. Some texts using this mode of analysis are Gunnar Myrdal, *An Approach to the Asian Drama* 1843–78 (1970); Rolf Goetze, *Understanding Neighborhood Change* (1979); Daniel Fusfeld and Timothy Bates, *The Political Economy of the Urban Ghetto* (1984); Duncan Kennedy, "The Effect of the Warranty of Habitability on Low Income Housing: 'Milking' and Class Violence," 15 *Fla. St. L. Rev.* 485, 512–513 (1987); and Lawrence Kolodney, "Eviction-Free Zones: The Economics of Legal *Bricolage* in the Fight Against Displacement," 19 *Fordham Urban L.J.* 551 (1991).

11. Samuels at 344–354 overstates Hale's sophistication on these issues. See Hale, *Freedom through Law,* 541–550. For a formal statement of the general proposition, see Duncan Kennedy, "Legal Formality," 2 *J. Leg. Stud.* 383–386 (1973).

12. Hale, "Coercion," 472–473.

13. Hale, "Bargaining," 628.

14. There is therefore some exaggeration in Hale's statement that "in fact the property rights are part of a legal arrangement whereby the law curtails the liberty of different individuals in different degrees, and the justifiability of the particular arrangements depends on the justifiability of the economic results rather than the reverse." Hale, "Economics and the Law," in *The Social Sciences and their Interrelation* 140 (W. Ogburn and A. Goldenweiser eds. 1927).

15. See Singer, 499–503. Hale himself *almost* makes this connection many times, insisting over and over again that the issues in tort, property, contract, and constitutional law are "policy issues" and involve "choice" (e.g., "Prima Facie Torts," 200–201). But he never seems to have adopted the *generalized* kind of internal critique represented by Felix Cohen, "Transcendental Nonsense and the Functional Approach," 1935 *Col. L. Rev.* 809. He seems indeed to have believed that there is an appropriate role for judges in protecting "normal" market functioning, while leaving distributive intervention to the legislature ("Coercion," 624–625; "Prima Facie Torts," 196, 218). This fitted the political context of the New Deal, the Nine

Old Men, and reactionary state judiciaries. But in hindsight the idea of facilitating "normal" functioning seems question-begging, given Hale's own insistence on the pervasive market-structuring role of law, and the general realist insistence that legal issues are policy issues. See Duncan Kennedy, "Form and Substance in Private Law Adjudication," 89 *Harv. L. Rev.* 1685, 1756–60 (1976).

16. Duncan Kennedy, "Comment on Rudolph Wietholter's 'Materialization and Proceduralization of Modern Law' and 'Proceduralization of the Category of Law,'" in *Critical Legal Thought: An American-German Debate* (C. Joerges and D. Trubek, eds. 1989).

17. Quoting from Hale's unpublished papers, Samuels describes his "basic paradigm" as follows: "The results do not take a completely 'predetermined' pattern from the coercive powers which condition it'; since '[e]ach individual is subject to compulsion, in that he must make a choice between loss of one liberty or another,' the results are also a function of the acts of will or choice on the part of the individuals and groups. Whatever the structure of coercive capacities, the process is at least a partially open and not a closed one." Samuels, 291.

18. Foucault, *History,* 92–96; see also idem, *Discipline and Punish,* 26–27.

19. In a brilliant unpublished essay, "Foucault for Lawyers," Al Katz argued that the realists should be understood as "disciplinary" and "normalizing" legal theorists, in the mode of criminology, industrial psychology, and so forth. One can find some support for this reading in Hale, *Freedom through Law.* For Foucault as an antidote to Fish, see Alan Hutchinson, "Part of an Essay on Power and Interpretation (with Suggestions on How to Make Bouillabaisse)," 60 *N.Y.U.L. Rev.* (1985).

20. Foucault, "Intellectuals and Power," 213.

21. Foucault, *History,* 17–35.

22. Foucault, *Discipline and Punish,* 30.

23. Id. at 277. "In fact, power produces; it produces reality; it produces domains of objects and rituals of truth. The individual and the knowledge that may be gained of him belong to this production." Id. at 194.

24. Foucault, "Two Lectures," 105.

25. Foucault, "The Subject and Power," 792.

26. For example, in the chapter on panopticism in *Discipline and Punish,* which to my taste is his single most brilliant production, the factory or workshop is listed along with the prison, the hospital, etc., at 203, 203–204, 205, 211, 215, 218, 219, 224.

27. Id. at 221. See also id. at 224–225.

28. See, e.g., Foucault, *History,* 92–96; *Discipline and Punish,* 26–27, 219,

285–292; Nietzsche, "Genealogy, History." 148–152; "The Subject and Power," 780–781, 790, 793–795.
29. Foucault, *Discipline and Punish*, 222–223.
30. Foucault, "Two Lectures," 95–96.
31. Id. at 96.
32. Id. at 97.
33. Id. at 106.
34. Id. at 107.
35. Id. at 105.
36. Id. at 106. For another version, see *Discipline and Punish*, 221–222.
37. Foucault, "Two Lectures," 108.
38. Mark Howe, *Justice Oliver Wendell Holmes: The Proving Years* 80 (1963).
39. Foucault, *History*, 92–97.
40. Foucault, "Two Lectures," 105–106.
41. Id. at 95.
42. Id. at 96.
43. Id. at 84–85.
44. Id. at 99–101.
45. Foucault, "Intellectuals and Power," 213.
46. "The contract may have been regarded as the ideal foundation of law and political power; panopticism constituted the technique, universally widespread, of coercion." Foucault, *Discipline and Punish*, 222.
47. Foucault, *Discipline and Punish*, 228.
48. Id. at 30.
49. Id. at 217.

4. Sexual Abuse, Sexy Dressing, and the Eroticization of Domination

1. The works that I particularly experienced this way, and to which I feel most indebted, are Andrea Dworkin, *Intercourse* (1987); idem, *Right-Wing Women* (1982); Shulamith Firestone, *The Dialectic of Sex: The Case for Feminist Revolution* (1970); Robin Morgan, *Going Too Far: The Personal Chronicle of a Feminist* (1977); Catharine A. MacKinnon, "Feminism, Marxism, Method, and the State: Toward Feminist Jurisprudence," 8 *Signs* 635 (1983); Frances Olsen, "Statutory Rape: A Feminist Critique of Rights Analysis," 63 *Tex. L. Rev.* 387 (1984); and Robin West, "The Difference in Women's Hedonic Lives: A Phenomenological Critique of Feminist Legal Theory," 3 *Wis. Women's L.J.* 81 (1987). See generally *Against Sadomasochism: A Radical Feminist Analysis* (R. Linden et al. eds. 1982). For more references, see notes 15–26 below. I also want to acknowledge the influence on

my thinking of two articles by Elizabeth Schneider: "Equal Rights to Trial for Women: Sex Bias in the Law of Self-Defense," 15 *Harv. C.R.–C.L. L. Rev.* 623 (1980); and "Describing and Changing: Women's Self-Defense Work and the Problem of Expert Testimony on Battering," 9 *Women's Rts. L. Rep.* 195 (1986).

2. Jane Gallop, *Thinking Through the Body* (1988); Judith Butler, *Gender Trouble: Feminism and the Subversion of Identity* (1990); Mary Joe Frug, *Postmodern Legal Feminism* (1992). See generally *Pleasure and Danger: Exploring Female Sexuality* (C. Vance ed. 1983).

3. See, e.g., Ferdinand de Saussure, *Course in General Linguistics* (C. Bally et al. ed., R. Harris trans. 1986); Claude Lévi-Strauss, *The Savage Mind* (1966); Jean Piaget, *Play, Dreams, and Imitation in Childhood* (C. Gattegno & F. M. Hodgson trans. 1962).

4. See, e.g., Jacques Derrida, *Of Grammatology* (G. Spivak trans. 1976); Michel Foucault, 1 *The History of Sexuality: An Introduction* (R. Hurley trans. 1980). I am following in the footsteps of David Kennedy, "Spring Break," 63 *Tex. L. Rev.* 1277 (1985).

5. See Gary Peller, "Race Consciousness," 1990 *Duke L.J.* 758 (1990). Some other works in 26 *New Eng. L. Rev.* (1992) that seem quite similar in perspective to my own are Lama Abu-Odeh, "Post-Colonial Feminism and the Veil: Considering the Differences"; Dan Danielsen, "Representing Identities: Legal Treatment of Pregnancy and Homosexuality"; Karen Engle, "Female Subjects of Public International Law: Human Rights and the Exotic Other Female"; Susan Keller, "Powerless to Please: Candida Royalle's Pornography for Women"; and Karl E. Klare, "Power/Dressing: Regulation of Employee Appearance."

6. Cf. Alan D. Freeman, "Legitimizing Racial Discrimination through Anti-Discrimination Law: A Critical Review of Supreme Court Doctrine," 62 *Minn. L. Rev.* 1049 (1978).

7. The works that have most influenced me are Guido Calabresi, *The Costs of Accidents* (1970); Richard Posner, *Economic Analysis of Law* (2d ed. 1977); and Steven Shavell, "Strict Liability versus Negligence," 9 *J. Legal Stud.* 1 (1980). There is a bizarre common "origin" to modern law and economics and poststructuralism in the lectures of Walras and Saussure in pre–World War I Switzerland, the neutral, multicultural "hole in the doughnut" of Europe. Compare Léon Walras, *Elements of Pure Economics* (W. Jaffée trans. 1954) with Saussure, *Course in General Linguistics.* See Duncan Kennedy, "A Semiotics of Legal Argument," 42 *Syracuse L. Rev.* 75, 97 (1991).

8. Mass. Gen. L. ch. 209A, §§ 1–9 (1992).

9. See generally Oliver Wendell Holmes, Jr., "Privilege, Malice, and In-

tent," 8 *Harv. L. Rev.* 1 (1894); idem, "The Path of the Law," 10 *Harv. L. Rev.* 457 (1897). My perspective is also strongly influenced by Wesley Hohfeld's "Fundamental Legal Conceptions as Applied in Judicial Reasoning," 26 *Yale L.J.* 710 (1917). See generally Joseph Singer, "The Legal Rights Debate in Analytical Jurisprudence from Bentham to Hohfeld," 1982 *Wis. L. Rev.* 975.

10. Equal Employment Opportunity Commission, Guidelines on Discrimination Because of Sex, 29 C.F.R. § 1604.11 (1985).

11. In such cases, of course, the male abuser may undergo some legally generated sanction short of liability, such as arrest and pretrial confinement, or an extralegal sanction, such as the negative reaction of a supervisor as a result of the filing of a Title VII suit.

12. The principal influence on this discussion is Robert Hale, "Coercion and Distribution in a Supposedly Non-Coercive State," 38 *Pol. Sci. Q.* 470 (1923); and idem, "Bargaining, Duress, and Economic Liberty," 43 *Colum. L. Rev.* 603 (1943). See generally Chapter 3 of this volume.

13. See the works cited in notes 15–32 below.

14. See Lewis Kornhauser and Robert Mnookin, "Bargaining in the Shadow of the Law: The Case of Divorce," 88 *Yale L.J.* 950 (1979).

15. Morgan, *Going Too Far;* Dworkin, *Right-Wing Women,* and *Intercourse;* Andrea Dworkin, *Pornography: Men Possessing Women* (1989); MacKinnon, "Feminism, Marxism"; Catharine A. MacKinnon, *Feminism Unmodified: Discourses on Life and Law* (1987); idem, *Sexual Harassment of Working Women: A Case of Sex Discrimination* (1979); idem, *Toward a Feminist Theory of the State* (1989); Kathleen Barry, *Female Sexual Slavery* (1979); Diana Russell, *The Politics of Rape: The Victim's Perspective* (1975); idem, *The Secret Trauma: Incest in the Lives of Girls and Women* (1986). See generally *Against Sadomasochism;* Frances Olsen, "Feminist Theory in Grand Style," 89 *Colum. L. Rev.* 1147 (1989).

16. For a different white male response, see John Stoltenberg, *Refusing to Be a Man: Essays on Sex and Justice* (1989).

17. Herbert Marcuse, *Eros and Civilization* (2d ed. 1966); Wilhelm Reich, *The Mass Psychology of Fascism* (1946). See generally Paul Robinson, *The Freudian Left: Wilhelm Reich, Geza Roheim, Herbert Marcuse* (1990).

18. Carol Gilligan, *In a Different Voice: Psychological Theory and Women's Development* (1982).

19. Dworkin, *Intercouse,* 121–143, 149.

20. Rosemary Pringle, *Secretaries Talk: Sexuality, Power, and Work,* 92–96 (1988); James Spradley and Brenda Mann, *The Cocktail Waitress: Woman's Work in a Man's World* 144–148 (1975).

21. See, e.g., Susan Bixler, *Professional Presence* 126 (1991): "There is also a power aspect. Dating a superior or a superstar at the office has an allure. It is similar to a freshman dating a senior in high school. Sometimes it is almost a mentoring relationship, wherein the junior person learns first-hand from an executive. The junior person is exposed to positioned people, to exclusive locations, and high-powered situations where he or she normally would have no access." (Why do the words "he or she" in the last sentence of this quote seem like a copout?)

22. See Susan Cole, *Pornography and the Sex Crisis* (1989); Dworkin, *Pornography;* MacKinnon, *Feminism Unmodified,* 134, 137–138, 146, 148, 155, 161–162, 163, 171–172, 181.

23. See Antonio Gramsci, *Selections from the Prison Notebooks* (Q. Hoare & G. Smith trans. 1971); Karl Korsch, *Marxism and Philosophy* (F. Halliday trans. 1970); Georg Lukács, "Reification and the Consciousness of the Proletariat," in *History and Class Consciousness: Studies in Marxist Dialectics* 83 (R. Livingstone trans. 1971); Jean-Paul Sartre, *The Problem of Method* (H. Barnes trans. 1963); see generally Alvin Gouldner, *The Two Marxisms: Contradictions and Anomalies in the Development of Theory* (1981). For a collection of references to the playing out of this debate in legal theory, see Duncan Kennedy, "The Role of Law in Economic Thought: Essays on the Fetishism of Commodities," 34 *Am. U. L. Rev.* 939, 992 n.58 (1985).

24. See, e.g., V. I. Lenin, *What Is to Be Done?* (J. Fineberg & G. Hanna trans. 1988) (1902).

25. "Sex feeling good may mean that one is enjoying one's subordination; it would not be the first time. Or it may mean that one has glimpsed freedom, a rare and valuable and contradictory event." MacKinnon, *Feminism Unmodified,* 218.

26. See *Coming to Power: Writings and Graphics on Lesbian S/M* (Samois ed. 1982); Nancy Friday, *My Secret Garden: Women's Sexual Fantasies* (1973).

27. West, "The Difference," 127, 144.

28. Christine Gorman, "Incest Comes out of the Dark," *Time,* Oct. 7, 1991, at 46.

29. See, e.g., Russell, *The Secret Trauma,* 167–168; Eleanor Miller, *Street Woman* 114–115 (1986).

30. MacKinnon, *Feminism Unmodified,* 93, 97.

31. For an assessment of MacKinnon's theory of Roe v. Wade, 410 U.S. 113 (1973), that skillfully translates the critique of structural Marxism into the critique of radical feminism, see Rosalind Petchesky, "Abortion as Violence against Women: A Feminist Critique," 18 *Radical America* 64 (1984).

32. Butler, *Gender Trouble*, 28.
33. See generally William A. Rossi, *The Sex Life of the Foot and Shoe* (1976).
34. See generally Regina Austin, "Black Women, Sisterhood, and the Difference/Deviance Divide," 26 *New Eng. L. Rev.* 877, 879–885 (1992).
35. Suzy Menkes, "*Vogue* Point of View: The Cutting Edge," *Vogue,* Jan. 1992 at 103, 110.
36. Susan Faludi, *Backlash: The Undeclared War against American Women* 169–199 (1991).
37. See Butler, *Gender Trouble,* 134–141.
38. Lynn Harris, "Behind the Bedroom Door," *Ladies' Home J.,* Nov. 1991 at 114, 119.
39. Julie Hatfield, "Defining Appropriate Dress in the Workplace," *Boston Globe,* Jan. 16, 1992, at 31.
40. Id.
41. The following article from the supermarket tabloid *Globe,* purportedly an account by "Cherie, 18, college freshman, Wake Forest, N. C.," reflects only the conventional view, since it has clearly been re-written in tabloid style and may well be an outright invention by a (possibly male) staffer:

    "CANDID CONFESSIONS: Extraordinary secrets of ordinary people. *Big itch was the best revenge on class witch:*

    "Last summer, a bunch of us high school seniors went on a two-week camping trip. We were in couples except for this tramp, Nina.

    "Nina was always trying to steal someone's boyfriend during the school year and she was no different on our little trip.

    "On the first night, my friend Donna and I caught Nina rubbing up against Donna's boyfriend Mike out in a clearing in the woods.

    "We read Nina the riot act, but she just laughed it off.

    "She kept wearing these high-cut shorts with no panties and a skimpy tube top with no bra. And when it came time to change into bathing suits for a swim, she'd find a bush you could practically see through to change her clothes behind.

    "After three days of this, the rest of us girls were getting edgy. Nina's sexy antics had our boyfriends steamed up and ready to pop. She was constantly rubbing up against the guys or dancing like a stripper to the radio. There wasn't one girl who wasn't afraid that her guy was going to sneak off into the woods with Nina.

    "Then, I caught my steady Jeff standing on the river bank and drooling as Nina splashed around in front of him—naked as a jaybird.

    "It was the last straw! That evening, while everyone was around the campfire, I crept into Nina's tent with an armful of poison oak. I opened her sleeping bag and rubbed the leaves all over the inside . . ." "Big Itch Was the Best Revenge on Class Witch," *Globe*, Feb. 18, 1991, at 29.

42. Barbara White, "More Guidelines from the School of Should," *Boston Globe*, Jan. 25, 1992, at 22.

43. Wendy Pollack, "Sexual Harassment: Women's Experience v. Legal Definitions," 13 *Harv. Women's L.J.* 35, 57n.73 (1990): "What is provocative? . . . Whenever a woman walked through the cafeteria, especially a young woman, the place would go wild . . . One woman in particular was a favorite target for this behavior . . . She wore the same white painters' pants that all the other painters wore. There was nothing in her dress or manner that welcomed the men's behavior. The only possible cause of this attention that I could identify was that she had blond hair.

    . . . I asked my fellow carpenters . . . 'What is going on here?' Their response was, 'She's just asking for it. Look at the way she wears those pants.' I was dumbfounded. Needless to say, the apprentice painter avoided the cafeteria after that."

44. Margaret Gordon and Stephanie Riger, *The Female Fear: The Social Cost of Rape* 6 (1991): "[M]any people know little about the crime [of rape] except the myths pervasive in our culture. Some of the more common are: . . . Otherwise decent men are spurred to rape by the clothing or behavior of women."

    The Hatfield story in the *Boston Globe* included the following: "'Dress is quite an insignificant factor in such attacks,' said Phillip Resnick, a forensic psychiatry professor at Case Western Reserve Medical School in Cleveland. 'Rapists say that they decide they're going to rape that night, and they select their victim largely based on opportunity: Is the woman alone? Is it a dark street?'"

    "*Myth:* 'The woman asks for it—she dresses in an inviting manner.' This is a common conclusion drawn by the harasser. It is also a rationalization that promotes harassment and retards solutions. Although there are individual cases to the contrary, limited studies available do not support a woman's dress style as a promotion of 'she asked for it.'" Lois Hart and J. David Dalke, *The Sexes at Work: Improving Work Relationships between Men and Women* 77 (1983). For a contrary view see Meritor Sav. Bank, FSB v. Vinson, 477 U.S. 57, 69 (1986).

45. Gordon and Riger, *The Female Fear.* 17 (1991).

46. *Working Woman* is probably trying to identify "traditionalist" respondents when it includes, in its survey about "sexual harassment in the workplace," "Do you agree or disagree with the following [state-

ment]? . . . Women bring harassment problems on themselves by dressing and acting provocatively." "Sexual Harassment in Your Office: The Working Woman Survey," *Working Woman,* Feb. 1992, at 14.

47. Janice Zazinski, "On the Clothes Women Wear to Work," *Boston Globe,* Jan. 25, 1992, at 22.
48. Leslie Martinich, "Link between Dress and Harassment? No," *Boston Globe,* Jan. 25, 1992, at 22: "There may very well be a link between dress that is interpreted as provocative and sex crimes by men, as the surveys cited by Julie Hatfield suggest, but it occurs in the minds of the perpetrators, not with the victims. Why must women continue to take responsibility for men's actions?"
49. Robin West, "Authority, Autonomy, and Choice: The Role of Consent in the Moral and Political Visions of Franz Kafka and Richard Posner," 99 *Harv. L. Rev.* 384 (1985); Mark Kelman, "Choice and Utility," 1979 *Wis. L. Rev.* 769.
50. West, "The Difference," 90–111.
51. Gallop, *Thinking Through the Body,* 92:
    "The Poetics Colloquium signified the world in which as a graduate student I had longed to make it. I was the only feminist speaker at the colloquium . . .
    "Writing this paper, I tried to make it possible to speak where the men were speaking, despite my body, but also in my body. Since I experienced my inability to transcend the body, where women were trapped, I had to think a way that the body was already 'poetic,' which is to say, belonged in the realm of high literary theory where I aspired to be . . .
    ". . . I dressed in a manner that bespoke the body as style, stylized sexuality. I wore spike heels, seamed hose, a fitted black forties dress and a large black hat. I was dressed as a woman, but as another woman. If my speech signaled an identification with a woman of another place, my clothes bespoke an identification with a woman of another time. I was in drag. My clothing drew attention to my body but at the same time stylized it, creating stylized body, what in the paper I called a poiesis of the body. The fit between the paper and the look, the text and the performance, was articulated unconsciously, and it worked."
52. Butler, *Gender Trouble,* 140–141:
    "Gender ought not to be construed as a stable identity or locus of agency from which various acts follow; rather gender is an identity tenuously constituted in time, instituted in exterior space through a *stylized repetition of acts.* The effect of gender is produced through the stylization of the body and, hence, must be understood as the mun-

dane way in which bodily gestures, movements, and styles of various kinds constitute the illusion of an abiding gendered self . . .

". . . The distinction between expression and performativeness is crucial. If gender attributes and acts, the various ways in which a body shows or produces its cultural signification, are performative, then there is no preexisting identity by which an act or attribute might be measured; there would be no true or false, real or distorted acts of gender, and the postulation of a true gender identity would be revealed as a regulatory fiction."

53. The norm of not dressing too sexily is a norm about where and when, rather than a straight-out prohibition of a type of dress. Sanctions against women who violate the norm keep the "spheres" separate. The relaxation of dress-code sanctions might change from both sides, and perhaps reduce, the sexual charge now associated with the contrasts between the various settings (daytime and nighttime street, movie set and back office, kitchen and boudoir, and so on). The consequences for those who derive pleasure from the contrast, and for those who invest in it ideologically, would be complex and far-reaching.

54. West, "The Difference," 90.

55. Marabelle Morgan, *The Total Woman* (1975) (brilliantly discussed in Dworkin, *Right-Wing Women*, 13–37).

56. *Pleasure and Danger: Exploring Female Sexuality* (C. Vance ed. 1983).

57. Consider bars with male strippers, and lingerie parties on the model of Tupperware parties. Barbara Ehrenreich et al., *Re-Making Love: The Feminization of Sex* 134–160 (1986).

58. See generally *Against Sadomasochism;* Sheila Jeffreys, *Anticlimax: A Feminist Perspective on the Sexual Revolution* (1990).

59. Kay L. Hagan, "Orchids in the Arctic: The Predicament of Women Who Love Men," *Ms.*, Nov./Dec. 1991, at 31.

60. Id. Another example: "If sexuality is socially constructed, it both changes and it can be changed . . . Of course, such processes take time, but the social-constructionist position opens us to the possibilities of transformation, including to the responsibility to account for our own sexuality." Michael Kimmel, "Introduction: Guilty Pleasures—Pornography in Men's Lives," in *Men Confront Pornography* 1, 6 (M. Kimmel ed. 1991).

61. Butler, *Gender Trouble*, 147.

62. Marny Hall, "Ex-Therapy to Sex-Therapy: Notes from the Margins," in *Gays, Lesbians, and Their Therapists: Studies in Psychotherapy* 91 (C. Silverstein ed., 1991).

63. This is what Roland Barthes, in his horrendously abstract semiology

of fashion, calls the "real vestimentary code," distinguishing it from the "written vestimentary code" of the discourse of fashion. Roland Barthes, *The Fashion System*, 34–35 (Ward & R. Howard trans. 1983). Throughout what follows, I use the written code as evidence of the real code. This approach would be problematic even if the discourse were that of the people wearing the clothes. In fact, the people producing the discourse are a small group of culture workers always subject to the suspicion that their vulgar monetary interests and more complex ideological projects influence what they say—in a direction oppressive to women. See Susan Faludi, *Backlash: The Undeclared War against American Women* 75–226 (1991). On the other hand, "fashion in the larger sense—as a means of seduction, as a vague consensus about what's attractive at any given moment, as the expression of some collective fantasy, as a code for information about ourselves—won't be laid to rest until we're all walking around stark naked (and what a dull world that will be)." Holly Brubach, "In Fashion: Sackcloth and Ashes," *New Yorker*, Feb. 3, 1992, at 79.

64. Molly Haskell, "Mad About the Boys: Big Screen Femmes Fatales Reflect Our Deepest Desires," *Lear's*, Jan. 1992 at 100.

65. "The Romance Report," *Ladies' Home J.*, Feb. 1992 at 118, 120, 121. "Racy, lacy lingerie—in pink or red—puts everybody in the mood!" Andrea P. Lynn, "Pour on the Passion! A Valentine's Eve Seduction," *Cosmopolitan*, Feb. 1992 at 187. "I knew it was over when . . . I heard that my friend Erin, who had a crush on my boyfriend, had taken him lingerie shopping with her the day I left for vacation.—Susan, twenty-six, writer, Philadelphia" Sue Campbell, "I Knew It Was Love When . . . I Knew It Was Over When . . .," *Glamour*, Feb. 1992 at 155.

66. Everyday dress practices, particularly those of the subcultures discussed earlier, respond to but also powerfully *influence* the "gender media images" described in the following: "there is an important way [in which] gender media images have become an essential for heterosexual sexuality. Since the capitalist patriarchal nuclear family has given way to a raft of alternative family forms, another material base is required to perpetuate the heterosexual 'masquerade' of the innate attraction between men and women. Since the contents of heterosexual desire are socially learned and there is no longer a hegemonic patriarchal family to provide the content of masculinity and femininity, there must be some other social arena which teaches males and females what the opposite sex desires from them. Thus, fashion and media images, once merely the perpetuators of images generated by the patriarchal family, have become the semi-autono-

mous social arena in which sexist and heterosexist desire are constructed." Ann Ferguson, *Blood at the Root: Motherhood, Sexuality, and Male Dominance* 118 (1989). This is the level of connotation or "rhetoric" in Barthes's semiology. See Roland Barthes, *The Fashion System* (M. Ward & R. Howard trans. 1983).

67. "If gender is a representation subject to social and ideological coding, there can be no simple one-to-one relationship between the image of woman inscribed in a film and its female spectator. On the contrary, the spectator's reading of the film (including interpretive and affective responses, cognitive and emotional strategies) is mediated by her existence in, and experience of, a particular universe of social discourse and practices in daily life. Thus, for instance, feminist criticism has shown that readings emerging out of a politically radical or oppositional consciousness can significantly alter the interpretation and the effects of filmic representation, as well as the spectator's self-representation, and may contribute to changing the social meanings and finally the codes of representation themselves." Teresa De Lauretis, *Technologies of Gender: Essays on Theory, Film and Fiction* 96 (1987).

68. Christine Gorman, "Sizing Up the Sexes," *Time,* Jan. 20, 1992, at 44.

69. Wendy Hockswender, "A Man's-Eye View of the Long Skirt," *N.Y. Times Mag.,* Jan. 12, 1992, at 38.

70. Brubach, "In Fashion," 81. These "descriptions" may be more or less up for grabs: "Beyond a few dim echoes of James Dean and ranch hands, however, blue jeans have no such powers of suggestion; they've been a fixture of our wardrobes for such a long time now that it's hard to regard them the way we do articles of fashion. So it's left to the manufacturers to create a context for jeans, something to trigger the consumer's imagination . . . [Calvin] Klein said, 'Jeans are about sex.' Jeans *are* about sex in some instances, but they're also about blue-collar jobs and white-collar pastimes" (id. at 81–82).

71. This whole approach is based on the analogy between dressing and other kinds of performance: "Recently, sexuality has been theorized as an assigned encoding (socially produced, not inherent), historically particular and heavily laden with the preoccupations of the time . . . [S]exuality exerts a strong influence on interpretation, and as Annette Kuhn notes, 'meanings do not reside in images . . . they are circulated between representation, spectator and social formation.' Spectators' ability to read impropriety into the stage appearance of the [Victorian] actress—to scandalize the idealized femininity—required knowledge of the referential context of female erotic topography . . . This lexicon can be rediscovered, allowing the visual performance text to be read through its historical codes . . .

". . . It is impossible to say whether the theater supplied visions that became invested with eroticism in the context of pornography, or whether the theater employed motifs already infused with sexuality . . . What is important is that because of the existence of this large body of literature documenting, justifying and enacting the erotic fictions associated with actresses it is impossible to claim that actresses were in control of all the signs they gave off. No matter how scrupulous their conduct was as private citizens, actresses had no authority or control over their public sign-making of bodily coverings, gestures, and spatial relationships lodged in a separate but symbiotically dependent source." Tracy Davis, *Actresses as Working Women: Their Social Identity in Victorian Culture* 106–108 (1991), quoting Annette Kuhn, *The Power of the Image: Essays on Representation and Sexuality* 6 (1985). The same idea can be used in the interpretation of representations of women: "[The bare-bottom thrashing of nuns during the French Revolution] constituted public political and religious humiliation, yet when they were translated into the visual realm, they entered the domain of the sexual and the pornographic, implied in the print by the exposed breast of one market woman thrashing a nun. The buttocks were pictured as the locus of desire in works ranging from Watteau's *The Remedy* . . . to the illustrations of pornographic literature . . . Within this context, the political prints that center on the bottoms of nuns, for example, can thus be placed in a chain of erotic behavior and imagery that focuses both on flagellation and on the erotic." Vivian Cameron, "Political Exposures: Sexuality and Caricature in the French Revolution," in *Eroticism and the Body Politic* 94 (L. Hunt ed. 1991).

72. Here is another example, from Davis, *Actresses as Working Women* at 109: "By freeing the torso from stiff boning, the costumes also signified a refusal to suffer and be still; the well-disciplined mind and well-regulated feelings that were associated with tight lacing gave way to connotations of loose morals and easy virtue, which also fuelled the misapprehensions of performers' accessibility and sexual availability favored by men."

73. Roger Trilling, "The New Face of Feminism," *Details,* Feb. 1992, at 75.

74. Consider Laura Dern's encounter with Diamond Tooth in *Wild at Heart* (Polygram/Propaganda Films 1990).

75. Michel Foucault, "Nietzsche, Genealogy, History," in *Language, Countermemory, Practice: Selected Essays and Interviews* (D. Bouchard ed., D. Bouchard & S. Simon trans. 1977).

76. Beth Wolfensberger, "Destination Romance," *Boston,* Feb. 1992, at

72: "Trashy or Sexy? Men, salesclerks report, gravitate toward black things, red things, sheer things, garter belts, and push-up bras . . . These are articles women seldom buy for themselves as most of them don't care to look like prostitutes when undressing in the gym. There is a time and a place for them, but if you are worried about sending the wrong message, stick to pastels, anything silk and simple, or robes."

77. Giacomo Casanova, *The Memoirs of Jacques Casanova* (1929).

78. Frank Harris, *My Secret Life* (1963); John Cleland, *Fanny Hill: Memoirs of a Woman of Pleasure* (1963); Pauline Reage, *Story of O* (Sabine d'Estree trans. 1965).

79. *Scorpio Rising* (1964); Hubert Selby, Jr., *Last Exit to Brooklyn* (1964).

80. Pamela Des Barres, *I'm with the Band* (1987).

81. E.g., Pat Califia, *Doc and Fluff* (1990).

82. Mark Seliger, "Heavy Metal Nation," *Rolling Stone*, Sept. 19, 1991, at 51–52.

83. "Great Style," *Elle*, Jan. 1992 at 20.

84. Maureen Orth, "Kaiser Karl: Behind the Mask," *Vanity Fair*, Feb. 1992 at 157.

85. *Mandingo* (Paramount Pictures Corp. 1979). See generally Patricia Collins, *Black Feminist Thought: Knowledge, Consciousness, and the Politics of Empowerment* 77–78, 166–179 (1991); bell hooks, *Black Looks: Race and Representation* 61–77 (1992). Why isn't there the close connection between white sexual stereotypes of black women and dress that exists for the others?

86. Lynn Harris, "Behind the Bedroom Door," *Ladies' Home J.*, Nov. 1991 at 119.

87. Grace Metalious, *Peyton Place* (1956).

88. *The World of Susie Wong* (Paramount Pictures Corp. 1958).

89. Susan Bordo, "Material Girl," in *The Female Body: Figures, Styles, Speculations* 127–129 (L. Goldstein ed. 1991).

90. Id. at 128.

91. *Paris, Texas* (Twentieth Century–Fox 1984).

92. Philip Roth, *Portnoy's Complaint* (1969).

93. David Steinberg, "The Roots of Pornography," in *Men Confront Pornography* 55–56, 57 (M. Kimmel ed. 1991): "I believe that these issues—sexual scarcity, desire for appreciation and reciprocation of desire, and fear of being sexually undesirable—are the central forces that draw men to pornography. While violent imagery, by various estimates, accounts for only three to eight percent of all pornography, images that address scarcity, female lust, and female expression of male desirability account for at least seventy-five percent of porn imagery . . .

"Finally, I think it is important to acknowledge that pornography provides a victimless outlet for the basic sexual rage that seems to sit within so many men, whether we like it or not. This is the rage that sadly gets vented at specific women through rape and other forms of sexual assault. It will not go away from the social psyche, pornography or no pornography."

94. Scott MacDonald, "Confessions of a Feminist Porn Watcher," in *Men Confront Pornography*, 35.

95. See, e.g., the movie *Street Smart* (Cannon Group 1987).

96. "Great Style," *Elle*, Jan. 1992 at 18.

97. *The Blue Angel* (Ufa 1930); Linda Wolfe, *The Professor and the Prostitute* (1986).

98. *Something Wild* (Orion Pictures Corp. 1986).

99. Catherine Texier, *Panic Blood* 14 (1990). In the following description, from Shakespeare's *Antony and Cleopatra* (act 2, scene 2), we have only the accessories, with the barge playing the part of the motorcycle in the quote from *Elle* above. But there is an answer to the dumb question.

> The barge she sat in, like a burnish'd throne,
> Burn'd on the water; the poop was beaten gold,
> Purple the sails, and so perfumed that
> The winds were love-sick with them; the oars were silver,
> Which to the tune of flutes kept stroke, and made
> The water which they beat to follow faster,
> As amorous of their strokes. For her own person,
> It beggar'd all description: she did lie
> In her pavillion,—cloth-of-gold of tissue,—
> O'er picturing that Venus where we see
> The fancy outwork nature . . .
> . . . From the barge
> A strange invisible perfume hits the sense
> Of the adjacent wharfs. The city cast
> Her people out upon her, and Antony,
> Enthron'd i'the market-place, did sit alone,
> Whistling to the air . . .

100. "[E]roticism itself remains ambiguous: it is at once the domain of women's mastery by men and, as Rousseau saw, the domain of women's mastery over men." Lynn Hunt, "Introduction," in *Eroticism and the Body Politic*, 12.

101. Molly Haskell, "Mad about the Boys: Big Screen Femmes Fatales Reflect Our Deepest Desires," *Lear's*, Jan. 1992, at 100.

102. But see id. at 98: "For all their apparent man craziness, the men's

women we like, and those who endure, are ultimately women with whom we identify and feel a sense of kinship. They are passionate, emotionally intense: We can't take our eyes off them, and they command the screen. They are not bimbos or pinups with vacant stares and wet lips but women with an instinctual awareness of what they're doing. They are individuals yet archetypal. And whether they'll admit it or not, they're looking over their shoulders at us, their competition, their sisters. In our imagination, we live together. They are our doppelgängers, our other halves."

103. Menkes, *"Vogue* Point of View," 110.
104. hooks, *Black Looks,* 160.
105. Pascal Bruckner, "Airbrush Dreams: A French Toast to American T & A," *Lear's,* Jan. 1992 at 66–67.
106. Lynn Minton, "What We Care About: A Fresh Voices Report," *Parade,* Jan. 26, 1992, at 5.
107. Hatfield, "Defining Appropriate Dress," 31.
108. Dalma Heyn, "The Intelligent Woman's Guide to Sex: Sex Is Not Enough," *Mademoiselle,* Feb. 1992 at 48.
109. Anne Wagner, "Rodin's Reputation," in *Eroticism and the Body Politic,* 235–236.
110. Id. at 235.
111. Id. at 230.
112. Id. at 235–236.
113. On the different interpretations of femininity as masquerade, see Mary Ann Doane, *Femmes Fatales: Feminism, Film Theory, Psychoanalysis* 25–26, 37–39 (1991); Butler, *Gender Trouble,* 46–54.
114. Butler, *Gender Trouble,* 136: "If the inner truth of gender is a fabrication and if a true gender is a fantasy instituted and inscribed on the surface of bodies, then it seems that genders can be neither true nor false, but are only produced as the truth effects of a discourse of primary and stable identity."
115. I argued earlier that this can happen because the woman wears clothing whose message of erotic availability is contradicted by the well-understood norms of the setting, so that she is neither available nor unavailable, but autonomous (male) and simultaneously the repository of body-power (female). This might be an example of what Judith Butler is talking about in the following passages: "In the place of a 'male-identified' sexuality in which 'male' serves as the cause and irreducible meaning of that sexuality, we might develop a notion of sexuality constructed in terms of phallic relations of power that replay and redistribute the possibilities of that phallicism precisely through the subversive operation of 'identifications' that are, within

the power field of sexuality, inevitable . . . If there is no radical repudiation of a culturally constructed sexuality, what is left is the question of how to acknowledge and 'do' the construction one is invariably in. Are there forms of repetition that do not constitute a simple imitation, reproduction, and, hence consolidation of the law . . . ?" Butler, *Gender Trouble*, 30–31. "If the regulatory fictions of sex and gender are themselves multiply contested sites of meaning, then the very multiplicity of their construction holds out the possibility of a disruption of their univocal posturing" (id. at 32).

116. "[B]oth visually and narratively, cinema defines woman as image: as spectacle to be looked at and object to be desired, investigated, pursued, controlled and ultimately possessed by a subject who is masculine, that is, symbolically male." Teresa de Lauretis, *Technologies of Gender: Essays on Theory, Film, and Fiction* 99 (1987).

117. See *Against Sadomasochism*. See also Sandra Bartky, *Femininity and Domination: Studies in the Phenomenology of Oppression* 51 (1990): "The right, staunchly defended by liberals, to desire what and whom we please and, under certain circumstances, to act on our desire, is not an issue here; the point is that women would be better off if we learned when to refrain from the exercise of this right. A thorough overhaul of desire is clearly on the feminist agenda: the fantasy that we are overwhelmed by Rhett Butler should be traded in for one in which we seize state power and reeducate him . . . Samois in effect advises P. to ignore in her own life a general principle to which, as a feminist, she is committed and which she is therefore bound to represent to all other women: the principle that we struggle to decolonize our sexuality by removing from our minds the internalized forms of oppression that make us easier to control."

118. Butler, *Gender Trouble*, 30.

119. Morgan, *Going too Far*, 301.

120. Id. at 232.

121. Id. at 237 (emphasis added).

122. Id. at 235.

123. Susan Keller, "Review Essay: *Justify My Love*," 18 *Western St. U. L. Rev.* 463, 468 (1990): "Madonna's [*Justify My Love*] video runs the risk of reinforcing the stereotypes of male power precisely by showing that women get that power only by dressing up as men, and of teaching rather than revealing the alternative meaning of the closing epigraph; that pleasure may derive from violation. It is a necessary risk, however, if we want to challenge the assumptions of gender."

124. Ferguson, *Blood at the Root*, 116.

125. Id. at 215.

126. MacDonald, "Confessions," 40.
127. Id. at 41. He adds: "In [some] instances the fantasy is in punishing resistant women for their revulsion. Of course, the punishments—usually one form of rape or another—often end with the fantasy woman's discovery of an insatiable hunger for whatever has been done to her. This frequent turnabout appears to be nothing more than a reconfirmation of the stupid, brutal myth that women ask to be raped or enjoy being raped, but—as sadly ironic as this seems—it could also be seen as evidence that, in the final analysis, men don't mean harm to women, or don't wish to mean harm to women: their fantasy is the acceptance of their own biological nature by women. I've always assumed that porn and rape *are* part of the same general problem, though I've always felt it more likely that porn offers an outlet for some of the anger engendered by men's feelings of sensual aesthetic inferiority, than that it serves as a fuel for further anger. But I'm only speaking from my own experience. I've rarely spoken frankly about such matters with men who use porn" (id. at 42).
128. *Wall Street* (Twentieth Century–Fox 1987).
129. Signe Hammer, "The Rape Fantasies of Women: Up from Disrepute," *Village Voice*, April 5, 1976, quoted in Robin Morgan, "The Politics of Sado-Masochistic Fantasies," in *Going Too Far: The Personal Chronicle of a Feminist* 230 n.1 (1977). Morgan comments: "It . . . provokes the startling thought that assertive women in general and feminists in particular might be especially prey to such culturally implanted self-punishing devices" (id.). But it seems to me wrong to see the "devices" as "self-punishing." The self-punishment is in guilt about one's fantasy, which is pleasure, whether it involves punishing or being punished.
130. Reage, *Story of O.*
131. The work that seems to be most clearly inspired by some such idea is the trilogy by A. N. Roquelaure [Ann Rice], *The Claiming of Sleeping Beauty* (1985), *Beauty's Punishment* (1986), and *Beauty's Release* (1987). For yet another take, see Jessica Benjamin, *The Bonds of Love* 51–84 (1988).
132. Keller, "Review Essay," 468.

Index